600

7915

10 ⁰⁰

# THE SIENESE PAINTERS
## OF THE TRECENTO

# THE SIENESE PAINTERS
# OF THE TRECENTO

BY

EMILIO CECCHI

TRANSLATED FROM THE ITALIAN BY
LEONARD PENLOCK

WITH 256 REPRODUCTIONS IN COLLOTYPE

FREDERICK WARNE & CO,. LTD.
LONDON AND NEW YORK

PRINTED BY THE CASA EDITRICE D'ARTE " VALORI PLASTICI " — ROME — ITALY

Arti Grafiche Panetto & Petrelli — Spoleto (Italy).

# CONTENTS

# THE SIENESE PAINTERS OF THE TRECENTO

I F certain well-defined limits and aims were not at once imposed upon the following essay dealing with the chief Sienese painters of the fourteenth century, the reader would be
justified in distrusting it for its brevity, if on no other ground.
The vastness of the subject alone would make it impossible
to discuss a single artist belonging to the school in a volume
of this size. We will therefore say clearly at the outset that
it is not our intention to insist afresh upon a mass of general
information which has long since been duly sifted and apprai-
sed, but to describe the formal principles and the historical
development of Sienese painting during the first half of the
fourteenth century, availing ourselves largely of the more
convincing publications in critical literature which have
appeared in recent years. A similar presentation, if we are
not mistaken, was in the mind of Van Marle when he began
his study of the development of the Italian schools (1924),
but it cannot be said that he has always succeeded in rendering his intentions plain. Again, in spite of such valuable ad-
ditions as the volume on Sassetta (1909), the *Essays* on Sienese painting (1918), and a number of notes and corrections
published in various periodicals, the outline of the Sienese
school traced by Berenson in 1897 must now be said to have
faded, memorable though the author's acuteness of observation, his conclusions – so considerably in advance of their
time – and the literary charm of his expression must always
remain. And the same remark will equally apply to the chap-

7

ters dedicated by Adolfo Venturi to Sienese art (1907); their merits are no less conspicuous, though of a different order. The greatest advance in critical researches bearing upon Sienese painting, even if this progress has been subject to periods of interruption, has been made during the last twenty-five years.

By this statement we do not, however, mean to subscribe to the stereotyped view that with the exception of references made by ancient chroniclers and scholars, Sienese painting – for sculpture the case is different – remained practically unexplored and unappreciated. The artistic antagonism between Siena and Florence did not prevent Vasari, for instance, from paying homage to almost all the important artists of the Sienese tradition; and a single page like that in which Lanzi traced the characteristics of the Sienese school in contrast with the school of Florence is of itself evidence of the most delicate comprehension.

"A blithesome school amongst a blithe people is the Sienese," Lanzi says, "and in the choice of colours and in the expression of faces it conveys such joy that some foreigners have been so far taken by it as to prefer it even to the Florentine." After this, Lanzi goes on to point out the constant obedience of Sienese art to devotion, " so that all the best work of the school is for the public in the churches," and hence "the gay aspect whereof I spoke " is all the more manifest and accessible. " The Florentines are greater philosophers, but the Sienese are greater poets ;" for " the latter are endowed with a special talent for invention and allegory, enabling them to animate the ancient legends with new fantasies: and all this with a readiness, a sprightliness, and what one might almost call an improvisation so singular that their vivacity of temperament has perhaps hindered their perfection in design, which is not their strong point, as you might say it is that of the Florentines."

In these notes by Lanzi we seem to read a graceful foreshadowing of the expressions " imaginative design " and "illustration" which have been applied with such conspicuous success to Sienese painting. Berenson, indeed, has complained in times more near our own that the students of Sienese art are " too few to have gone farther than the mapping out of the main outlines and distributing the known materials more or less coherently among the various dominions and districts; " but it seems impossible to deny that, with the exception of Pietro Lorenzetti and Barna, a very characteristic place has always been assigned to the Sienese in the annals of Italian art. The motives underlying this admiration may indeed have been more or less clear; yet it must always have been evident that artists like Simone or like Ambrogio Lorenzetti succeeded in gathering and distilling the essence of a world of sentiments and passions then already on the verge of passing away, and that they expressed it in the mode of an impassioned and ornamented commemoration, which, devout as it was, had all the acquired preciousness of a self-pleased beauty—a beauty not always or entirely to be explained as the result of an intention to make the work of art into a rite, into the richest possible offering that could be laid upon the Divine altar. For if, in one point of view, the characteristics of this school are intensity and freshness of religious sentiment, we shall find in it a no less clearly pronounced precocious elegance that can bear comparison with the most dexterous refinements achieved by later times.

It would, then, be an error to claim for Sienese taste that it remained fixed in a single inspiration, from the first dawning of Duccio towards the close of the thirteenth century, right down to the sunset of its artistic civilization, and that Siena was a sort of enclosed garden or "nursery," completely shut off from all the other existing schools, yet containing an abundant growth of pictorial personages, all of the first rank. There is some truth in the theory that artistic developments have their hour of greatest purity and intensity at their beginning, but it is more difficult to justify it in the case of Siena than elsewhere.

Although in the golden period, which may be reckoned as extending from 1285 to the pestilence of 1348, intercourse and exchanges with other schools were not wanting, they were not of a kind to disturb the natural development of Sienese painting, and their extent was always limited. Later on, circumstances changed. Foreign artists began to work in Siena more frequently. The influence of Florence and of central Italy generally made itself more strongly felt. Even Sienese artists of reputation, like Sassetta, when they worked away from home – Sassetta's *St. Francis in Ecstasy* (plate CCXLVIII), painted for Borgo Sansepolcro, is an instance of this – seem bent, as Lanzi has pointed out, upon being less Sienese, and, when they felt themselves guaranteed by the preferences of the locality, allowed their individual genius free rein. Thus the simplicity, the organic character of the first decades of the fourteenth century, gave way to an intricate rhythm, heavy and disordered; archaism, eclecticism, antiquarianism, became the order of the day, until with Matteo di Giovanni, Guidoccio Cozzarelli, and Neroccio di Landi the Sienese tradition ends. Yet when we recall the fretful, chilly Madonnas of these last artists, with their brocades and velvets and gold, the chubby Infants toying with coral rosaries while the angels look at them very much as a factor's boy might look at the " young master," and the bloodless female saints half-buried in their baroque provincial expensiveness, who would not wish to forget the dictates of taste, the exigencies of style, and all that painting had produced in the early Trecento at Siena, and so enjoy without scruple one of the most florid and romantic periods of decadence to be met with in the whole history of art ?

\* \* \*

With regard to the first historical relationships of the school, it is enough to point out that, during the second half of the thirteenth century, Byzantine internationalism, variously modified by Romanesque and Gothic elements, underwent a process of differentiation resulting in four great regional branches of which Cimabue, Cavallini, Giotto, and Duccio were the respective representatives.

Berenson, when he published reproductions of the *Throned Madonnas* in the Hamilton and Kahn Collections (plate I), ascribed them to an artist of Constantinople who worked somewhere about 1200. That the two paintings have a deep æsthetic significance admits of no question; yet we doubt whether there is any adequate reason for supposing that they set out from the Bosphorus as part of a merchant's cargo or the plunder of a returning Crusader, and continued their travels until eventually they reached Calahorra on the confines of Old Castile and Navarre, where they were found, and whence they subsequently passed to the above-mentioned American collections. The schools of Cyprus furnished Venice and other trading centres of the Mediterranean with pictorial furniture in abundance, and Vasari informs us that after 1250 "the rulers of Florence summoned certain painters of Greece to that city with the express purpose of bringing back to Florence the art of painting, which was rather lost than gone astray " – a fact which shows that the tendency of taste in Italy at the time was still prevalently and officially Byzantine. If, as some students believe, the origin of the Hamilton and Kahn panels is to be sought, not at Constantinople or in Cyprus, but in an Italian city, then the old tradition, represented by Vasari, according to which every painting before Giotto's time, no matter by whom executed, was called Byzantine, receives a most striking confirmation – at least in its general outlines. Such paintings as the " paliotto " of Assisi (Toesca, *Storia dell'Arte italiana*, I, fig. 692) and that of the Vatican Gallery, the work of a Byzantine or Italo-Byzantine hand, testify to a perfection which cannot lightly be dissociated from the idea of a constituted, active school; and this being so, the supposition that several decades later an artist like Duccio needed to serve an apprenticeship in Constantinople will appear highly improbable.

11

Perhaps, in comparison with Florence, the condition of things at Siena at no time permitted the employment of Byzantine masters of outstanding merit. No trace can be found in Siena of monumental mosaics, and Siena elaborated Byzantine influences blended with traces of the Romanesque; but we find there applications, although on a provincial scale, of most of the types known to Byzantine iconography – types hieratic or cursive, archaic or of more recent style. Thus the *Madonna* of the Opera del Duomo (Venturi, *Storia dell'Arte italiana*, V, fig. 28) and the *Madonna* of Tressa correspond to ancient types, while the thirteenth century gave us, first, the so-called " paliotti" of Berardenga and San Pietro in Banchi (plates II and III); next, the ΟΔΗΓΗΤΡΙΑ of Guido of Siena and his school; and lastly, the type of the "Motherly Madonna " with its greater expression of kindly feeling.

\* \* \*

Much of the importance formerly attached to the question whether Siena preceded Florence in the new pictorial developments or whether the priority belongs to Florence disappears as soon as we bear in mind the uniform prevalence of the Byzantine tradition until far on in the second half of the thirteenth century. Even a convinced upholder of Florentine pretensions like Vasari recognized, as we have seen, that in Florence the art of painting had rather perished than gone astray. It would seem that at the period to which Vasari refers (1250), Guido and his followers had already announced a new art at Siena. Lanzi, however, corrected certain reticences in the account of early Sienese art left by Vasari and Baldinucci, remarking with his wonted sagacity that no great reliance can be placed on the alleged novelty of Guido, if only on account of the scanty remains of his work which have come down to us. His *Madonna*, formerly in the Church of San Domenico (plate IV), was largely repainted by a follower of Duccio; the *Madonnas* of Arezzo and Florence are reduced to the modest quality of copies, not executed by the artist; and although the *Madonna and Child* in the Gualino Collection and a few other paintings whose authenticity is anything but convincing have been added, purely by way of hypothesis, to Guido's repertory, the personality of the innovator emerges from the whole complex still vague and ill-defined. Even the attempt made by Van Marle, who is one of the critics most bent upon accentuating Guido's personality, fails to give us any satisfactory critical definition of its real nature. What he seems to discern is a mere dry and showy repetition of the Byzantine canon, accompanied, especially in the ornamentation, by Romanesque elements. With Guido and his school, we are still, so far as artistic novelty is concerned, within the sphere of a Coppo di Marcovaldo reaffirming on Sienese soil after Montaperti the Byzantinism whose origins lay in Florence, where the influence of choicer models may well have led to a calligraphic refinement altogether wanting to the productions of Guido's school. Nor must we neglect to mention the apt remark of De Nicola that if we admit – as we must – the date 1221 for Guido's *Madonna* (plate IV), it becomes impossible to discover any ordered, rhythmical advance in Trecento painting. From works far more Byzantine than Romanesque in character, such as the Berardenga "paliotto," (1215; plate II), we suddenly pass with Guido to the full formula of Italo-Byzantine painting, and thus the products of Guido's school continue down to a date (about 1260) far too late after the master's death.

In spite of the descriptive catalogue published by Sirén, and until the materials collected by Offner make their appearance, an exhaustive collection of the figurative *data* illustrating Sienese art in its beginnings and during the twelfth century remains an unsupplied want. But while we may reasonably expect that fresh researches will cause many details to appear in a new light, it is clearly idle for us to indulge to-day in fantastic conjectures, or to solicit our scanty pieces of evidence in the hope that they may give us information which it is not in their power to supply. Still, it would seem that at a certain moment a more elegant imitation of Byzantine models took place in Siena, and that this imitation followed closely the models found in illuminated manuscripts (Van Marle). The "paliotto" of San Pietro in Banchi (plate III) and another "paliotto" with episodes from the life of the Baptist (Toesca; I, fig. 698) appear to confirm this view. The central figure of the "paliotto" of San Pietro enters into the canon of Guido and of the artists named after him, while in its six compartments we find iconographic motives closely akin to those used by Duccio – for example, in the *Nativity* and in the *Call of St. Peter* (plates III and XXV). As the researches of Van Marle and other students on the subjet of Duccio's iconography have shown, there is no limit to the lists of similar analogies easily discoverable in Byzantine miniatures, frescoes in Cappadocia, French miniatures of the twelfth century, and bas-reliefs by the Pisani. The Madonna of the *Annunciation*, in the "paliotto" of San Pietro, however, bears signs of something beyond a mere iconographical precedent; for the movement of this figure, contrasting with the vehemence of the angel, whose movement repeats a Byzantine scheme, may be termed entirely Ducciesque.

The two diptychs (plates VI and VII), usually attributed to followers of Guido, hint, on the other hand, at a ruder style of painting. Observe the unwonted breadth of their structure – this being particularly noticeable in the second – and that airiness characteristic of popular art. Whether or not they are both by the same hand, and whether the second diptych (plate VII), representing Blessed Andrea Gallerani the Eleemosynary, preceded the other – in which, according to Van Marle, the artist betrays the imperviousness of old age to new ideas by his slavish imitation of Byzantine models – are points of doubtful certainty and of no great significance.

The Crucifix before which the Blessed Andrea is shown in prayer has been thought to present affinities with a small panel now at Budapest (Venturi, *Storia*, V, fig. 13), owing to the presence in the latter of the same wavy Romanesque decoration which occurs twice in the diptych (plate VI) below the figures of the two tyrants. The saint wearing a cap (plate VII) is a realistic note carrying us more than a century further on to Andrea Vanni's likeness of Gallerani (Van Marle, II, fig. 87), where the ecstasy of Simone Martini is translated into the lowly devotion of the populace.

So far, then, we find ourselves, on the whole, in the presence of works which do not as yet reveal the characteristics of the Sienese school; and this remark applies equally to works by Vigoroso and other artists which bring us down to somewhere near 1280. When Sienese characteristics do from time to time appear, it is only in fleeting glimpses, reflections of more or less distant sources; until, in the midst of this scantly harmonious and almost contradictory production, there rises up the naive yet refined beauty of the *Rucellai Madonna* and the *Gualino Madonna* (plates VIII to X) and the first paintings of Duccio – the last slightly earlier than the other two.

\* \* \*

The question of the *Rucellai Madonna* (plates IX and X) appeared to have been definitely settled by the conclusions at which De Nicola arrived in 1911. Although the opinions expressed by Van Marle were somewhat different, he, too, gave a convincing summary of the whole discussion in 1924. The question, however, has lately been re-opened by Lionello Venturi, who attempted to assign the *Gualino Madonna* (plate VIII), recognized by almost all critics as the work of the artist who painted the *Rucellai Madonna* (plates IX and X), to Cimabue, provoking thereby a keen dispute which well illustrates the complicated background lying behind the developments of native and orientalizing tendencies in Florence up to about 1280, and which indicates further the point of time and

15

the works in which the various fields and traditions first began to be clearly distinguished. Lionello Venturi sums up the results of his examination of the *Gualino Madonna* by pointing out that the painting marks the culminating point reached by Italian colourism in the twelfth century. " In its brown and purple, its blue and gold," he says, " it maintains the Byzantine tradition; but in its harmonies of lilac and rose, of pale yellow and light blue, it reveals a new sensibility, perhaps prepared by the miniaturists. If the *Rucellai Madonna* were not veiled by her century-old patina, she, too, would live with an equally chromatic life." Strange, however, that this spring-time colouring should appear but once in the entire production of Cimabue, and never have struck root at all in Florence ! " It is the trumpet-call of fresh and youthful life:" yet, once more, the call awakened no echo in Florence, and we shall look in vain to these two Madonnas to find a link in form and colour with the wholly diverse art of Giotto. Only fifty years later do we discover a colour of this intonation, this musical intention, in Florence, and then it is in the most Sienese of all the Florentines – Bernardo Daddi. We find it again after Daddi in Angelico, but Angelico derived it – apart, naturally, from his own temperament – from the miniaturists and from Lorenzo Monaco; and their origin was in Siena.

It is indeed true that the two Madonnas betray remarkable iconographical affinities with the *Madonna of the Servites* at Bologna, and even closer resemblances to the *Madonna of Mosciano ;* yet these works belong in only a very vague way to the circle of Cimabue, and cautious critics are content with saying of them, what might equally well be said of the *Rucellai* or of the *Gualino Madonna,* that " they maintain the grandiosity of Cimabue while adding to it a new graciousness." May we not rather conclude, accordingly, that they are not Florentine, but Sienese with Florentine elements, such as we should expect to find in the work of an artist, who was Sienese in sentiment, but had felt the influence of Cimabue, and was careful in giving proof of his skill in Florence towards

16

the year 1285 not to depart too far from the models and from the taste in vogue there at that time ? It is only incidentally that their pictorial expression tends towards the plastic, sculptural quality of the Florentines; in colour and line it is far closer to the musical quality of Siena. Florentine art was already by this time abandoning the last *scoriae* of Oriental tendencies; whereas it was precisely these which appear to reassert themselves and form the basis of painting in Siena.

Toesca has remarked how the severity of Cimabue is attenuated in these paintings by the perfect coherence of their style, exactly propotioned to the greater warmth and luminousness appearing in the tones of the drapery and in the flesh-tints of the faces. To this we may add the further consideration that the painter of the *Rucellai Madonna* could not have been ignorant of Duccio's works. It was from them that he derived not only the Gothic elements already appropriated by Duccio, but the decorative grace which in his more subtle presentation offers so marked a contrast to the monumental uncouthness of the Florentine. To this subject, however, we shall return later on, adducing particular reasons why the *Rucellai* and the *Gualino Madonnas*, together with the *Madonnas* of Mosciano and in Santa Cecilia at Crevole cannot be assigned either to Cimabue or, generally speaking, to any Florentine artist, nor yet to Duccio, as some writers – Venturi, Strzygowsky, Van Marle, and others – appear to suggest.

* * *

A detailed examination of political and religious events and of the changes in manners which accompanied the formation and growth of Sienese taste lies outside the scope of this essay. Those events fall within a period extending, roughly, from Siena's victory over Florence at Montaperti (1260) to the loss of power by the two chief Arts a century later. By a kind of historical paradox, Siena's victory marked the beginning of the rise of Florence; the collapse of the Arts, on the other hand, was attended by a multitude of disorders and the first symptoms of Sienese decline.

With regard to the religious character of Sienese culture, from the earliest legendary Saints in Roman and mediæval times – Victor, Ansanus, and Soror, founder of the Hospital " della Scala " – down to St. Galganus, Giovanni Battista Tolomei, and the Blessed Andrea Gallerani, there exists a copious hagiographical literature; and still more extensive is the list of lesser personages bound up in one way or another with local devotion. Not, however, that we can establish any parallelism between religion and painting in Siena. The golden age of Sienese painting had already reached its term when in the second half of the fourteenth century the spring-time of the mystical literature which flourished more abundantly at Siena than perhaps in any other part of Italy blossomed out in the Blessed Giovanni Colombini, in St. Catherine and her disciples, and in St. Bernardine. How deeply struck were the roots of Sienese mysticism we may learn from Feo Belcari and from other writers of lives and *laudi*, and again from Bernardino Ochino, the friend of Michelangelo and Vittoria Colonna. In Ochino the seed-plot of Siena widened its borders, entwining itself with the first shoots of the Reformation. The doctrine of Christ's human nature propounded by Socini shows us Sienese mysticism fallen into heresy; but in Brandano it reassumed the sternness and ardour of the primitives; and finally, amid the fully developed naturalism of the nineteenth century it gave back a reflection of the lightning-flash of ancient prophecy in the tragic preaching of Davide Lazzaretti.

This religious literature delayed the arrival of the Renaissance at Siena, or, rather, it fostered an archaïsing spirit; and hence, while profane studies were by no means neglected, the Renaissance did not assume in Siena the definitely scientific character it bore at Florence. On the other hand, the widely diffused mysticism of the Sienese tradition in no way hindered the existence of that crude individual and social experience which we find portrayed in the sonnets of Cecco Angiolieri, nor again a wildly ostentatious display of which the *lunari* composed by Folgore of San Gimignano are typical. The passion of Angiolieri with its icy coldness and fury recalls Villon's faculty for the *macabre*. Individual hate, growing to exasperation in the narrow limits of provincial life, here finds vent in an imaginative ferocity that could hardly have existed in centres of wider activity or superior culture, where personal quarrels are either kept in their due place and suffocated, or at all events transcend their contingent character. Cecco's plebeian virulence seems only to find relief through its very exaggeration, in much the same way that a grotesque lyricism will at times burst forth from the mad verbosity of certain swearers. Something of the same spirit may be seen in Taddeo di Bartolo's representation of the various vices and their punishments in his paintings of the *Inferno* (plates CCXXXVIII and CCXXXIX), when compared, for instance, with the *Inferno* of Nardo di Cione in the Strozzi Chapel. Nardo himself was far from being untouched by Sienese influences, but he uses the " receipt " for Dantesque allegory with all the literal subserviency of a minor artist whose chief concern is to show by " documents " that he merits his place in a learned tradition. Bartolo, on the other hand, abounds and superabounds in atrocious inventions and comments; and although his paintings were executed as late as 1393, they teem with the kind of horrors and obscenities to which an artist belonging to some other region of Italy might have given expression a century earlier, and this with an insistence upon naturalistic and sexual allusions to which we shall only find a parallel in the sculptures of certain Indian temples. Folgore's sonnets in praise of luxury and pleasure are seasoned with humour and cheap philosophy. Satirical references to St. Francis, anti-clerical jibes worthy of the local chemist's shop, are scattered through them. Can any trace be found in this picture of sensual life with its hatreds and

19

factions of a graver, more melancholy mood — the mood which springs from satiety and remorse, with that background of sentimentality and vague mysticism which almost always underlies the seeming insatiability of the eroticist and the voluptuary ? In Florence a subject-matter like that of Folgore's sonnets would speedily have been turned into a tale or short story, as being the substance out of which characteristic, clearly defined figures are moulded; but at Siena the same materials were wrought up with a note of festive lyricism into a kind of procession, a burlesque and coloured pageant.

We find ourselves, so to say, in a new abbey of Thélème, capable of being moved, according to the season, from the plain to the hills or along the shore, and frequented by *bourgeois* of middling culture, who rather enjoy an easy ostentation of foreign style. And how easy and innocent it all was we may gather from Folgore's sonnets to the Virtues: they are written with the very ink he used to mix up his curious compounds of legend, epic, and chivalry.

Florence — austere, cold, speculative — was able to elude any inclination towards mysticism and religion in too many ways. The Florentines were too " philosophical " for mystical speculation. Their civilization unfolded itself in the plastic arts no less than in literature with a monumental affirmation of human personality, both in the presence of nature and of religion itself. To this the possible deficiencies of Giotto, and of Masaccio and Michelangelo after him, as religious illustrators are due; but their sense of human personality is overwhelming. Their moulds can only produce images of heroes, and these heroes are fated to withstand the divine. Hence we find in Florence an unwearied interest in science, a vigorous method even in the practice of the arts, precocious humanism, and a passion for the antique. Yet in Florence the antique never became an object of superstition and fetichism, as it did elsewhere. And for the same reason. So too in the plastic arts we find in Florence a tradition prevalently sculptural, chiefly bent upon defining the mass of bodies and their movement,

20

with the exaltation of the human machine and all its energies as its goal, sublimating them until they should transform the world. The robust intellectualism of Florence was founded experimentally upon the observation of the real; but this observation was never self-complacent, nor did it mirror itself in art until an abstract elaboration of its findings had been accomplished. It is on this account that the painting of landscape with a descriptive or merely ornamental significance is rarer in Florence than elsewhere, occurring only in secondary artists.

In Siena, on the contrary, we find a multiform tendency, always at one in its unvarying contrast with the virile Florentine style — a tendency towards the visionary and the fabulous, and directed at times towards minute points of naturalistic curiosity. In the higher forms created by Duccio, Simone, and the Lorenzetti, we have the picturesque suggestiveness of religious narrative, the exalted vehemence of the sacred drama, and human beauty divesting itself of the body in the ecstasy of devotion, until it becomes, as it were, a crystal wherein Divine beauty is discovered, radiating outwards. Then, as those forms decline, we have the fantastic, legendary element, constantly adorning the *genre* inventions of Sassetta and Giovanni di Paolo, and, lastly, landscape — this being not seldom understood in its more elect acceptation as the expression of a certain religious or pseudo-religious wonder exhaling directly upon nature and the spectacle of the world.

\* \* \*

Although we have no intention of reviving old theories concerning " the beautiful in nature " and the " imitation of the real," applying them at this point in a question-begging sense, it is a fact, however, that the natural aspect of the country around Siena, and especially in the narrow triangle of which the angles are represented by Certaldo, Chiusi, and

Montalcino, was not only the most appropriate for receiving the cypher of Byzantine landscape, as this had been handed down by so many examples in Sienese tradition, but was also peculiarly adapted for interpretation by the imaginative spirit and with the spatial sense possessed by these painters of miraculous episodes. How often, as we wander over the *crete* towards Arbia and Asciano, we seem to find ourselves in a landscape by Duccio! There are the same bare, cindery, low hills, stamped with the dark metallic intaglio of leafage and crowned by some stunted tree swaying almost imperceptibly as it crackles amidst the silence of the sky – low hills, eaten away by deep erosions like so many cabalistic diagrams in a geological script.

To avoid all suspicion of forcing description to serve our immediate purpose, we might here quote from the pages that have been dedicated by naturalists – Targione-Tozzetti and Fisher, for example – to this region of mobile ground, " parched and fissured in summer, a vast expanse of viscid slime in winter." " In this strange land, formed out of a labyrinth of low hills and mounds, and furrowed by hollows with muddy streams, vegetation has not time to thrive. Only a few blades of grass spring up on the barren soil, so desolate and constantly shifting, where the landscape acquires a look of unspeakable sterility and dreariness." Small valleys and places of retreat for recollection and solitude make it a diminutive Thebaid (plate CLXI) – hummocks with quaint shapes as of pineapples, prickly like cactuses or actinias – miniature obelisks, prisms, and stones, sharp-edged like knife blades, that break off in flakes and fall to the bottom of the valleys spotted with greenish mould. The suggestion of a skeleton-nature is heightened by the contrast between the black of the trees and the livid hue of the ground, and by the strange patterns traced by shrubs and lichens. It is a scene for witchcraft and penitence, a haunt for supernatural visions appearing in an elemental landscape penetrated by a strange power of hallucination. Not to mention Duccio, who has inlaid this landscape in his Byzantine gold and enamelled it with greens as vivid as that of the *cetonia* and with deep mysterious blacks, observe the effects achieved by Simone in his *Guidoriccio* (plate CXIX), by Giovanni di Paolo in his *Madonna* (plate CCLII), and by Sassetta in the two episodes from the *Legend of St. Anthony the Abbot* (plates CCL and CCLI). The landscape of the Lorenzetti is perhaps less characteristic and follows these forms less frequently; but in the above-named artists, in whom the correspondence is closer, even the intonation of colour is attuned to the scene. If this is not always quite so noticeable in Duccio, bound as he was to an abstract conception of colour and with his pictorial vision fixed in paint exalted to the preciousness of jewels, in the others we notice at once the greens, now pale, now vivid, the yellowish grey, the silver, the dove-grey and subtle violets that mark the living landscape. Giovanni di Paolo, in the predella of the *Legends of the Virgin and San Galgano* (Accademia of Siena, n. 198), has created some of the most remarkable examples, giving them all the transparency of an aquamarine gem – landscapes of a chalky substance, white and grey, with streams in the distance and calmly undulating torrent-beds disposed for the walks and meditation of his patriarchal saints. He is never more pleased than when he can mark one side of the picture with a spiral or fan-shaped shell, such as are turned up every day in these Pliocene beds at the first touch of the spade. Ashen clay, amaranthine willows, green grass – what more or better could we desire in order to recall the palette of Neroccio di Landi or of Matteo ?

\* \* \*

The foregoing attempt at a rapid characterization of religious, literary, and natural conditions may serve to convey something of the Sienese mood and its tastes, and, as we have seen, during the greater part of the fourteenth century the

23

condition of the arts at Siena was such as to secure the longest possible continuance, the greatest integrity, for them. Hence Della Valle and Lanzi are guilty of exaggeration when they claim that it was only subsequent to Matteo di Giovanni and Francesco di Giorgio that painting was practised at Siena by other than " national " artists. "There was an enactment," Lanzi writes," to the effect that every stranger who desired to work in Siena should pay a florin and give good and sufficient security, besides, up to the amount of twenty-five *lire*. This stipulation was well thought out. On the one hand, strangers were not excluded – in which case Siena would have incurred the reproach of inhospitality – and, on the other, they were hindered from claiming commissions for paintings in Siena to the prejudice of native artists." According to Della Valle, a somewhat similar provision was in force in order to prevent extraneous professors of philosophy, medicine, and law from establishing themselves at Siena.

Now, while it is true that these measures were dictated by considerations of economic competition, from the point of view of æsthetics, the "safeguard" of the florin and the twenty-five *lire* in no way prevented Matteo di Giovanni or Francesco di Giorgio from borrowing from Castagno, Donatello, Paolo Uccello, Pollaiuolo, Girolamo of Cremona, and Piero della Francesca; and, with all due respect for the Sienese taxes, it is impossible to deny the fact of artistic exchange, even in the case of the painters with whom we are at present concerned. If, speaking generally, the opportunities and efficacy of such exchanges appear to be necessarily greater in our time with its wealth of exhibitions, reviews, and photographs, it may nevertheless be true that the exact contrary was the case in what would be considered the most impervious decades of the fourteenth and early fifteenth centuries, when rarity of opportunities for seeing pictures intensified search and study in a corresponding degree. Difficulties of communication not only heightened curiosity as to what was being done elsewhere, but gave an intense, impassioned poetry to the achievements of culture. Even when journeys were made, it was not always possible to return a second time to re-examine a work so as to understand it in all its bearings; and the necessity of making notes, measurements, and graphical memoranda implied a deepening of observation and an immediate beginning of elaboration and adaptation of the work to individual taste. Nowadays, on the contrary, the very abundance of the facilities offered by art reviews, shows and reproductions, lessens the significance of the relative experience. Our heaps of printed paper and photographs form a kind of disordered emporium or pandects of confusion, whereas then scanty materials, painfully gathered together one by one, constituted for each artist a *Thesaurus* or *Regia Parnassi*, whether destined for his individual use or for transmission from master to pupil. Thus we find Duccio, one of the most traditional painters and the least eager for novelty, studying not only Byzantine models but French miniatures of the twelfth century or, at all events, such art products as had given currency to some of their iconographical discoveries. These reached Siena through the agency of merchants, especially from Provence and Champagne. Moreover, Duccio profited by the inventions and applications thought out by Giovanni Pisano – if, as Sirén observes, the Crucified Christ of Gothic type, with the legs drawn up and the loin-cloth knotted at one side – a type which we find in the central panel of the *Maestà* (plate XXXIX) as well as in the triptych in the Accademia of Siena (Alinari, 36684) – appeared for the first time in the pulpit of Sant'Andrea at Pistoia (1301) and in the pulpit of Pisa. For though the Accademia triptych is assigned, not to Duccio, but to his workshop, the attribution does not alter the fact of the transference and the borrowing of forms. The same arrangement of the legs occurs in the *Crucifix* by the pseudo-Masarello di Gilio, dated 1305 (plate LXIII), and leads us to draw a similar conclusion.

Nevertheless, it is important to remember that the in-

4

dependent existence of the Sienese school, considered as a homogeneous stylistic development – and this alone justifies such a study as we have here undertaken – was at no time compromised, least of all during the first half of the fourteenth century. Its spiritual " constant " remained undestroyed – the force, that is, which results in a coherent æsthetic formula, while it leaves the manifestations of single personalities entirely free. That Byzantine influence played a large part in its first determination we have already seen; and if the results were more efficacious in Siena than elsewhere – than in Apulia, for instance, or in Sicily, or at Florence, though the most choice examples of Byzantine art flowed thither – this was because the climate of fantasy and sentiment was peculiarly favourable to it. Similarity of interests provoked a choice and adaptation of analogous expressive means. But, when we speak of Eastern influence and of Siena as a mystical Eastern island lying in the midst of Tuscan classical tradition, it is well to remember that no worthy art would have been produced in Siena at all, had not that influence been transformed into something both new and native.

With regard to the foundation of fact underlying this relation to the East, in addition to the hints already thrown out in the course of our remarks, we would beg leave to refer the reader, not to the hypotheses framed by modern writers who have taken it up at a more or less great distance of time, but to the words of one of our old scholars – writers who were in no way inclined to repeating fashionable or exotic foibles, but who were animated by the most scrupulous regard for local matters. " The Levant," writes Della Valle, " was to the Crusaders a new world. The milder climate, the advancement of the arts, the study of manuscripts, the exercise of agriculture and trade, all alike tended to soften the manners of the Crusaders, who communicated to their various countries on their return *les débris des sciences et des arts qu'ils trouvèrent dans l'Asie*. With a view to keeping up their intercourse, many of them established themselves in

26

Syria, at Damietta, and elsewhere; and in this way there began a flourishing commerce between East and West which lasted for two centuries. In the thirteenth century, Messer Guido del Palagio (of the family of the lords of Cerreto) with nine hundred crusaders from Siena took an honourable part in the capture of Damietta, while the Salimbeni and other Sienese families distinguished themselves likewise in other crusades. Siena chiefly owed her greatness to this revolution of things. Guido and the other Sienese returned home laden with spoils and fresh knowledge; and painting, sculpture, learning, science, and the arts, all made excellent progress after this epoch."

* * *

All this, however, would have amounted to little, if material relationships had not found support in spiritual analogies. Hegel has touched upon the similarity presented by certain attitudes of the spirit of India – or, more generally, of the East – to the spirit of the Middle Ages; and the subject was taken up and developed by Spaventa in a public lecture, delivered on November 23, 1861, at Naples, as an introduction to his course of philosophy held at that University. I could have wished not to include a page of metaphysics in these notes on art, but it appears to me that the point could with difficulty be expressed and suggested better than in Spaventa's compendious style. " I may," he says, " be mistaken, yet it seems to me that there is the same relation between the mediæval spirit and the new nature – I mean the nature which reached its maturity in scholasticism – as that which may be traced between the Indian spirit and immediate or what I will call " natural " nature. The object is fantastical in India, and it is fantastical in the Middle Ages. In both it is given by the religious representation and inseparable from it; in both you find the same schematism, the same collection of determinations which never really succeed in determining the object as it is presented to the intellect; and in both there is the same confession of the insufficiency of all the categories, and their annihilation in the indeterminate Absolute.''

The oriental and the mediæval spirit, unlike the Greek and the Tuscan classical spirit, were thus incapable of transforming vague, impersonal divinities into an Olympus inhabited by determinate, living individualities. They alternate between an empirical, sensual reality and a completely empty, abstract unity, and the two extremes co-exist in the same consciousness without inter-penetrating or passing beyond the generic abstraction (purely negative in oriental and mediæval religions; ennobled by asceticism and piety in Christianity) which necessarily springs from transcendence.

That Walter Pater was influenced by Hegel, though on a plane nearer to that of art criticism, appears probable; it is certainly remarkable that, writing at a time (1873) when the knowledge of Sienese painting was far less advanced than it is at present, Pater drew a parallel between the Orient and Angelico. To Pater's contemporaries Angelico clearly offered the most characteristic example of an art designed to '' suggest the transcendent.'' The parallel interests us here because it seems to fix a point which arrested Berenson's attention when he attemped to reach a formal theory of pictorial expression, starting from general considerations upon the Orient and mediæval Christianity. His chief effort in this direction will be found in the volume dedicated to Sassetta, for though nine years later, in the *Essays* on Sienese painting (1918), he promised to return to the relations between Sienese art and the extreme East, so far he appears not to have carried out his design.

After various considerations illustrating the tendency of Western art to degenerate into science or to provide a merely empirical transcription of reality, and after pointing out the preponderating share given by it to modelling rather than to line, with the result that it tends towards the architectonic and the monumental, Berenson inquires into the means by which the art of design, whose immediate object is a visible representation, can give us a suggestion of the invisible and express a religious inspiration. Such means, he thinks, would be the following:

1. The use of spatial composition. This was carried to perfection in the Italian tradition by Perugino and Raphael.

2. The avoidance of chiaroscuro and modelling, and the employment of contours alone – by contour being understood not merely lines defining a form, but lines rich in energy and vitality, capable of seizing movement-values suggesting the incorporeal, that is, life set free from matter – something, in short, which approaches the farthest limits of the capacity of visive art to evoke a spiritual reality.

3. A combination of both these expedients of technique, by setting figures suggestive of incorporeal life amidst spatial effects evoking the other world and the infinite. No European school, Berenson continues, has come closer to the oriental schools than the Sienese during the fourteenth century and the early decades of the fifteenth, but the relation between certain tendencies is so mysterious that one single tendency carries with it the complex result of all the rest. " Thus, Sienese design, when it reaches to height of great art, not only tends to avoid modelling in the the round and to procure its effects by pure line, with values of movement alone; tends not only, as follows upon pure line, to flat colours, but – and this is not so easily explained - tends as well towards colour schemes similar to those in use in old Chinese and Japanese art. "

Stated in this way, Berenson's theories may seem somewhat mechanical, and, in any case, they need to be confirmed by an examination of the widely differing and personal quality in the work of each single artist. But, however this may be, Berenson's presentation of the problem of Sienese art in terms of imaginative design must be considered opportune, in so far as it is precisely the failure to value its linear essence which

29

has led to attempts at explaining the natural development of the Sienese school by reference, especially, to the late and extraneous influences of Gothic linealism.

\* \* \*

And now, at last, let us consider in what precisely consisted the new element whereby Duccio transformed the Byzantine tradition and laid the foundation of the Sienese. Vasari, who did not succeed in seeing the *Maestà* – although, as Lusini remarks, down to 1776 it was quite easy to see it in the Cathedral, near the altar of St. Sebastian – Vasari contented himself with repeating Ghiberti's statement that it was a work executed almost in the Greek manner, though with a considerable admixture of modern features. Lanzi merely observes that " Duccio shows Greek influences, but his *Maestà* almost marks an epoch in art." Della Valle, writing in 1782, has considerably more to say, particularly with regard to the *Maestà*. " The manner," he begins, " is that of Guido of Siena " – we cannot blame him for judging the manner of Guido chiefly by his *Madonna* (plate IV) which had been largely repainted by a pupil of Duccio – " the manner is that of Guido of Siena, but now much softened and improved. Some of the countenances are not wanting in grace, though most of them display the trouble and confusion of the age in which they were painted. The limbs have not the dryness that characterizes the Greek manner of those days." He reproves the defects in certain perspectives, but admits that " many modern painters have learned and copied more than one lesson from the compartments of this panel, which was destined to be the rule of art for many years." Again, he praises the scene of *St. Peter's Denial* (plate XXXVII) for the liveliness of the expressions, the *Mitte manum*, and " certain figures of old men with motions full of spirit and great meaning in their eyes and their faces." " Giotto," he says, " certainly never designed feet in this way, nor planted them so well." This last sentence, however, would rather need to be inverted. Selvatico (in 1856) considered Duccio superior to Cimabue and even to Giotto, though only in respect of " the delicacy and grace of the countenances " – a remark which may be interpreted as a faint recognition of Duccio's felicity in illustration. "What truth, what elegance," Selvatico exclaims, "in the countless heads that fill his great panel in the primatial church of Siena! Perhaps Angelico alone has reached such perfection in painting the heads of women."

It is, however, to Schnaase (1876) that the merit of the first penetrating characterization of Duccio's art appears really due. In the *Virgin in Glory* he traces signs of the school of Cimabue, but treated with greater freedom and delicacy. He notices the wrinkled expressiveness in the heads of the old men and the striving after poetical beauty in the faces of the young. He has acute remarks on the finely narrative quality of such scenes as the *Entry into Jerusalem* (plate XXXII), the *Washing of the Feet* (plate XXXIV), and *St. Peter's Denial* (plate XXXVII); and also with regard to certain counterbalancing details, such as the "used up" worldly figures of Herod and Pilate in contrast with the vulgar virulence of the Pharisees and the suavity and submission of Christ, and the apparition of the Angel as opposed to the statuesque group of the *Marys at the Sepulchre* (plate XLV). And, he says, although we have no proof that Duccio drew from the antique, and must rather infer the contrary, the group of the Marys is nevertheless reminiscent of classical sculpture even in the treatment of the drapery. (Here it may be remarked parenthically that we fail to see why Nicola Pisano is allowed, with good proof, to have borrowed from Roman and perhaps from Etruscan sculpture, while these sources should have been closed to Duccio.) Lastly, Schnaase notes the Byzantine influence perceptible in Duccio's colour and composition, without, however, finding in it a sufficient explanation of his originality, when we consider that the *Maestà* gave conclusive expression to the pictorial aspirations of the whole thirteenth century after a slow

process of ripening of which we can only imperfectly reconstruct the various stages. For Duccio achieved an efficacy in
each attitude and gave a new emotion to faces and expressions,
and these qualities are not explained even by attributing them
to naturalistic observation and the study of the real. In conclusion, Schnaase's remarks on the suggestive, mysterious
character of Duccio's landscapes, the setting of his episodes
and so forth – effects obtained by balancing details in composition one against the other with a perfectly harmonious taste
adapted to the expression of religious feeling – seem to anticipate Berenson's theories of spatial composition.

With Schnaase's pages before them, it cannot but appear
strange that some critics should have gone back even beyond
Ghiberti. Pératé, for example, observes that only " *le génie
grec parle dans les petites compositions évangéliques du maître
siennois,*" while Langton Douglas distinguishes a preliminary
Byzantine and a final Gothic manner with a Roman phase
between the two – a distinction which seems to be a rough formula for a process of fermentation carried out not merely
with ingredients of extraneous culture but by the operation
of a far more intimate and vigorous leaven.

A fresh step in the interpretation of Duccio was taken by
Berenson in his *Central Italian Painters* (1897). " A pictorial
dramatist, a Christian Sophocles, somewhat astray in the realm
of painting " – so Berenson describes him – Duccio interpreted the sacred stories with " a simplicity, a clearness, a
completeness " so perfect that even the rudest of his contemporaries could grasp their meaning, and with a sumptuousness
so resplendent as to allow his pictographs to be " offered up as
a sacrifice, along with all the rest of the furnishing and actual
decoration of God's holy house." Nor was he merely "sublime in
his conceptions, deep in feeling, and skilful in transcribing them
in adequate forms "; he " lifted his spectators to his own level
of perception." The versatility of his interpretation found expression equally in the ecstasy of the *Marys at the Sepulchre*
and in the *genre* episode, almost touched with humour, of *St.*

*Peter's Denial*, and to all his subjects he lent varied qualities of grouping, movement, and realization of space. Nevertheless, his excellence in composition depends largely upon the fact that he found ready to his use the motives and feelings of the extraordinary revival of antique art which began at Byzantium in the ninth and lasted on into the thirteenth century. " Duccio, properly regarded, is the last of the great artists of antiquity, in contrast to Giotto, who was first of the moderns. Duccio's motives, types, and attitudes are still the old art-alphabet of Hellas, made cursive and somewhat debased. His old men are the last descendants, in unbroken line, of the Alexandrian philosophers; his angels, of Victories and Genii; his devils, of Silenus. As Giotto compares with Giovanni Pisano, so does Duccio with Giovanni's father, Nicola, only that Duccio was far more subtly antique."

" The last of the great artists of antiquity " – Berenson's formula met with success. Weigelt adopted it almost as it stood; so, too, did Van Marle, though he modified it slightly by calling Duccio the last and greatest of the Italo-Greek artists, the painter in whom Byzantine severity was replaced by a gracious and wholly Italian melancholy. Venturi also employed a similar mode of expression when he declared that " Duccio engemmed the antiquated forms of Byzantine art and gave them Italian beauty." Gielly, who has endeavoured more recently to trace the characteristic principle of this beauty, or, in other words, the motive of Duccio's novelty, thinks that it is to be found in the artist's striving after truth and in his observation of nature – qualities which both enriched his inventions and transformed his technique.

* * *

Such a view seems to agree none too well with Berenson's remarks upon Duccio's fidelity to the motives inherited from Byzantium – a view which has been confirmed in the main by Van Marle's minute researches into Duccio's iconography.

The truth is that as a rule Duccio is more independent than Giotto; but that, like Giotto, he remains substantially traditional. The Pisani, Cavallini, and Taddeo Gaddi made many more innovations in iconography than did Duccio and Giotto (Van Marle), and in not a few instances where Duccio departs from the Byzantine tradition, an Italian version will be found intermediate between that tradition and his own. It is to this Italian version that Duccio attaches himself. The figure of Herod throned among his counsellors in the background of the *Massacre of the Innocents* (plate XXVII) is contrary to the Byzantine tradition, but it had already been introduced by the Pisani at Siena and Pistoia. The *Transfiguration* has a parallel or, most probably, an immediate precedent at Siena in the first compartment of a panel published by Venturi (*Storia*, V, fig. 89). According to Byzantine tradition, the *Marys at the Sepulcre* were two, and not, as in Duccio's painting, three (plates XLV and XLVI), but Duccio's innovation, which, in point of fact, goes beyond the question of number, has antecedents in the *Madonna of Santa Maria Maggiore* at Florence, attributed by Sirén to Coppo di Marcovaldo (Sirén, figs. 85, 86), in a *Crucified Christ* by Barone Berlinghieri, and in other paintings of the Pisan school (Sirén, figs. 22, 50, 54).

Speaking of Duccio's *Temptation* (plate XXXI), Van Marle observes that his Satan betrays Gothic influence, as being represented in diabolic and not, according to the almost invariable Byzantine tradition, in human form. To us, however, the point most worthy of emphasis is rather the infinite discretion shown by Duccio in Gothicizing and Satanizing his Satan, a discretion shown again in the *Descent into Limbo* (plate XLIV), where the demon is a slightly worse edition of the Vatican Pan (Loevy, fig. 282). And here an observation already quoted from Berenson is illuminating. Duccio, Berenson remarks, always made the fullest possible use of Greek materials in expressing the grotesque and the monstrous; his Satan has more of a Silenus than of a devil. If we may conceive – and it is not difficult to do so – a peasant of those days unearthing

34

with his spade some fragment of pottery from the underground
Etruscan burial places in the neighbourhood of Siena and Volterra,
and Duccio having opportunity to study it, it would be impossible to imagine a more successful transposition of a satyr into
Satan than Duccio has effected here. All he needed was to add
a pair of bat-like wings, while retaining the characteristic
compression of the loins in the attitude of the nude form. To
complete the transformation, Duccio has given his figure of
the Tempter an arched horse-tail at the bottom of his spine,
similar to the tails of satyrs playing under pergolas in Hellenic
pottery.

But this is not all. We would not ascribe to definite
Gothic influence even the elements of Gothic architecture, or of
Gothic grafted on to Romanesque, that occur in the scenery and
interiors of the episodes from the life of Christ in Duccio's
*Maestà* – the gateways with their towers and battlements
(plate XXIX), the pointed double windows ornamented with
tracery (plate XXX), the castles and *campanili* grouped together as if in a market-square, and the " baptistery "
(plates XXXI and XXXII). Apart from the constant tendency
to confuse iconographical influence in the raw state with stylistic influence properly so-called, this was a kind of architectonic
background which fell well within the compass of the artist's
natural observation. But there is a further observation to be
made. A painter who really aimed at securing appropriateness
and truth in his subjects would have endeavoured to place the
figure of Christ in the architectural setting of a Roman
colony in the century of Augustus or in the landscape of
Palestine, as these might have been described by returning
merchants and pilgrims. Such preoccupations were happily
unknown to Duccio's time, although, with the help of certain
togas and breastplates, he half-heartedly endeavours to suggest the costumes of the Roman functionary and legionary of
about the year 33 A. D. For Duccio, the life of Christ takes
place in the immediate visible reality of Siena, where architecture itself was in process of change. A devout artist is

naturally disposed to bring the figures of religion into the every-day life beside him; and Sienese painters were bound by law, and, apart from law, by their natural tradition, to "manifest to ignorant folk who know not letters the wonderful works wrought by virtue and by the power of faith." In this way they were obliged to give their visual conceptions a character of the greatest perspicuity, and not lead spectators astray by far-fetched subjects or borrowings of an abstruse kind.

\* \* \*

That the moral qualities and practice of Duccio fully re-sponded to the demands set forth in the Sienese statutes we are assured by Della Valle on the testimony of Mancini. Thus we are told that Duccio " wedded his artistic skill to the Christian piety for which he was so greatly honoured," and that he was " most tenderly affectioned towards his native place, as is shown by the pavement of the Cathedral, for which it is said that he received only a trifling remuneration." Without re-peating from Milanesi and Weigelt all the circumstances that relate to the dates of his various commissions, payments and contracts for paintings on the *cassoni* of the Sienese Mu-nicipal Archives (1278), for the *Madonna* in Santa Maria No-vella at Florence, identified by some writers with the *Rucellai Madonna* (1285), for a panel and predella for the altar in the Casa dei Novi at Siena (1302), and for the great *Maestà* (1308), we may assign Duccio's birth to a date nearer to 1260 than the year 1250, for the later date agrees better with his known status in 1278 when he was still a young painter engaged in trivial tasks. It is well known that the *Maestà*, for which the contract was drawn up in 1308, was finished and placed triumphantly in the Cathedral in 1311. Lastly, the question of the rejected inheritance allows us to date his death somewhere about 1318. Sundry other pieces of information, however, give a bolder light and shade to this picture of the artist's life, apparently so calm and patriarchal. We hear of fines, large and small, which Duccio had to pay: once in 1280, and five times in 1302. On one of these last occasions the fine was inflicted for causing a public disturbance; in the other instances, for debts. The civic authorities, indeed, request the artist's technical opinion, and he is found sitting on the commission appointed to advise the Council; but he refuses to take the oath of obedience to the Captain of the people, he demands payments on account and has to be pressed before he will consign the works for which he has entered into contract, and in a variety of other ways it is clear that he was often in financial straits, although he figures as the owner of a house, and was able to purchase consignments of wine and, later, vineyards.

On account of these incidents Van Marle was led to describe Duccio, in contrast with the respectable figure of Giotto, as a precursor of the Bohemian artists of Montmartre. This is too great a leap; and such it would be even if we contented ourselves with a Montmartre chronologically nearer to Duccio – the Montmartre, shall we say, of Villon? All of Duccio that finds expression in his artistic production, in the recollections – perhaps a trifle optimistic – of Mancini, in his dedication for the Madonna of the *Maestà*, " *sis Duccio vita te quia depinxit ita* " – a ritual dedication, if you will, yet one that seems to vibrate in this second verse with heartfelt emotion – all this leaves the figure of Duccio – not so schematic, indeed, as Mancini would wish, in matters of devotion and civic respectability – but at all events innocent of the charge of dissipation. As we remarked with regard to the poets of Siena, certain outbreaks of temperament, a certain waywardness of conduct and defiance of convention, might well be woven on to the delicate, imaginative disposition that formed the groundwork of the Sienese spirit. In this way the vine-leaves trailing festoon-fashion round the biography of Duccio lend it an added charm; they awaken a memory of the vine growing beside the mast and the rowlocks of the ship in the Greek hymn, and the recollection is accompanied by a sense of rural repose.

\* \* \*

As we should naturally expect, it was through that part of his work which best lent itself to the formation of a canon — the features and gestures of his Madonnas, angels, and prophets - that the influence of Duccio made itself specially felt. All these characteristics are summed up in the painting on the front panel of the *Maestà*. To this theophany and to certain lesser works we propose to return later on when we shall have a more convenient opportunity to consider them in close relationship to the immediate development of the school. Now let us pass at once to the scenes from the lives of Christ and of the Virgin (plates XXIV to LVI), for it was in these that Duccio's genius found its most characteristic expression and was destined to make no further advance.

We have already seen a Sienese precedent for the *Nativity* (cf. plate III), far closer to it, indeed, than the frequently mentioned mosaic in Santa Maria in Trastevere by Cavallini, or the fresco in the upper church of Assisi, or the mosaics of Palermo (Colosanti, *Arte bizantina*, plate 34; Venturi, *Storia*, V, figs. 117, 149), and it is easy to perceive how the scattered elements of tradition have been organised and completed in Duccio's presentation (plate XXV) with a view to securing the result at which the artist and his patrons chiefly aimed — an intense presentation of the sacred events in terms of painting.

The rigid centrality of the Divine Infant is emphasized by the angle of the roof with the star hanging upon it, by the diagram of the sky, and, we would dare to say, by the vivid crescent, more reminiscent of the horns of the moon than of the attributes of the ox. The Madonna surrounds the Child, and the world is inserted round them as if in concentric zones, the stable being enclosed by the rocks, and the rocks by the band of sky. Heavenly and earthly actors have their part in the scene, yet in such a way as not to disturb the warm isolation of the Madonna and her Child; they do not intervene, not even the poor St. Joseph, who sits there, thoughtful, upon a stone outside. The angels gaze at the sky, and a few of them into the stable, greeting the miraculous event with a choral thrill that will be repeated later in the *Crucifixion* (plate XXXIX) in far different tones. The shepherd with the white beard, standing against the lintel, watches a far-away constellation, and against that vertical line his gaze seems directed into infinite distance. Passing over the scene of the women washing the Child, notice the sheep, and compare them, for instance, with the sheep in Giotto's *Sacrifice* and *Vision of St. Joachim.* In Giotto these representatives of nature express no more than the indifference, the listlessness, of nature itself. Some sheep are asleep; others, unmindful of the angelic apparition, crop the grass; and the two rams butting their heads appear to have no other purpose than that of forming a sharp symmetry with the cusp of the kneeling St. Joachim. In the *St. Joachim retiring among the Shepherds* the sheep issue with their wonted indifference from a sort of pen like a hut in a war-zone, following the young men with the osier baskets; a small dog runs to welcome the aged saint, who looks at him good-naturedly yet without conviction. To a Florentine, you would say, a dog is always a dog, and it is nothing more. In Duccio, on the other hand, the flock is gathered together in an unmoving ecstatic group, and seems to be actually intent upon the miraculous event, according to the description of the *Protoevangelium* of St. James – " And behold the sheep that were led to pasture, went not forwards but stood still," and again, " I saw the mouths of the kids at the water, and they drank not." It matters not whether these passages were known to Duccio; he has expressed the amazement of nature at the moment of the miraculous birth, the participation of created things – sentiments, these, touched with Oriental colour. Moreover, Duccio may well have studied the motive of the flock in the pulpit of Siena Cathedral, where the inspiration from the *Protoevangelium* appears certain, though the treatment is more anecdotic. In Nicola's composition, the head of the animal shown looking upwards pierces through it, and so creates an impression far less lively than that of Duccio's white sheep with her muzzle resting against the crib and seemingly trying to get a discreet view of what is going on inside.

In the *Massacre of the Innocents* (plate XXVII), a modified version of the motive of Herod in the pulpit at Pisa (1307), Nicola Pisano's inventions reappear at Siena in the episodes of the women and the murderers, but Duccio's composition has greater freedom and clearness, and is less broken up by dramatic gestures. On the faces of the mothers we can see already the characteristic *rictus* which will be carried to spasmodic intensity later on by Pietro Lorenzetti. In contrast with Nicola Pisano's treatment, however, we may note a less pronounced " rotundity " in Duccio's presentation of the Roman accoutrement worn by the executioners. In the scene of *Christ disputing with the Doctors* (plate XXVIII), the winged and naked marble *amorini* set in the niches above the columns are a forcible reminder of classical antiquity. There is no need for us to repeat Berenson's observations upon this scene, in which the domestic anxiety felt by Joseph and Mary loses none of its evidence by being kept subordinate and to one side. In the *Woman of Samaria* (plate XXIX) and *Christ on the Way to Emmaus* (plates L and LI), the chief suggestiveness of the scenes arises from the vast space behind the figures — legendary horizons, whose silent solitude is heightened by their contrast with the city pavement, worn smooth and polished by the passing of many feet.

The *Entry into Jerusalem* (plate XXXII) was destined by its wealth of incident and movement and by the novelty of its landscape to linger in Sienese tradition as a success often rivalled but never surpassed. Notwithstanding all the help he could borrow from the expressionism of the Lorenzetti and from his own taste for vehement, eloquent action, Barna could add nothing to this scene, not even in his handling of the animal part of it, although this was one of the effects in which popular

opinion always held him specialized. And in spite of all its
grandiose qualities, Giotto's interpretation at Padua remains
scanty and evasive. Giotto gives us a scene of private homage,
not, as here, the exultant joy of a city, manifested in the complex yet perfectly clear rhythms of the crowd – the disciples
marching in a serried platoon, the boys with olive-branches
running ahead like outriders and colliding with the crowd of
citizens who have come to the city gates. In Giotto's fresco
the towers are deserted, and the city is shut up in itself, aloof
and almost hostile. Duccio, on the contrary, with his incidents of the spectators and the curious lookers-on, has created
the illusion of an entire city shouting " Hosannah ! " The
movement spreads to the neighbouring streets and round
about the baptistery-shaped ascent. It has been already remarked by Berenson how by means of the perspective of the
walls and the half-opened door in the foreground the artist has
compelled us to take a fixed position as spectators of the scene,
thus intensifying our share in the effects of space and movement
by making us consciously attentive to them.

The *Healing of the Blind Man*, the *Washing of the Feet*
(plate XXXIV) and the *Seizure of Christ* (plate XXXVI) present other group-scenes, each of which, in spite of the artist's
insistence upon them, is individualized without any danger of
falling into the commonplace, owing to their being almost
always rendered with a sweeping general impulse of wonder,
grief, fear, or the like. Last of all, in the *Crucifixion* (plates
XXXIX to XLI), we have a sublime scene of counterposi-
tions, from the group of the women to the group of the Jews.
The cut of the ground, marked by the fissured rocks of the
*mons scissus*, accentuates the suggestion of upheaval and
landslide – if the expression may be allowed – conveyed by the
gesticulating mass of soldiers and elders, one of the last of
whom, in the right-hand corner of the painting, has fallen
to the ground, while a second figure, moving backwards, leans
over him. If anything in painting could suggest conviction –
the wavering conviction of the accusers and the ministers of

justice – and the sense of baffled hatred penetrating that conviction, Duccio has found the most striking expressions to render it here. On the opposing side stand the group of women – homogeneous forms, almost identical in the similarity of their head-dress and their bearing, like a rudimentary Church cemented by the vision of the Divine suffering. The figure of John – calm, Roman, monumental – so different from the melo-dramatic figures of the Evangelist scattered throughout the entire history of painting – reminds the spectator of a shepherd protecting a terrified flock and making no display. The column of his body, firm and sure, is like a bastion shutting out the vile populace of sophists and executioners whom we see cursing and accusing each other. And the tumult of the angels' wings engarlanded about the Cross unites the earthly drama to the drama of heaven.

We have purposely insisted here upon the intensity with which Duccio seizes the significant features of a scene and gives them pictorial expression, because Van Marle has recently represented the artist's gift as consisting chiefly in his skill in ornamenting and almost in illuminating the sacred texts rather than in telling their story. Duccio is not, perhaps, so highly endowed with dramatic sense as Giotto and Pietro Lorenzetti, but he yields to none in his delicate subtlety of interpretation, in the limpidity and the linking together of his various motives. If we had space enough at our disposal, we might easily prove the truth of our assertion by analysing the passages from one situation or mood to another, the complex gradation of the figures and the architectonic environment in the ten compartments describing the journeyings of Christ from Annas to Caiaphas, to Pilate, to Herod, and back to Pilate once more. In this last episode (plate XXXVIII), where we see Christ on the point of being handed over to the executioners, the meek, solemn figure under the ironical gaze of the soldiers of the guard stands out with the same vivid whiteness that, two centuries later, will gleam against a darker zone of shadow in Tintoretto's *Ecce Homo*.

But there is little, even in Duccio's repertory, that for narrative point can surpass the scene of *St. Peter's First Denial* (plate XXXVII). St. Peter denies with a certain emphasis, stretching his feet out towards the fire with a marked interest, as though by exaggerating the act he would invite the company not to disturb him and to desist from further questions. The woman, shown from behind in the act of stopping for a moment, interrogates Peter with the air of one who is certain about what she is saying, and expects that he will answer with a lie. Notice the hand already laid upon the banister of the stair: it is in itself the complete expression of the movement of a person quitting the scene in order to go about her business: if I were not afraid of appearing too subtle, I would say that the very apron rolled up round her waist indicates the woman's bustling haste to get back to her pots and pans. The perspective of the arm and the banister is at fault, yet the efficacy of the gesture is so great that we hardly perceive the error, and when we do, it in no way disturbs us. In this way a breath of comedy enters into the tragic event. In the panel – divided into two sections – of the *Third Denial*, while the soldiers buffet the blindfolded Christ, St. Peter is standing outside the door and the bystanders press him again: " Surely thou art one of them, for thy speech betrays thee." He hears the cock crow directly above his head, and the cock is exhibited, as if on an ensign, among the instruments and emblems of the Passion now hastening to its end.

A minute illustration of the appropriateness of the means employed by Duccio in representing the second narrative would keep us for too many pages bound to the *Maestà*, but we may point out in particular the following – the rigorous symmetry of the doubting Thomas, intended to concentrate attention upon the figure of Christ Who raises His right hand above His head as He uncovers His side, so that the figure acquires greater dimensions thereby; and in the *Prayer in the Garden* (plate XXXV), not only the group of the sleeping disciples and the spatial motives intensified by the blazonry of the trees on the luminous bareness of the background, but the way in which the figure of the praying Christ is inserted in a kind of niche formed by the ground – a vivid symbol of the essence of prayer, even divine, as involving the annulment of the individual and creating union with and adhesion to the transcendent; and, lastly, how the two trees standing in the foreground in front of the rocky niche with the kneeling figure, and the third tree placed above them and continuing the perpendicular of one of them, serve to isolate the scene and almost create the effect of flowers or palms set before a figure on an altar.

In the *Seizure of Christ* (plate XXXVI), as Berenson has pointed out, the middle tree has the function of marking and heightening the figure of the Redeemer hemmed in by the crowd – a like function being assigned to the cusp of rock behind the angel in the *Marys at the Sepulchre* (plate XLV). Berenson has further drawn attention to the glamour of beauty in the forest of parallel lines described by the lances and the staves of the torches against the sky, lines which themselves convey the sense of a multitude running up, as in the Pompeian mosaic of the Battle of Alexander. No less admirable to my mind is the rhythm of the diagonal fissures in the ground, accompanying the oblique, compact flight of the disciples, like waves of a movement retiring into the distance. In the *Deposition* (plate XLII) the artist was less successful. So far as we can judge from the painting in its now seriously damaged state, the arrangement adopted in the work-shop triptych belonging to the Accademia of Siena (Alinari, 36683, 36684) in which Joseph of Arimathea slides the body vertically down the Wood of the Cross, was one better suited to the grouping in a scene where the emphasis is on the vehement gesture of the Mother stretching out her hands to support the head of the dead Redeemer. The version in the *Maestà* is lacking in weight; the actions, deprived of their necessary contrasts, are left empty, and the whole scene is weakened by tears and grimaces.

According to Weigelt, the hands of pupils may be detected

in a few panels of the *Maestà* which narrate scenes from the life of the Madonna, and their inferiority has been recognized also by Van Marle. Take, for instance, the landscape in the *Burial of the Virgin* (plate LVI), and compare it with the landscapes we have already noticed. You are at once struck by a certain want of decision in the conception and by an excess in ornament and incident which may well be explained by the intervention of assistants. But without lingering over these details, it is more important for us to make one or two further remarks upon a few of Duccio's paintings of greater moment, and then pass on to speak particularly of his colour.

*  *  *

Turning first to Duccio's choice of episodes from Sacred Scripture and his tendency to give special relief to situations not frequently portrayed and in some instances decidedly rare – the episodes of the *Healing of the Blind Man*, the *Woman of Samaria*, *St. Peter's Denial*, and some others – we must not suppose that incidents like these represented the preferences of the Byzantine tradition; on the contrary, they are the situations in which the artist has shown the greatest freedom of invention. Rescued, as we may say, from the scraps of the marvellous story, these scenes were attuned to the idyllic and elegiac intonation, to the dreamy humility assumed by the supernatural in the mind of Duccio. In other words, the conception of the sacred transaction which he had formed was already far removed from to the geometrical, hierarchical, and triumphal conception of the painters of Byzantium. Thus the slight discrepancy of the proportions in the *Nativity*, a discrepancy so faint as to be almost imperceptible, has clearly been designed with a view to accentuating the importance of Mary – an analogous proceeding to that noticeable in the statue of the Virgin in the National Gallery triptych (Van Marle, II, fig. 5). Other instances of ritual indications rather than actual pictorial rea-

lities are the miniature figure held in the Redeemer's arms as
a symbol of the departed soul in the *Death of the Virgin* (plate
LV), and the branch of palm crowned with stars (plate LVI)
The figure of Christ is distinguished by the golden gleam of
His apparel only when introduced as a supernatural apparition (plates XLIV, XLVIII, LII, LIII, LV); as a rule the
linear ornamentation upon the hems of the robes of Christ
(plates XXXI, XXXII, XXXV, XXXVI) and of the Virgin
(plates XXIV to XXVI) suffices to distinguish these two chief
personages. Attributed to the so-called Gothic influence, this
mode of ornamentation breaks the fall of the drapery in figures
which are really designed with a closer uniformity to examples
taken from " classical " sculpture or from the sculpture
of the Pisani. Affinity to Roman sculpture and to the Hellenistic models continued by it is peculiarly marked in the figures
of Duccio's Prophets (plates XVI, XVII, XXV) and in the
greybeards who frequently appear in the various panels of
the *Maestà*. The handling of the curls in hair and beards is,
however, more dry, and the angles of the draperies are frequently more acute. As Duccio's anxiety to underline states of
feeling leads him to emphasize wrinkles and the curves of lips,
it would be interesting to discover the reason why he has given
many of his countenances that kind of flat-nosed, Socratic
appearance which was destined to re-appear in Pietro Lorenzetti and his followers as a definitely plebeian characteristic.
Still more interesting is the question as to how far the directly
Byzantine material which he had before his eyes influenced
Duccio's transformation of Roman and Hellenistic types, and
how far the so-called Ducciesque " realism " played a part
in the process. By " realism " I mean here that observation
of the actual which Gielly, for instance, considers to have been
the fundamental principle underlying the " renovation " accomplished by Duccio's art.

A few examples may serve to make this second question
clear. First of all, you will find in each compartment of the
*Maestà* at least one feature in which observation of real life is

46

attested by lines drawn with a scansion whose intention admits
of no doubt whatsoever – the foot of the Angel of the *Annunciation* (plate XXIV) firmly planted upon the ground; the
gestures, groupings, and perspectives in the *Entry into Jerusalem*
(plate XXXII); the nudes of the *Crucifixion* (plate XXXIX);
those of the *Christ laid in the Sepulchre* (plate XLIII); and
the poor, cured-looking leg which St. Peter holds out with
such shame from under his rags in the *Christ Washing the
Disciples' Feet* (plate XXXIV). This last instance by itself would
make all need of further illustration superfluous. On the other
hand, it is not less characteristic of Duccio that in certain other
details he will renounce all pretension to realism – *e. g.* the
conventional and approximative drawing of certain hands like
those of St. Catherine (plate XXII), and the unsteady balance
of many of his figures, so that in more than one scene you have
a sensation of danger, as though the whole construction were
seamed with cracks and had been left unfinished. It is true
that in the general relationship of the masses, the balance of
empty and fully occupied spaces, and the direction of group-
movements, Duccio's composition is always orderly and convincing, but it is internally disturbed by gaps and *hiatus*,
due, it may be, to that very striving after expression which
reaches its climax at points where the artist's observation and
his memory of the real come out most strongly. How are we
to reconcile these apparent contrasts? The answer is, I believe,
this. Duccio's realism in no way formed an organic method;
it was not even an embryonic mode of observation or a considered effort to render the facts which came within its view, as
was possible later for the Florentines, the lesser Sienese painters,
and the Flemings. It was simply a realism superimposed by
way of help or commentary upon an instinctive total vision,
and, as such, it welded itself without difficulty to the ideal
material which had come to light again from the subterranean
tradition, and into which the artist poured without stint his
own inventions, at once so naive and yet immortal.

In this way, Duccio's position closely resembled the position of the Pisani. Think of the *Crucifixion* by Nicola at Siena, with the old woman wiping her eyes; or of his *Paradise*, where the figures looking up to Heaven crowd together with the eager, inquisitive movement of peasants seeing an airship for the first time – and this in a scene requiring the most severe " hieratism." Similarly, in his *Nativity* at Pisa, Giovanni presents us with the motive of the woman touching the water of the basin with her left hand in order to make sure that it will not scald the Child, and with the detail of the she-goat scratching her head with her hind hoof. These and many other similar incidents, indubitably discovered or " controlled " by real life, blend with elements of Roman, Gothic, or other origins; but though the latter may at one moment have been completely absorbed and transformed while at another they remain, so to say, in the raw state, they have, in each case, been touched by the spirit animating the composition as a whole.

Furthermore, this variety is not a composed and intentional variety such as we may find in a tardy eclecticism or in styles already in process of disintegration; it is the multiform gathering together, at a different stage of consciousness, of elements taken from all possible experiences, and restored to health in such of their aspects as might otherwise have seemed wanting in vigour by the harmonizing energy of a new tradition already at the point of birth.

* * *

How greatly this achievement of harmony depended upon Duccio's colour must be obvious to every observer. Perhaps now a little darkened owing to the gums used by the artist in mixing his pigments, as well as dulled by the natural action of time and by subsequent glazing carried out here and there, the general tone of the colour has, nevertheless, still a gorgeous, almost barbaric quality, recalling the colour of Oriental mosaics and miniatures. In the case of Duccio, however, and, perhaps, in considering the work of the whole Sienese school, we must be on our guard against thinking of colour in any definitely structural sense, interpreting it rather as above all else a mode of ornament or of music. From De Grüneisen's remarks upon Duccio's obedience to the canonical, ritual colour of the Byzantines as well as to their iconography in his treatment of the dress and other attributes of the principal figures in these sacred scenes, it would seem that the artist was to some extent forced to compose to obligatory rhymes, although in modulating the various tones within the prescribed mode he had ample scope to allow his most daring personal tastes free play. In the mantles of the *Marys at the Sepulchre* (plate XLV), the scale of violets and reds lends itself perfectly to these musical variations without destroying the framework of the monumental group, though it is true that the Magdalene's red in the *Noli me tangere* (plates XLVIII and XLIX) appears heavy and dry in relation to the surrounding colours. Still, allowing for a slight darkening in the tints and the gold, what delicate, airy modulations there are in all the scenes from the lives of Christ and the Virgin, from the first to the last! What contrasts and passages of intense vividness – scarlets, peacock and emerald greens, silver, blacks, and metallic blues edged with gold! There is an exquisite crudeness and a taste for the unexpected that are truly Oriental – not to speak of panels like the *Crucifixion* (plate XXXIX), where the colour reaches an intense excellence equal to that of the composition itself.

Nor is it true, as is commonly stated – at least it is not true with regard to Duccio – that the gold ground forms " the extreme immobile limit of breathable space," a kind of compact border separating the figures, human and divine, from the universe of the colours. I would prefer to say that the gold is a kind of primordial synthesis of colour – an acute and therefore all the more inarticulate fermentation of the colour pressing and biting round the forms. The gold is a kind of Creation light irradiated by a fine incandescent dust, and in it every defect of aerial and linear perspective is attenuated.

On the other hand, although Duccio's contour can convey
lively notations of movement, and although in several works
– the Madonna with Adoring Franciscans (plate XI), the
Madonna of the Maestà (plate XIV), and the St. Agnes (plates
XXIII and LVII) – it is already drawn and spun like an
expressive material finding its highest meaning in its own modulation, it would be untrue to say that colour intervenes with
the definite function of intensifying or isolating the effect of
arabesque, as it does in Simone Martini. We do, indeed, find
the anticipation of this linear taste in Duccio, but it is instinctive, or at all events, unpremeditated. Thus while Martini will
stretch the rhythm of line to its utmost vibrations and draw
from every motive a series of musical variations, selecting the
colour appropriate to these effects, Duccio's colour keeps very
close in intention to that of the Byzantine and Cosmatesque
workers in mosaic. Apart from the novelty of the dramatic
expression, the Madonna with Adoring Franciscans (1278,
plate XI) affords the best instance of Duccio's closely linked
kinship to Byzantine colour, and at the same time it is an eloquent example of his gains from the work of the miniaturists.
The typical notes of dark blue in the Virgin's robe, the blood-red
of the cushion, and the light violet in the drapery of the Child
are evidences of his relation to Byzantine colouring; the expand-
ed curtain with its pattern of green and white, like majolica,
and the gold fringe, recalls the illuminated work of French
Gothic miniaturists.

\* \* \*

A more complex accent of colour was reached by Duccio
in his Madonna in Glory on the front panel of the Maestà
(plate XIV), where the very size of the figures and their serried
order led him to a less vehement treatment. Here we find him
employing a colouring suffused and harmonized by light and
shade, in order to inlay in the subdued groundwork the great

opals of the faces with their transparent shadows of greenish and
ashen hues. The theophanies of the mosaic workers offered abundant examples of groupings equally majestic, but not so calm. To
gain some idea of the variety of modes accepted almost contemporaneously by Italian art at the dawn of the Renaissance, we
may take the *Paradise* of Nicola Pisano, which Duccio had, we
may say, before his eyes, and from which he may perhaps
have drawn certain hints for the upper rows of angels and
apostles in the *Maestà*. Instead, however, of punctuating his
panel with diagonal gestures or with the twisting and twining
of pagan nudes, Duccio has introduced, upon a motionless,
ecstatic ground of angels and saints, rendered still more motionless by the rigorous symmetry of columns, niches, and haloes,
the broad and tranquil rhythm of the figures as they hasten
on either side to fall upon their knees, and so take up and prolong, almost with the function of a festoon, the gradation of
the throne and the Madonna's mantle. Van Marle has critici-
zed adversely the detail of the ten niches with figures of Apostles, but it rather appears to me that they lighten the mass
which would otherwise have been too densely packed by the
ranks of angels and saints – an effect noticeable in Nicola – and
that they have the further advantage of introducing a vertical
movement which serves to modify and give value to the super-
human stature of the Virgin, at the same time heightening the
delicate episode of the angels leaning upon the back of the
throne and looking on – a conception which had been slowly
matured from Guido to Coppo and to Cimabue, and handed
on from Cimabue to Duccio himself (plates XI and XIII). Tradition affirms that the face of the Madonna was repainted by
Ambrogio Lorenzetti, and De Nicola has suggested that to enjoy
the splendour of this *Madonna in Glory* unimpaired, we should
have to imagine the figure of the Virgin substituted by that of
the *Madonna of Montepulciano*. The uniformity of the various
physiognomies, while it increases the sense of immobility,
ecstasy and rapture, in no way excludes a harmonious liveliness
of expression – in other words, it conveys no suggestion of

abstractedness, but rather that of a sublime kinship realized by the common share in a beatific state, as when St. Augustine speaks of the classical, statuesque beauty that bodies will assume after the Resurrection in the City of God.

The features of the four protectors of Siena – SS. Ansanus and Savinus on the right, the bishop Crescentius and Victor on the left – are more individualized than those of the other figures, as though they were nearer to the human beings for whom they intercede at the heavenly throne. And while Savinus and Ansanus announce the type of Simone's saints, figures of chivalry and romance, St. Agnes and St. Catherine, clad in mantles like empresses of Byzantium, anticipate the saints in the polytych of Pisa, who appear enclosed in a profile of supernatural elegance. Hints of a similar transfiguration occur again in Duccio's *St. Agnes* – a painting at one time held to be contemporary with the *Maestà*, but which betrays evidence of a further degree of formal development and may therefore be regarded as the final expression of Duccio's art (plate LVII).

But it is in the angels of the *Maestà* rather than in these figures of virgins and saints that Duccio seems to have expressed his personal ideal of beauty; and so strong was the enchantment exercised by the type he thus created that few Sienese artists succeeded in freeing themselves from it even after the lapse of many decades. Not to mention less significant artists in whom a literal application of the type was scarcely to be avoided, we meet with it again in Pietro Lorenzetti and his followers at Cortona, Arezzo, and Siena (plates CXLIX, CLII, CLIV), in Lippo Vanni (Van Marle, II, fig. 299), in Paolo di Giovanni Fei, and in others. Only the originality of Simone Martini was able to transform the type almost immediately, or, at all events, after the *Maestà* of 1315, where we find it already greatly modified. The angel of the *Annunciation* plate (XXIV) has, it is true, been likened to the Νίκη Ταχυδρόμος, but the angels of the *Maestà* are compounded of a very different essence from that of rhythmical speed. With their calm light of alabaster tone, these angel faces express a kind of ecstasy arising from delight at what they hear or see, as though they were intent upon solemn music, while their immense eyes, with wide and slightly swollen lids, are fixed upon the vision of the divine. Forms, temples, and cheeks are rounded in gigantic and sumptuous curves, and yet this almost soft serenity has a note of implacability, a suggestion of fate. It is the meeting of a beauty steeped in sentiment, like the impassioned beauty of a woman, with the sovereignty of the angel or the cherub, and creating together a sort of sexless idol. The divine melancholy of adolescence and youth never found expression in a form more simple or more weighted with the memory of distant civilisations and far-away mysteries.

And now, before leaving the *Maestà*, let us return once more, as we promised, to the *Rucellai Madonna* (plates VIII to X). For, if our comparison of the *Rucellai Madonna* with the Madonnas of Cimabue led us, first of all, to think of a Sienese artist enriched by Florentine experiences, we shall find, when we compare the *Rucellai Madonna* with the *Madonna* of the *Maestà* and with other Madonnas by Duccio closely akin to it, that the weight of the scale is by no means in favour of its attribution to Duccio. The attitude of the Child in the *Rucellai Madonna* is indeed almost identical with that of the Child in the *Madonna with Adoring Franciscans* (plate XI), and so are certain details of the throne. The angels in this last panel hold up the drapery exactly as in the *Gualino Madonna* (plate VIII). Moreover, the arrangement of the drapery in the panel with the Franciscans might almost seem to be a simplified version of the drapery in the *Rucellai Madonna*. The same characteristics of Sienese goldsmiths' work are noticeable in the decoration of the dresses and in the haloes ; and even the physiognomy of the Child, with that slight turning-up of the nose, is not unlike in the *Rucellai Madonna* and in the *Maestà*, although traits of this kind are frequently to be be found even in school-products (plate LX), and the Child of the *Maestà* has a more massive look than the Child of the *Rucellai Madonna*. But the treatment of the hair is different:

finely drawn out in the *Rucellai Madonna* ; bolder and more wavy in the *Maestà*, as in almost all the paintings by Duccio. The ear of the Rucellai Child, again, is more curved. But what most of all makes it impossible to fix upon Duccio is the tormented delicacy of the type of the *Rucellai Madonna* – those long, slender, fleshless limbs with their evanescent veils of colour; the extremely light draperies falling in extraordinarily close, capricious, serpentine folds (De Nicola), and the quality of the painting, thin and slight, and without that soft fullness which we noticed in Duccio's faces. On the other hand, it is certain that no artist draws so close to Duccio as the painter of the *Rucellai Madonna* and the Madonnas usually classed with it, not only in certain characteristics of form, but also in the high level of their æsthetic perfection.

\* \* \*

The direct influence of Duccio in Siena and its neighbourhood – by neighbourhood I mean the region towards the Maremma, since the development of painting northwards was less pronounced – extended from 1290 to shortly after 1320. By the second of these dates even the work of minor artists who were more faithful to the formulæ left by Duccio was already penetrated by artistic currents flowing from Simone Martini and Pietro Lorenzetti. That Duccio's authority and prestige did in fact begin to make themselves felt very early is shown by a fact to which we drew attention above. The master of the *Gualino Madonna* and the *Madonna of Mosciano*, who afterwards gave us his masterpiece in the *Rucellai Madonna*, was undoubtedly familiar with Duccio's paintings – a view held by De Nicola and by Toesca – and he had furthermore appropriated elements of the so-called " Gothic linealism " originally elaborated upon a Byzantine basis by Duccio himself.

Within the limits necessarily involved in an *excursus*, we

may class the artists who depend most closely upon Duccio in the following order:

1. Pupils and imitators whose historical names are known – Mino, Masarello, Guarnieri, Giovanni di Duccio – and others whose personality was distinguished by conventional names – the " Master of the Badia at Isola," " the Master of Montalcino," " the Master of Città di Castello " (plates LVIII to LXIII).

2. Ugolino di Neri, commonly known as Ugolino of Siena (plates LXIV to LXVII).

3. " Ugolino Lorenzetti " – to use the designation coined by Berenson to indicate a master formed chiefly under the influence of Ugolino of Siena and Pietro Lorenzetti, and, according to De Nicola, to be identified with Biagio of Siena or Biagio di Masarello, an artist mentioned in documents of 1320 and 1363 and re-baptized by DeWald as the " Master of the Madonna of San Pietro Ovile " (plates LXVIII to LXX).

4. Segna di Buonaventura, who, with his followers, represents the transition of the school from Duccio to Simone Martini (plates LXXI to LXXIII).

To the pupils and imitators of Duccio mentioned in the first group – Mino, Masarello, and the rest – no certain works can be assigned. Even some of the paintings which might with reason be referred to them, as the polyptych reproduced in plate LVIII – especially the central panel – and the *Madonna* reproduced in plate LX, only differ from Duccio's works in being slightly inferior, while they repeat or adapt his schemes and facial types. The *Madonna* of plate LX is in the general effect of the face and the hand closely akin to the *St. Catherine* of the *Maestà* (plate XXII) and to the *Madonna* of the polyptych reproduced in plate LVIII. Van Marle proposes to identify the artist with the unknown restorer of Guido's *Madonna* (plate IV), the panel which gave rise to the prolonged controversy concerning the precedence of Siena over Florence in the revival of painting.

It is not, however, possible for us, in the space at our

disposal, to give even an approximate list of works painted by artists belonging to this group, nor to point out the characteristics by which they might conveniently be divided into either workshop-products or works executed by followers. Our attention is claimed by products of more composite nature and greater originality. In the *Maestà* of the " Master of the Badia at Isola," a painting at San Salvatore di Badia, near Colle, we have a fusing of the Madonna in Duccio's *Maestà* with the *Rucellai Madonna.* Here the elements borrowed from Duccio are associated with a still more archaic feeling in the forms of the Cosmatesque throne, taking us back to Byzantine art at the close of the thirteenth century. The same spirit, with a similar arrangement of the figures and accompanied by an even greater wealth of Ducciesque features, appears in the " Master of Città di Castello "; only here the increased length of the figures, the redundant drapery, and the silhouette of the kneeling Dominican introduce us to characteristics found in the repertory of Ugolino of Siena, while in works of probably late date, like the dossal in the Accademia of Siena (n. 33; reproduced by Van Marle, II, figs. 50, 51), a certain plasticity and a sense of volume are more noticeable and have caused some to think of the influence of Pietro Lorenzetti. It is especially in his expression of plasticity that the "pseudo Maestro Gilio " has affinities with the " Master of Città di Castello," and hence it has been thought that the hand of Pietro Lorenzetti at the early Byzantine phase of his career can be detected in the *Madonna* attributed to the first-named artist (plate LXII).

\* \* \*

The extent to which Ugolino of Siena drew from Duccio is best shown by a simple comparison of Ugolino's *Deposition* (Van Marle, II, fig. 65) with the corresponding panel in Duccio's *Maestà* (plate XLII). Except that the group of the lamenting figures has been slightly thinned out, Ugolino's composition appears at first sight to be a direct copy. Even Duccio's mistakes in perspective are reproduced in Ugolino's version of the Entombment. We may therefore suppose that, like Segna at Massa Marittima, Ugolino had been commissioned to supply the Florentine Church of Santa Croce with an " equivalent " of Duccio's *Maestà*, the fame of which must have spread throughout all Italy. This circumstance, together with the other paintings which Ugolino is known to have executed at Florence, and the activity of Simone Martini at Naples and Assisi, of Barna at Arezzo and Florence, of the Lorenzetti at Arezzo, Cortona, Assisi, Florence, and elsewhere, goes to prove that for the first half of the century, at all events, Siena was able to beat Florentine competition, and sometimes within her very walls.

But while Ugolino kept thus closely to Byzantine and Ducciesque iconography, he introduced new elements of style. Compared with the St. John the Baptist in Duccio's *Maestà*, the figure of this saint in one of the panels of the Santa Croce *pala*, now at Berlin (Van Marle, II, fig. 61), presents a more vigorous, dramatic expression, the facial type being rendered more imperious by the perpendicular line of the nose, which, as again in the St. Francis (plate LXVI), accentuates the curvature of the frowning brow.

In both these figures the limbs and the general bearing tend towards length. Nor does the hand show the somewhat soft and casual tapering of the hands painted by Duccio; the modelling and curves are more skilful, and there is a more exact and telling scansion in the joints of the phalanges. This corresponds to Ugolino's fondness for multiplying linear incidents in the folds and angles of his dresses, while at the same time he endeavours to obtain a vigorous movement beneath their voluminous drapery. In this taste for dramatic movement De Nicola detected the influence of Giovanni Pisano; Berenson, in other respects, that of Pietro Lorenzetti; and as the latest information we possess with regard to Ugolino belongs to 1337, since the *Madonna of San Casciano* (plate LXVII) was painted

after 1335 (De Nicola), we may accept their views. But, assuming
this date to be correct, the small figure of the donor kneeling
at the feet of the monumental Madonna – the " dantino,"
as they call him at San Casciano, from the resemblance to the
figure of Dante – can make no claim to the honour of being
one of the first " portraits " of the Trecento, since, without
going beyond the limits of the Sienese school, Simone's
likeness of Robert of Anjou at Naples is earlier by some fifteen
years. Nevertheless, it is one of the first figures studied from
life, for the modelling of the face is no longer a result of minia-
ture-like outlines but is created by a broad texture of lights
and shadows.

\* \* \*

A careful analysis of the *Nativity* (plate LXVIII) and its
attribution to a painter for whom he invented the name of
" Ugolino Lorenzetti " were the work of Berenson, who performed this task with inimitable industry, isolating Ducciesque
traits in the attitude of the hands of the Madonna, in the trian-
gular opening of the cave, and in the pose and drapery of St.
Joseph (*cf.* plate XXV); elements borrowed from Lorenzetti
in the angels and in the slender columns, floreated capitals
and leafy cornices; and, lastly, a vivacity of movement in the
figure of the shepherd, recalling a romantic painter of two
centuries later – Lorenzo Monaco.

As a result of the efforts of Perkins (1913), Berenson (1917)
and De Nicola, who has accepted Berenson's argument, various
paintings have gradually come to be attributed to this supposi-
titious " Ugolino." DeWald, on the other hand, has attempted a
more complex exposition of the question. Among the more
important of these paintings which had never found a convincing attribution, but which fit in fairly well with the characteristics and influences alluded to above, are the following: the
so-called Triptych of Fogliano with SS. Ansano and Gal-

58

gano (plate LXIX) appearing in the guise of youthful warriors and rustically pompous in their martial attire; a *Crucifixion* in the Louvre (Berenson, *Essays*, fig. 11), and a second *Crucifixion* in the Berenson Collection, slightly earlier than the Fogliano Triptych, which is usually dated about 1325 (plate LXX). The artist's derivation from Duccio is best seen, however, in two polyptychs: the first in Santa Croce at Florence and the second formerly in Sant'Agostino at San Gimignano (Berenson, *Essays*, figs. 6, 8). None of these works, it is true, comes up to the *Nativity* in artistic merit, but the latter painting alone is probably sufficient to place " Ugolino," as Berenson observes, on the same level as Lippo Memmi, even though his standard of execution varies and betrays a propensity towards experiment. On the whole, the list of works attributed to " Ugolino " after expert scrutiny seems to point to an artist who started from Duccio and aimed straight at Bartolo di Fredi or, at all events, in the direction of Barna, while he remained strangely insensible to the influence of Simone Martini. This is the more surprising as about the year 1335 – the date assigned by Berenson to the *Nativity* – we should have expected to find Martini's influence far stronger than that of the Lorenzetti. " Ugolino " adapts elements borrowed from the Lorenzetti to the Ducciesque scheme, adding, however, a certain suggestion of archaic, popular art, which never failed to arouse interest at Siena and reappeared at the very end of the century in Bartolo and Taddeo.

* * *

Segna di Buonaventura was an artist of a less rare species. Traces of his life and work are to be found in documents between 1298 and 1326. At times he has even been mistaken for Duccio, as in the *Crucifixion* of the Crawford Collection (plate LXXI), but only for Duccio in his workaday, mechanical hours. Even a hurried comparison with the *Crucifixion* in Duc-

59

cio's *Maestà* (plate XXXIX) will show how weakly Segna has here interpreted his master's motives, in spite of certain feeble attempts to secure variety, as, for example, in his figure of the Magdalene with her arms raised – though this, too, may be merely a memory of Assisi.

A still more striking testimony to Segna's faithfulness to Duccio will be found in what De Nicola has called his " free copy " of parts of the *Maestà* – a work executed for the Cathedral of Massa Marittima somewhere about 1316 and now reduced to a pitiable state. Here the deformation of the figures in the sense of length shows that Segna was not unacquainted with Ugolino di Neri, though he has none of the gloomy, angular vividness of the latter, being rather lifeless and methodical, and displaying the monotonous correctness of a conscientious workman. In the numerous *Madonnas* and *Crucified Christs* turned out by Segna and by his sons Niccolò and Francesco as well as by other members of his school, the use of formulæ is constantly repeated: some are borrowed from the *Maestà*; others recall the *Rucellai Madonna*; others, again, are best summed up in Ugolino's *Madonna of San Casciano* (plate LXVII), as, for example, the arrangement of the kneeling donors; and, lastly, there is the type of the *Crucified Christ* (plate LXIII). This process continued right up to the first contamination of these surviving mannerisms, as we may term them, by the new modes introduced by Simone Martini – modes which copyists gladly welcomed and applied in a vulga rendering (Van Marle, II, fig. 105), with a facility that corresponded exactly to their own want of dramatic sense and originality.

A passing reference might be made at this point to the rapid spread of the Sienese tradition to Perugia, where it is represented by the artist who painted the *Madonna* in the Art Gallery and the *Maestà delle volte* (Venturi, *Storia*, V, figs. 31, 32), and, later, by Meo di Guido; but we prefer to leave the crowd of lesser *epigoni* on one side and take a better leave of Duccio's art.

\* \* \*

In adopting the language of Byzantium, the classical language of universal Christian art, in order to transform it, Duccio really seemed to have discovered a vein of native *graecitas*. In other and greater artists, the materials of a visualised narrative which had become invested with a ritual character were either wrought up into a religious and civic monument, or else, as in Giotto, welded into a kind of dramatic synthesis. Duccio, by a natural instinct to which we owe the intensest productions of his art, seized legend afresh in the very act of its formation, in a reality wherein every element of court gesture and worn out elegance was purged and restored to a primordial intonation.

It is as though he were giving expression to an age of shepherd or sea-faring kings, at a time when little cities were building upon hills lately shorn of their forests, with the sound of the scalpel ringing in the clear morning, and with the gods still walking through the world. Image of the beginnings of society under placid laws, there breathes through Duccio's work the perfume of a time of renewal. And hence it is that in Duccio's narrative the life of Christ seems like the unconscious upspringing of a myth in a popular, domestic environment – a myth laden with tenderness and fantastic, cherished in the midst of a brotherhood, of which the members are all known amongst themselves, each trusting the other and giving mutual support to their moods, their imaginings, and their dreams. It is the kind of environment described by Renan in the first chapters of the *Apôtres* or in his account of the Mediterranean journeys of St. Paul, and closely akin in spirit to the dawn of the Renaissance in the springtime of the Franciscan movement: *Depuis les poèmes homériques, on n'avait pas vu d'œuvre pleine de sensations aussi fraîches. Une brise matinale, une odeur de mer, si j'ose le dire, inspirant quelque chose d'allègre et de fort.''* With some slight modifications, these words might be applied to Duccio. There is in the deep breath, the oriental suggestion, of his painting, a sense of sails spread out to the wind, of journeyings by sea, of calm havens lying below little settlements, at once citadels of the faith and schools of art.

Duccio's painting has its splendid moments when his inspiration touches more moving themes – the *Christ and the Woman of Samaria* (plate XXIX), the *Crucifixion* (plate XXXIX), or the familiar appearances of the Risen Saviour while the disciples were still in hiding or scattered abroad. In the *Christ on the way to Emmaus* (plates L and LI) this Greco-antique illusion, as we may call it, is strangely intense. The wayfarer clad in goat-skin with the wide hat seems a figure taken from some rustic description, and recalls the scene of Ismene approaching Œdipus and Antigone in the Sophoclean drama; while the disciple pointing to the gate of the silent city against the golden background of the sky at sunset will awaken the poesy of the episode for all time, lending it a sweet and suggestive irrefutability that no other celebration of Emmaus in the painting of centuries has equalled.

\* \* \*

Almost eighty years had to pass after Giotto's death before artists like Masaccio and Angelico made their appearance in the Florentine school, and even then they failed to reach the importance and the greatness of Giotto. In the meantime, apart from the fact that many Sienese painters – Ugolino, Martini, Barna, the two Lorenzetti – were summoned thither, the influence of Sienese painting upon the painting of Florence can be clearly seen. It should not, indeed, be exaggerated, but it is undeniable. After a first more purely Giottesque phase, Bernardo Daddi arrived at Florence in time to apply certain characteristics of form and the most recent developments in colour reached by Ambrogio Lorenzetti. In Nardo di Cione Sienese influence is less pronounced but still unmistakable; nor is it without significance that not merely old Vasari, but a student like Della Valle, even though his artistic sense may at times leave something to be desired, attributed to Simone the frescoes painted by Andrea of Florence in the Cappella degli Spagnoli. Cavalcaselle, however, has attributed them to Lippo Memmi – that is, to an orthodox follower of Martini – working in collaboration with Andrea of Florence and lesser Sienese artists. So clearly predominant in these frescoes appeared the characteristics of Sienese colour and the Sienese gift for illustration, however clumsily applied.

At Siena the place left vacant by Duccio was at once taken by an artist in no way inferior. Already at the time of the Master's death the *Maestà* of Simone Martini (1315) was there to prove that Duccio's artistic heritage had been gathered and was being administered to advantage. We say "heritage" from the habit of linking up artistic facts, but in reality it would be impossible to conceive a more complete break than occurred at the very outset of Simone's career, in spite of the fact that the natural coherence of the school remained intact. Pietro Lorenzetti, who was practically contemporary with Simone and had served the same apprenticeship, restless by temperament and naturally inclined towards daring expressions, shows himself faithful to Duccio – not, indeed, in his *Madonna* in the Collegiate Church of Casole, a work more Byzantine than any by Duccio (De Nicola), but certainly at Cortona and at Arezzo (1320) – and this after fifteen years at least of artistic activity. Simone, on the contrary, calm, self-assured, elegant in his profound novelty, freed himself from the fetters of his school-training almost without our perceiving how he accomplished it, and suddenly appears before us completely formed.

The Vatican *Saviour* (plate LXXXI), which some critics consider with good reason to be the first work by Simone which has come down to us, clearly continues the type of Duccio's Christ, as is shown by the joining together of the eyebrows by a thin line of downy hairs. Further reminiscences of Duccio occur in the St. John, St. Agnes, St. Peter, and in other saints of Simone's *Maestà* (plate LXXV), as well as in the angel bearing a lily. Some figures, however, are entirely changed. It is, nevertheless, true that frequent partial restorations have caused a general deterioration of the *Maestà* and render such comparisons only possible within certain limits. In the same way, the colour, in spite of a prevailing airiness and solemnity of tone in its tints of shaded rose and faded blue, and in the worn, sombre mantle of the Virgin, is now no more that a pale reflection of its former beauty. Where the testimony of Simone's *Maestà* is valuable is, above all, in the arrangement, and this betrays at once the difference between his taste and that of Duccio. Instead of a throne conceived in a modified Romanesque style, Simone gives us a throne with pointed gables and fretted tracery suggesting the windows of a Gothic cathedral; and the motive of the niches with figures of Apostles, which crowned Duccio's composition, is now replaced by a grandiose canopy, red, black, and white, with ribbons streaming like oriflammes, while the Apostles themselves have come down to take an actual part, as Van Marle remarks, in the act of homage. Notice also how the Madonna and the two female saints nearest the throne are crowned with diadems passing over their foreheads and giving an effect of lowness as in French sculptures and in those of Giovanni Pisano. The division of the folds of drapery, again, especially in the mantle of the Madonna, is carried out with an intuition so complex and so mature as to have no relation to the marginal arabesques of the mantle of Duccio's Madonna; and the motive of the offering of flowers (plate LXXX) is entirely new. Furthermore, though it has been argued that in its present state the *Maestà* is merely a precious worn-out tapestry, concerning the full pictorial reality of which we can at best form vague conjectures, still, apart from the novel beauty of the facial types – particularly those of the female figures (plates LXXVII to LXXIX) – enough is left for us to perceive the precision of the means employed by Simone in its structure. As an instance of our meaning, we may point to his placing along a vertical line the slightly bent head of the

Virgin, her hand, her column-shaped knee, and the upright Child;
thus creating an effect of severe frontality which is at the same
time secretly diversified and dissimulated. A similar arrangement
will, it is true, be found in Duccio, but in him it is less deliberate and sure. And when Lippo Memmi and his father repeated
the same motive in the *Maestà* of San Gimignano, (plate LXXIV),
their excessive insistence upon Simone's expedient only re-
sulted in stiffness, and the sumptuous architecture of folds about
the knee of Simone's Madonna became in Lippo's fresco — and
we say it without in any way forgetting its considerable merits —
the trumpet of a phonograph with its mouth resting upon
the ground.

* * *

There is a tendency to exaggerate the importance of the
Gothic factor in Simone, and even to antedate its manife-
station, no less than the Byzantine element in Duccio. It is
clear that when cultural influence of this kind is an established fact — it matters not whether the influence be Gothic
or Byzantine or any other — our attention ought chiefly to
be directed towards understanding the individual characteristics whereby the artist has given concrete expression to his
own particular " Gothicism " or " Orientalism," as the case
may be, and towards distinguishing the several works in
which these personal characteristics appear. The painting of
*St. Louis crowning Robert of Anjou* (plates LXXXII and
LXXXIII) will serve to illustrate the point we wish to make.
Van Marle, while fully recognizing the famous curves at the
borders of the drapery, is nevertheless unable to pronounce
the painting typically Gothic. This hesitation does honour
to Van Marle's taste, but it leaves altogether unexplained the
perplexity he feels in not being content to regard the painting
as purely and simply "Martinian." Had he viewed it in this
way, he would have had no need to create the entirely non-

existent problem of a conflict between Byzantine and Western modes in this first period of Simone's activity, and a consequent triumph of the former a few years later in the polyptych of Pisa (1320), a painting which Van Marle calls Ducciesque, though in reality it is not so. We have already attempted to show why it is not possible to speak of a contrast between the Oriental Byzantine position and the Mediæval Gothic position, but only of a difference in their respective points of view; and so it follows that there can be no necessary contradiction between the two corresponding categories of style. Art grew up at Siena amid the riches of both these civilizations. Crusaders and merchants brought the oriental heritage to Siena and kept it alive there; traders, æsthetes, wealthy amateurs, and scholars welcomed to Siena the inventions of French culture and sent into France the products of local art in exchange.

When Aldobrandini of Siena, a physician who practised at the Court of Provence, died at Troyes, his manuscripts passed to the Library of the Arsenal at Paris. Folgore, Siena's lettered buffoon, celebrated the exquisites who adopted French usages and manners. Stage inventions taken from French mystery-plays were copied in Sienese popular drama. The Court of Naples, to which Martini was summoned and where knighthood was conferred upon him, was a French Court. Robert of Anjou, when he visited Siena, was received with the greatest honours imaginable. If it is impossible for us to determine the extent to which Simone – an artist so refined and rich in reflexes, and the representative of the most lucid and settled phase of stylistic consciousness reached by art in Siena, and, it may be, beyond it, during the fourteenth century – may have been influenced by Gothic culture through suggestions conveyed directly by miniatures, ivories, statues, costumes, and so forth, this at least we may unhesitatingly affirm, that not for one single instant can we possibly be tempted to mistake the spirit and the forms of Simone's art when it presents itself unimpaired and living, for the spirit and forms of Gothic art. Only at a very late date and, especially, after

Simone's journey to Avignon – in the *Annunciation* and in parts of the Antwerp Polyptych – do we find traces of a certain harshness due to the presence of elements not completely absorbed; and then we are in the period of his decline, the period when Pietro Lorenzetti influenced Simone's art to an equal degree with Gothic. In æsthetic appraisement, indeed, we must be ever on our guard against confusing the traces or *scoriae* of culture with genuine creative qualities. For if we allow ourselves to indulge in experiments of æsthetic chemistry, we shall constantly find ourselves bewildered by discovering that a painting which exhibits signs of Gothic quality is not Gothic after all, as when the torso of a young Indian ascetic or a profile from a Persian miniature comes unexpectedly before us, framed in the curves and flourishes of so-called Gothic linealism and adorned with the lilies of France (plate LXXXIII).

To the victory thus won by Simone in uniting two of the chief currents in æsthetics and culture in that age, welding them together in a new and Italian pictorial reality – the victory won by the knight Simone, friend of French kings and of popes living in exile upon French soil – we might perhaps find an historical parallel in the enterprise to which the Western Church addressed herself in order to assert her position against Byzantium. It was through France, whom she had instituted the ideal heir of the Roman Empire, that the Church aimed at wresting from the Orient the last treasures of Hellenic learning and beauty by the exploits of the Crusades. Such a parallel would enable us to establish further points of contact and opposition between the mediæval spirit – the spirit of chivalry – and the Byzantine, Oriental spirit; but, as it would only prolong under another form and with great risk of complications the chemical experiments to which we alluded, we prefer to limit ourselves strictly to the sphere of figurative comparisons. Returning, then, to Duccio, we notice how he transfused into the iconography and colour of the Byzantines the spirit of the new religious and communal civilization.

It was characteristic of this spirit that it read and interpreted the forms of Byzantium in exactly the same way as contemporary writers in the vernacular – the authors of the *Novellino*, for instance, or the *Fatti di Enea*, – read and interpreted the histories of the ancient "knights," the heirs of Troy and founders of Rome. In this way, Duccio succeeded in creating a popular idiom out of a choice vocabulary of words heavily weighted with science and æstheticism. With Simone began the organization of this idiom, its transference to a plane of consciousness and coherence, its development into syntax and poetics, its transformation into a learned tongue. And hence at first sight there appears to be an impoverishment in Martini's subject-matter, the impoverishment which always accompanies the change from naive to controlled and reflex forms. In the first place, his "narrative field" is obviously more limited than that of Duccio. Even when Simone lays himself out to narrate – for example, in the chapel of San Martino or in the Naples predella (plates LXXXIV and LXXXV) – you feel that he is not carried away by the event, like a painter of epic or drama, who, in giving you the episode as it actually happens and while it happens, hardly allows you to perceive that he is selecting and isolating a particular episode. Simone's procedure is different. He gathers up the sense of each event in an ecstatic appearance, after first carefully removing every element not wholly in accord with his calm sublimity of tone; and the result is a diagram of resplendent symmetries. Simone is a lyrical poet and a poet of learned lyric. It was his mission to set the new tradition in comely order and to fit it to a limited number of sentiments and modes of expression.

In this point of view we might make use of the parallel which has been drawn in every age between Simone and Petrarch. Their mutual friendship, the portrait of Laura, the distich written in Petrarch's own hand below the miniature painted by Simone – all these seemingly give colour and support to the comparison. Martini and Petrarch were both artists of great mastery. They were both stylists rather than creators; both were inspired by a desire to imagine angelic forms; both were in touch with French culture; and they were both, we may add, artists who exercis ed an incalculable influence upon European art in all its manifestations at a decisive moment of its formation. But in all else it is impossible to conceive two temperaments more completely at variance. You have Petrarch with his crystalline style: restless, unstable, rippled with contradictions, tumid with sighs; Simone detached and secure in his lofty melancholy. Few artists have equalled Simone in plunging their visions into intimate and burning sentiment; and even among those who were naturally drawn towards expression, few have been able to render, as he and some modern painters have done, what may be called the sense of their own relation to that expression itself. Yet this, too, was accomplished by Simone in a way so impassible that he seems to engrave with a diamond point some truth of science – a mathematical relation or the parabola of a star.

\* \* \*

Line was the essential element whereby Simone achieved the miracle of these transfigurations; and line was the principle of the lyrical, rhythmical order which he introduced into the Byzantine treatment of colour. As music develops and contains the colour of sounds in lines of movement sometimes reaching a vividness that can evoke real plastic gestures, so the rise and fall of line has in Simone something of the quality of a musical subject translated into visive terms. For, not only does Simone's line unwind itself so as to delimit harmoniously zones of different chromatic resonance, creating therewith the most dainty tapestries of colour; not only does it succeed in describing admirable spatial arabesques; it is possessed of a whole series of intrinsic meanings communicated by the varying degree of tension with which it is set in vibration. Its movement, calm and rounded as almost always in the Sienese, presents inflections that are supreme in their intensity and their heaviness or lightness. It is not a question of what Berenson (in another connection) has called line functioning so as to convey values of volume and movement and give plastic evidence to the representation, but of a function determined by the simple effects of the movement and swiftness of the line itself – its difficulty in setting itself free, its joy of expansion; it is an interior modulation like the rhythmic beat in the rendering of a musical phrase. The solidity and what we may call the " plausibility " of bodies and volumes, the charm of colour, and the descriptive beauty of facial features, are all alike subordinated to this first principle of Simone's art and act in function of it; they afford the " sensible " substance wherein its virtue can be displayed; they constitute, as it were, its range of sound, its quality of resonance. What they create is the suggestion of a universe transfigured into chromatic splendour and ardent feeling, and hence their effect is like that of the gorgeous velvets and brocades, the scintillating lights, the audience of superb beauty descended from ancient lineage, meeting together at the performance of some great music in an act of ritual exaltation, when all the varied elements become saturated with the music as it rises up and penetrates them, the music sceming to fuse itself with them into one sole reality, one single block of electrified substance.

Speaking of certain sublime subtleties in Botticelli's linear decoration, Berenson, it may be remembered, used a somewhat remote comparison to the extreme high notes of the violin. We say remote, because the impression of daring, of peril, of icy solitude, that you receive from sounds trembling upon the furthest limits of sense seems to offer no close analogy to Botticelli's treatment of line with its want of long and sustained modulation. Rather, his expression was of another order – nervous, convulsed, repetitive, and with an incessant movement of lines like tongues of flame now combining and now divided by the wind; his rhythm, that is, is fitful and broken. But apply the same image to Simone's design, and you have an apt illustration of its majestic, crystalline " bowing " and its rounded yet vertiginous phrasing in a world of expression beyond which nothing seems to exist save light alone.

Another characteristic of Simone's drawing to which we can only make a passing reference after our discussion is that it does not usually derive its intrinsic quality from any concern with illustration – the constant source of those incidents and breakings-off which dominate the course of Gothic line. We may notice, lastly, the unfounded character of the claim put forward by Dami that Botticelli was a direct derivation from Simone – a view which is disproved by a number of other considerations into which we have not space to enter here. It is true that both artists make an essential use of line, but in spirit and in style they could not have been wider apart.

* * *

Apart from mural decorations which have now for the most part perished, Simone left no paintings in Siena, or, rather, those which he did leave, like the *Annunciation* of 1333, were far too precious not to awaken a desire for their removal in process of time elsewhere. At Pisa, Naples, Assisi, and Orvieto he worked at points of intense irradiation, and he was, as has been said, an artist not merely of Italian but of European rank. This is a fact that needs to be borne in mind if we would rightly appreciate the force and directness of Simone's influence, which far outweighed that of Gothic upon himself. It made itself felt not only in Naples — the centre for contemporary exchanges with French culture, where Simone supplanted the tradition of Cavallini and had pupils and followers of his own — and at Avignon, through the agency of Provençal disciples, but can be traced in every place where the new art appeared, modifying and purifying international Gothic in so far as the latter was capable of receiving the teachings of its law.

Born, in all probability, as Vasari relates, somewhere about 1284, Simone grew up in the atmosphere of Duccio, even though in a material sense Memmo di Filippuccio, his future father-in-law, may have been his master. The principal dates in Simone's career are the following:

1315. He signs the *Maestà* of the Communal Palace of Siena.

1317. He paints at Naples.

1320. He paints the polyptych for the Church of Santa Caterina at Pisa.

1322 or thereabouts (Berenson, *Essays*, p. 21). He paints the altar-piece for the Dominican Convent at Orvieto.

1328. He dates the fresco of *Guidoriccio.*

1333. Together with his brother-in-law, Lippo Memmi, he finishes the *Annunciation*, now in the Uffizi Gallery.

From 1328 onwards, even if the frescoes at Assisi are to be assigned to a subsequent date, Simone must have spent a considerable period of time at Siena. According to Della Valle (*Lettere Senesi*, II, p. 98), in whose days the painting still existed, he there painted in fresco a Madonna in Glory upon the façade of the palace above the steps of San Giovanni. The decision of Benedict XII to summon Simone to Avignon was perhaps due to Cardinal Jacopo Stefaneschi. After obtaining leave from the Genoese government, the artist, accompanied by his wife and his brother Donato, set out in February, 1339. At Avignon he worked in Nôtre Dame des Doms and made the acquaintance of Petrarch; and there he died in July, 1344.

The paintings in which Simone has left the most exact and intense if not the fullest expression of himself are: the *St. Louis of Toulouse* (plates LXXXII to LXXXV); the *Madonna and Child* (plate LXXXVI); the *Polyptych of Pisa* (plates LXXXVII to XCVIII) – all these belonging to the three years from 1317 to 1320; the *St. Catherine* (plate C), and the

*Annunciation* (plates CXXV to CXXVIII). These paintings bear the same relation to the Assisi frescoes as does the chamber-music of a great composer to his symphonies. For although the frescoes at Assisi maintain the purity of the artist's style, while adapting it to newer intentions, the most secret accent of his inspiration will probably be best discerned in the first-named works.

\* \* \*

We cannot, after all, be astonished when we find the writers who discourse of Simone Martini left almost bereft of speech, as if stricken dumb by admiration, when they come to the sovereign work of all – the *Polyptych of Pisa*, with its four-and-forty figures engraved upon gold; the enchantment already felt to be well-nigh excessive in the *Madonna and Child* (plate LXXXVI) at Palazzo Venezia is multiplied here a thousand-fold. How, indeed, is it possible to analyse Bach's Preludes or the Motets of Palestrina one by one, or, if the image be better suited to Simone's art, a sequence of plain-chant versicles and responsions, without feeling at a loss for words ?

In the general arrangement of his pictures, Simone's need of order and symmetry led him to an archaism in some ways more pronounced than that of Duccio, and, consequently, he was obliged to have recourse to a still closer alliance with geometry. His sense of line and space, again, was so exalted that it assumed decisive values even in its most attenuated inflections, despite the apparent imperturbability of his drawing. Thus the humility of *St. Mary Magdalene* and of *St. Catherine* (plates LXXXVIII and XC) is expressed, not so much by the expression of their faces or gestures, as by their scarcely perceptible leaning against the column, as if they would withdraw backward from the glory confronting them. So, too, in the figure of the *Baptist* (plate LXXXIX),

notice how the patient drooping of the shoulders is in keeping with the low forehead, the hallucinated eye, and the
prominence given to the right hand as it is raised to declare
the future–theology and prophecy in Chinese shadows, as a
humourist might say.

Again, unlike Duccio's emotion, which embodied itself
in the narrative of earthly and heavenly adventures, the emotion of Simone never escaped to an historical horizon, a succession of events, existing outside itself; it is an ascending,
vertical emotion, which accomplishes its cycle within itself,
just as conscious perception, when it is perfect and mature,
is neither illuded by the colour of a legend nor appalled by
the terrors of a drama, but is simply meditation and vision.
Simone's figures are rarified, accordingly, in a kind of plastic
abstraction, in which the requirements of scansion are reduced to the smallest possible limits. It would seem as though
the infinitesimal modulation of distances, just the light and shade
effects necessary to give variety and harmony to the columns
of a building, met their needs. Or we might think of a garden
adorned with marble figures and containing nothing else except
fountains rising in silent obelisks and a succession of immense
flowers unencumbered by leaves.

Simone's world is a realm of magic, a continuous transfiguration always identical in its modes and yet ever new, like
the changes of a motionless flame fed and kept burning by
fresh essences constantly poured into it. How strange, then,
that there should be critics who see in the figures of this polyptych with its countless inventions and its inflexible "measure"
nothing but monotony and symptoms of languidness! To mention but a few of the inventions that unceasingly pass before
us, think of the grey gold enwrapping St. Catherine, with her
hair of an albino blonde that never saw the light; and, in the
adjoining panel, the purple book held by St. Peter Martyr,
seemingly a conventual shield, *sable* and *argent*, and quartered
*gules*. Or notice those dark-flaming counterparts, the Baptist
and the Magdalene, giving light to the blue robe of the Virgin,

while this in turn shows up in still closer contrast with the orange and red of the Child's tunic. And, outside the seven principal compartments, upon which it was but natural that the artist should lavish his most studious thought – the St. Mary Magdalene of the predella (plate XCV), with her mantle irised like a pigeon's throat, her snow-white wimple, and the light of her hair appearing through the veil; the Saint Ursula (plate XCVIII) in red of graduated tones and with a wide cross of gold upon her breast and mantle; the St. Gregory (plate XCIV), with that mitre as of a Buddhist saint, his chasuble of red, and his book of emerald colour; the Evangelist at his side in a violet mantle showing, where it opens, the tunic of lighter violet beneath it; the other Bishop next to the Magdalene with a mantle like fresh grass and worked in gold; and the St. Thomas Aquinas (plate XCVII), from whose book with the incandescent words Francesco Traini evidently learned to " read " painting.

Now, an art like this, with its predilection for types of extreme elegance, for figures which seem the stuff of dreams, and with its deep delight in embroidery, enamels and gems, was, indeed, bound to convey at last an idea of almost sickly delicacy, of an industriousness at once feminine and nunnish. And this is what actually happened in the case of artists who indulged in excessive decoration without possessing Simone's gifts. Stefano of Zevio, Gentile of Fabriano, and certain French primitives are instances in point. With Simone, however, the vigour of his style is all the more marked where the expression is sweetest and the medium most delicate. For the calm richness of their gold and ivory and enamel confers upon these figures an impassibility as of idols; and they seem in some mysterious way to have acquired strength and become invincible since they have warred down time in forms so slight. At times some lovely work of art will come forth from the dust of centuries and bear witness to a beauty of exquisite refinement, yet consumed by an age-long tradition of dominion and splendour. The *Queen Nefertiti* of the Berlin Museum is one such example;

the darkening of the tints heightens the effect of the white enamel eyes and intensifies the impression as of a fetich or an ikon. It is to works of art like this that we shall find the figures painted by Simone in the *Polyptych of Pisa* most closely akin.

\* \* \*

If in his Madonnas and virgin saints Simone has gathered together the varied aspects of womanly beauty, wisdom, and devotion, enclosing them in a contour of delicate and sublime cadence, and if he has given us in his men saints, as it were in a sort of visual repertory, the ideal of the knight, the gentleman, and the monk, in *Guidoriccio* (plate CXIX; 1328) on the contrary he has magnified the type of might and lordship – the knight who abandons polite pastimes, decorative company, court music, books of hours, and enters the military field. That the artist should portray his personage in a profile view was in accordance with the spirit of Sienese tradition. We have other examples of it in the portraits of King Robert at Naples, in the mitred donor at Orvieto, the head of the Emperor at Assisi, and the " dantino " at San Casciano. Here the device was rendered still more necessary both to stamp the likeness of the captain as with an indelible die, and also to allow the artist scope for a grandiose linear treatment of his figure and of the caparisoned war-horse against the horizon shut in by the two fortresses. In the lower part of the fresco, where the somewhat convulsed curves of the horse-trappings introduce the still less connected movement of the courser's legs, we have an instance of Simone's skill in presenting an arabesque upon a spatial field serving at once to delimit it and to set it in relief. At the same time, however, we are made conscious of the danger to which such a presentation was exposed when combined with a living movement and with the suggestion of an action not set abstractly in rhythm with it and, so to say, not " danced."

Horse and horseman tower against the background of the horizon like a metaphysical mask consisting of two busts. The eye of the charger looks out from his trappings of gloomy yellow stamped in black, like the eye of some monstrous beast. White banners, shields of broken white and black, fortifications on the bastions, and shafts of lances cut themselves out glacially upon the leaden sky. Sure of his trenches, which seem like designs taken from some ancient treatise on the art of war, the *condottiere*, well-nourished and cruel, exhibits himself from under his bonnet of white and red as the one sole will in all that lonely field.

\* \* \*

In the Chapel of St. Martin at Assisi Simone not only worked as painter but also designed the glass for the windows. According to some writers, he even acted as architect and adapted the form of the Chapel and its mural space to harmonize with his conception. However this may be, he certainly displayed all the wealth of his art in blending the clear design and glowing colour proper to illumination with the majesty of fresco. Of his frescoes painted some years earlier in the Church of the Incoronata at Naples (cf. A. Venturi, *Storia*, vol. V, figs. 519, 520), little or nothing is now known to us, and this remark is perhaps still more true of the frescoes he was to paint later on at Avignon. Thus the very excellence of the Assisi frescoes, while satisfying the loftiest æsthetic ideal, only increases our regret for these works that have perished.

Leaving the consideration of the dates at which the Assisi frescoes were painted to another part of our inquiry, we will first of all bestow a passing glance upon the half-length figures in the embrasures of the windows, amongst these being the Moorish saint and the two hermits (plates CXIII to CXV). The latter of these, with their crutch-shaped staffs, have evidently come down from some legend of the forests wherein knights-errant, stricken harts, and stags of St. Hubert bearing the image of the Crucified Lord between their antlers are wont to rage. The figures of women saints inside the arch – the four figures of men appear deteriorated – betray signs of an unusual effort after volume and statuesque effects, and need not detain us. For what we desire chiefly to emphasize in the *Legend of St. Martin* is the extent to which, over and above the qualities of design and composition, Simone's subtle treatment of colour has helped in this presentation of events so eminently characteristic of himself – a presentation, that is to say, of a number of ecstatic situations.

Little now is left of the *St. Martin and the Beggar* (plate CI) beyond the sweeping curve of the horse turning to look behind him and repeating as he does so the broad gesture of the Saint giving away his cloak, and the attitude of the shivering beggar. But in the *Christ appearing to St. Martin in a Dream* (plates CII and CIII), the whole of the lower zone, with the chest of the colour of wine-lees, the greenish coverlet stamped with red squares, the white of the bed-linen, and the ultramarine of the background, forms a play of colour such that to find its equal in taste we should need to go to the choicest miniature of the epoch of Timur. Wearing the cloak which St. Martin had bestowed in alms, Simone's Christ seems, as He converses with the angel, to allude to the neighbouring scene representing the Saint's meeting with the beggar, and the attitudes of the two figures convey a suggestion of conspirators or accomplices engaged in some sacred plot.

A still higher pictorial note is reached in the *St. Martin in Meditation* (plate CVIII). The motionless blues of the background are here attuned to the costume; and although the colour has perhaps been slightly deepened by time, yet its cold intensity seems to intensify the inaction and suspension of the principal figures. The monk touching the meditative Saint upon the shoulder is so closely linked up by the black and white of his habit to the setting – except for a touch of red, entirely in blacks and whites – that he exists merely as a graphic or narrative element, introduced on account of the logical interest of the story, without becoming a complete pictorial reality. You would expect to find the word " *Silentium* " written here as at the entrance to a monastic enclosure; and far from interrupting the solitude of the seated bishop, the figures of the two acolytes serve to guard it. In a more complex passage – the fresco of the *Obsequies* (plate CXI) – we have the same concentration of colour directed towards the point of chief interest. The blue catafalque imposes the wonted note of frozen immobility. Beginning from the black-hooded figures on the right and going on to the blue of the figure standing behind the bishop, there is a slow passing of deep, cold tones over the nocturnal sky and the shadows of the arches. From these notes the scale descends to the white albs of the ministrants and the rosy cowl of the priest with the grey hood, and so at last to the subject of the highest illumination – the gold and silver tints upon the officiating bishop and upon the body of the dead, while the delicate dove colour of the acolyte bending to kiss the bishop's hand introduces a shade of tender penitence among these resplendent glories. Even the minutest annotation in colour, like the blue veil worn round the shoulders of the youth holding the torch and relieved against the grey of the monks' habits, has its due part in describing the curve of sombre relations which begins with the blue of the vaulting and passes on to the sky seen through the windows until it finally reaches the black hoods, thus bending the entire painting like a curved shell so that the light is concentrated upon the figure on the bier. Notice, further, how the composition is gently rounded by the gradual curve from the head of the mitred celebrant to the youths placed at either end of the catafalque, the movement of line sustaining the inflections of the colour.

In spite of the damaged state of the fresco, a similar intention to direct the definition of colour upon the protagonist, by reducing it to vacancy at the extremes of the painting, is clearly visible in the *Miracle of the Mass* (plate CIX), the episode which balances pictorially the scene of the *St. Martin in Meditation* (plate CVIII) on the opposite wall of the chapel. Here the altar frontal is red; the white altar cloth repeats the values of the cowl of the kneeling server. The Saint occupies the centre of the composition, and the light of the torch and the hands elevating the Host are at the *foci* of the parabola. The unwearied sequence of vertical lines in the plumb-line of the altar cloth, the frontal, the celebrant, the torch, and the acolyte forms a real " elevation," suggested by the insistent rhythm of parallels. And observe, again, how this rhythm is bound up with that of the fresco below – the *Knighting of St. Martin* (plate CIV) – where the painting is dominated by the vertical lines of the column and the principal figures. Nor is this all. In these two frescoes the rhythm is rendered all the more insistent by their proximity to the empty angle of the chapel – a parallelepiped of darkness, beyond which the perpendicular lines and the shafts of the windows, slender like organ-pipes, resume the theme.

This scene of the *Knighting of St. Martin* and that of *St. Martin leaving the Army* (plates CVI and CVII) have less need of comment, as they possess a more obvious narrative quality. Here Simone's manner tends rather towards that of miniature, without, hewever, losing its calm and breadth. In the first of these two scenes, the most delicate incidents of colour are used to effect fine gradations or to create insets of paint, as in the group of minstrels and the long tunic of the flute-player wearing a cap. In the second, we may point to the Emperor with his medal-like profile and azure mantle, and to the huge soldier with the parti-coloured cap and the green tunic that makes so vivid and elegant a contrast to the violet robe of the Saint. The slender cross held by St. Martin – it is no less frail than that of Constantine in Piero della Francesca's fresco – seems in its material slightness to hint at the invisible might of its protection against the loneliness

of the barren wastes towards which the Saint directs his foot-
steps. Observe also how the painting is cleft diagonally beyond the seated Emperor by that oblique mass of green with
the inner distances of the valley stretching far away – a
scene of cabalistic suggestions. This linear falling-away introduces and prolongs the sense of parting, of separation from
the world and setting out through the wilderness, the contrast
between the encampment of the army which the Saint has
left behind him and the church of the faithful towards which
his journey lies.

In this way Simone has fitted the structure of the episode
and its narrative purport to the vision and the action of the
spectator. Similar considerations might be made with regard
to other scenes in the legend, as, for example, the *Death of
St. Martin* (plate CX), where the recollectedness of the colours
against the dark ground strikes a deeper note of mourning
than in the *Obsequies* (plate CXI). The rose and scarlet brocades of the knights in their attitudes of reverence evoke an
echo of legend and fairyland – that element of phantasy to
which all the painters of Siena down to their last representatives, Neroccio and Matteo, at times recur, as though to a
typical cadence in singing.

* * *

The upper parts of the *Christ appearing to St. Martin*
(plates CII and CIII) and the *Death of St. Martin* (plate CX)
together with the five half-length figures of saints in the right
transept of the Lower Basilica – St. Francis, St. Clare, St.
Elizabeth of Hungary, St. Louis, and a youthful saint bearing
a lily (plates CXVI to CXVIII; Anderson, 15406) – as well
as certain portions of the frescoes in the Chapel, have given
rise to a discussion whether Donato Martini, Simone's brother, may not have collaborated in them. Authoritative
critics like Berenson – we refer to his lists published in 1908 –

appeared not to admit this collaboration, but to attribute the entire cycle to Simone. Furthermore, it may be remarked that some of the above-named figures, notably the St. Francis, and the St. Clare, and the Angel of the Uffizi *Annunciation* (plates CXXVI to CXXVIII), sum up the whole repertory of Simone and its characteristic splendour, as they appeal to popular taste. None of the critics – Venturi and Van Marle, for example – who are dissatisfied with the attribution of these figures entirely to Simone has so far spoken in terms that go beyond a certain feeling of doubt, though it is difficult to explain this hesitation regarding Christ with the Angels, and, more particularly, the St. Martin carried to Heaven by Angels (plates CIII and CX). As Venturi observes, the lengthening of the faces in these figures is carried to the extreme, as though they were viewed in a convex mirror, and the grace of Simone and his golden luminousness fall into mannerism. Even the five half-length figures, superior as they are to these parts of the frescoes in their quality, betray a lack of Simone's precision in texture. Thus the saint next to St. Clare, holding a lily, is listless and wan; the expressions are generic and uniform; the cut of the almond-shaped eyes is stereotyped; and so, too, is the perpendicular line joining the forehead to the elongated nose. The tints, also, even allowing for their considerable deterioration, are more cloudy and suffused than is consistent with Simone's wonted use.

The effect of Simone's colouring with what we have called its lyrical, musical qualities is all the more striking when we compare the frescoes of St. Martin's Chapel with those of the Upper Basilica. In respect of colour, Giotto gives the impression of being a rustic, aloof and inarticulate. It matters not which of the last named frescoes were executed by him or by his pupils, their general effect is the same–an effect of monumentality and dramatic power, the whole arrangement being thought out with a view to expressing volume and character. And the colour is rude and summary, dashed down Capuchinwise. Contrast with this impulse, assurance, and spontaneity the art of Simone. Here you have a measured art, an art thoroughly based and carefully thought out, an art which will have soon accomplished its course and consume away. In Simone the vital sap already grows chill and thickens; in Giotto it is still acrid and springing. Again, Giotto is not restricted by his subjects, so as to feel respect for them not only as artist but also as a man. He has even a certain capacity for mockery, as in his scene of St. Francis unexpectedly appearing to the friars who lift up faces pink like melons. Simone, on the contrary, never departs from a grave composure in portraying his personages – musicians, courtiers, and warriors; and he will ennoble them with a thoughtful and almost reverent attention even when they seem to lend themselves to less solemn treatment (cf. plates CV, CVII, and CXII).

It is only after a complex process of distant contaminations, when Simone's portraits had succeeded in influencing French painting and had supplied a number of characteristic models to Jan van Eyck and Hugo van der Goes – models destined more than a century later to awaken great excitement at Florence with the Portinari altar-piece – that we can speak truthfully of " realism "; and hence it is difficult to understand how critics have raised this question either with reference to the *St. Louis crowning Robert of Anjou* (plate LXXXII), or to the small figure of the kneeling donor in the Orvieto polyptych, (plate XCIX), or, worse still, to the fresco of *Guidoriccio* (plate CXIX). The last is something in the nature of an heraldic paradox; heraldry has firmly established and entrenched itself in the landscape.

*  *  *

A second question, regarding the collaboration of Lippo Memmi, is suggested by the polyptych formerly at Orvieto and now in the Gardner Collection (plate XCIX), and by a second polyptych in the Museum of the Opera at Orvieto. The latter is a mutilated work, signed and dated 1322 ( ? ), with figures of the Madonna and Child, St. Peter, St. Mary Magdalene, Trasmondo Monaldeschi – bishop of Sovana and donor of the painting – St. Dominic, and St. Paul, who holds out his unbound Epistles like a pack of playing-cards (Alinari, 25977, 25978, 25978A). That Memmi collaborated in this second polyptych, at least in the figure of St. Peter, appears to us possible. Amongst other things, we find that Martini almost always poses his figures in such a way that the line of the neck, upon which the head rests in a markedly characteristic manner, follows the exact vertical line cutting the centre of the base. Memmi, on the contrary, seems to be afraid of carrying geometry so far; the line of his necks more frequently intersects the perpendicular at an angle, and consequently the verticality of his figures is shifted from the middle of the arc. Compare, as an instance of this, Memmi's *Madonna*, also at Orvieto (Alinari, 25975A).

In these two polyptychs, as Berenson has remarked in his *Essays*, we have one of the first examples in Simone of a pointed Gothic frame; but in order to see Simone's love of line meeting and blending intimately with elements of true Gothic we must have recourse to the central figures of the *Annunciation* painted in 1333 (plates CXXV to CXXVIII). From this point onwards we may watch the growing complication of Simone's personal linealism, already abstract and carried to the most acute precision imaginable, by a new element that was calculated to do it violence, to rob it of its elasticity, and to arrest its impetus and power of recovery. Like all cultivated, reflective artists, at his best moments Simone was wont to draw profit from his vast artistic experience, but in other and less happy hours he was a victim of the destiny that always lies in wait for science when it is not absorbed by inspiration. Henceforwards Gothic infiltrations, elements of an alien and cultural character, may be detected with increasing frequency in his paintings, until at last we find them mingled with borrowings from the elder Lorenzetti in a quest for expressions of dramatic feeling in faces and gestures (cf. plates CXXX and CXXXI).

In placing the vase of lilies between the Angel and the Virgin Simone followed the conventional arrangement of the scene. But we need only go back to Duccio's *Annunciation* (plate XXIV), where the earthenware crock seems to have been borrowed from household use, to perceive the distance that separates the earlier rendering from this sensibility, so dazzled by its love of the curious and precious. Not even in contemporary works painted by artists no less rich in decorative taste than Simone, as, for instance, in the *Madonna and Saints* by Ambrogio Lorenzetti (plate CXC), or in later works like the *Nativity of the Virgin* (1342) by Pietro Lorenzetti (plates CLXXVI, CLXXVII), do we find furniture so choice and elaborate as this flower-vase with its acute sense of stylization and a provocative intention to set free angular and twisted lines as an accompaniment to the metallic, tongue-shaped leaves set upon the stalks of the lily. A hint at this kind of taste, however, appears in the Magdalene's vase of ointment in the Gardner Polyptych painted in 1325 (plate XCIX). Barna, though he borrows from Simone in the *Adoration of the Magi* (Alinari 37262) and in the *Marriage Feast at Cana* (plate CXL), tends, nevertheless, to simplify his model, and we shall look in vain for examples of similar stylization in Paolo di Giovanni Fei (cf. plate CCXXVIII). Indeed, it may be said that they were altogether unknown in Siena until several decades after the close of the century – a fact borne out by the simplicity of the vases and furniture appearing in the Polyptych of Asciano, painted in 1430 by an artist so fantastic and splendour-loving as Sassetta (Plates CCXLII and CCXLIII), although in the *Adoration of the Magi* (Lombardi, 2810), which is of almost contemporary date, we find a singularly rich exhibition of elaborate small ware.

Not that I would speak ill of the Angel of the *Annunciation* (plate CXXVI) – a figure which has always succeeded in melting even the hardest hearts – and, still less, of the Virgin who turns with such touching bewilderment towards him at the sound of his message. Berenson has well said that " as you look at the angel's mantle, it is as if you were seeing the young sunlight upon driven snow." And his wings of iridescent colour, still faintly beating, that strip of the Scotch tartan mantle seemingly caught and held fast by the swiftness of his flight, the branch and crown of olive, and, above all, that face ! It seems as though the adornment, the luxury, and the latest fashions of all the latitudes had met by appointment upon the gleaming marble pavement to compose so rare a beauty; and yet it is a beauty already undermined and secretly threatened by the very excess of its exquisite elegance.

Had Simone been born in a severer tradition, we should perhaps have found him turning henceforwards to a genuine abstractness of line almost entirely devoid of figurative intention. Thus in Michelangelo the values of modelling are sometimes presented in a purely architectonic scheme of masses in movement without any relation to figures as such. So, too, line will assume a function essentially dramatic in Oriental landscapes and compositions. Simone, however, made no such advance. He kept instead to the development and the complication of arabesque, bending it to the expression of feeling carried to the furthest possible limits. Nor was it easy to reach them in a culture so avid of emotional refinements as that of Siena.

In this fidelity to arabesque, this " marking time, " as we may call it, Simone offers an example of a process directly opposed to that of many artists who yield in their formative period to the seductions of romantic expression but in their mature works accept a rigorous restraint. As for Simone, the result is well illustrated by comparing his paintings at Naples and Pisa – I will not say with the delicate *Annunciation* formerly in the Stroganoff Collection (plate CXXIX) or with the Liverpool *Holy Family*, painted in 1342 and reproduced by Van Marle (vol. II, fig. 160), where we may observe a curious rounding and almost a brutalized modification of the facial type – but with the *Polyptych of Antwerp*, in which the figures in the scene of the *Annunciation*, and, particularly, the Virgin with her snake-like sinuosity, have a rigidity that rather suggests sculpture in a polychrome material not altogether obedient to the artist's hand than painting (cf. Venturi, *Storia*, vol. V, figs, 512 and 513); or, yet again, with the scenes of the *Passion* now distributed between Antwerp, Berlin, and Paris.

Thus, when Venturi tells us that " not only the colour but the soul of Simone had now caught the flame; his design is freer; the proportions of his faces have lost their former length," we cannot but feel that this is indeed to make the best of the residuum of Simone's art. Not, of course, that all its virtue suddenly disappeared – that was impossible – but his art now began to assume an ambiguous quality which becomes increasingly noticeable the further Simone departs from the solemnly ecstatic and almost ritually prescribed manner of the frescoes at Assisi in search of a new type of painting, at once crowded, gesticulatory, and violent. And this being so, a growing concentration in colour may well seem somewhat inadequate compensation. The *Crucifixion* and, in a still higher degree, the *Deposition* (plates CXXX and CXXXI) are the best of these later paintings. In the latter we may notice the rhythm of the arms stretched out to receive the body of the Redeemer against the line marked by the two windows, and the answering gesture of the lamenting Magdalene, whose arms seem to describe a niche for the body itself. As to the remaining works, it is enough to say that in them Simone aimed at shortening as far as possible the distance that separated his own art from the manner of the first Flemings and Germans a century later – from Rogier van der Weyden and Hans Memling.

The activity of Simone and his pupils at Avignon perhaps interests us more as one of the many instances of Sienese irradiation in Europe during the early fourteenth century than for the direct traces of paintings left by Matteo of Viterbo and other assistants in the Popes' Palace and elsewhere. Matteo and the Sienese artistswere by no means the only craftsmen who worked at Avignon at this period. There were painters, besides, from Arezzo and Florence; and in addition to a number of Frenchmen who have been identified singly by Michel, we find a certain Resdol from Vienna, a German named Deboslat, and Hertsnabel, an Alsatian. The last three all continued to work in Avignon until almost thirty years after the death of Simone.

At one time the practice of annexing *sic et simpliciter* the whole group of Sienese artists, and even Simone himself, as soon as they set foot on the soil of Avignon, was a favourite proceeding with certain French historians, who appear to have confused temporary domicile with artistic dependence upon France. Although Michel and Durrieu more recently have adopted a less "Tartarinesque" attitude, Gielly still maintains the earlier position, though he admits that Sienese models exercised a vague influence upon the fishing and hunting scenes painted by a French hand in the Pope's Wardrobe. But, as we have already said, the question cannot properly be envisaged in this way. Simone's work was already done by the time he left Siena, and, except in rare instances like the Stroganoff *Annunciation*, it never afterwards recalled the splendour of Naples, Pisa, and Assisi. The evidence for Simone's independence of French influence during his years of formation and for his subsequent reactions to French Gothic will be found in his activity considered as a whole, and especially before 1333; it is useless to search for it in the last phase of his art out of Italy.

\* \* \*

The polyptych of *Beato Agostino Novello* (plates CXX to CXXIV, painted about the same time as the great *Annunciation* or perhaps a little later, would afford still clearer proof that Simone's inspiration had gone astray, at all events to the extent noticed above, if we were not forced to recognize that Lippo Memmi bore a large share in the execution. Even in those parts where Simone's majestic rhythm is least blurred – the central figure (plate CXX) and the group of women accompanying the child raised to life (plate CXXIV) – the drawing lacks the nervousness of the Uffizi and Stroganoff *Annunciations*, and the line falls with the dull fluidity that is always characteristic of Lippo.

Although earlier critics were accustomed to speak of Lippo as a painter who merely gave currency to schemes invented by his brother-in-law, and the space at our disposal precludes us from dedicating more than a passing notice to him, we nevertheless feel that this view does him less than justice, despite the fact that his chief merit does not go beyond a certain dignity, slightly vacuous and uniform, and the sureness of hand which we associate with the attentiveness of a copyist rather than with the thrill of invention. Lippo's highest achievements, like the *Madonna* (plate CXXXIII). or the *St. James* (plate CXXXV) with the dark green mantle lined with yellow, and the red robe and book – a marvellous example of Martinian colours transferred to dignified mannerism – or, again, his small *Crucifixion* (plate CXXXVII) and certain parts of the Orvieto polyptych (cf. plate CXXXII) invariably convey the impression of a reflex art, derived at first from Simone and later on from the Lorenzetti. When, on the other hand, Lippo attempts the grand style – not, indeed, in the *Maestà* of San Gimignano, a work of collaboration, nor in the *Madonna with St. Michael* (Alinari, 9563), also at San Gimignano but now repainted like a doll, and so useless for any comparison – but in the *Santo Ansano and Santa Julitta* (plate CXXXVI) or in the figure of *Beato Agostino Novello,* he at once becomes obtuse, ill-tempered, *refrogné.* And how poor he is in surprises, how terribly correct, how dull! His *rôle* was pre-eminently that of the scholastic and conservative, and so it fell to his lot to provide the Martinians of the second half of the century – Andrea Vanni and Paolo di Giovanni Fei – with an interpretation of Simone's sublimity reduced to the level of a school-manual. In all Lippo's abundant output we shall look in vain for one of those unexpected inspirations of genius that sometimes enliven the life work of a second-rate artist, like the *Madonna of San Casciano* in the first half of the century or the episodes in Lippo Vanni's polyptych of *St. Dominic and St. Sixtus* in the second – not to mention the works which Barna's rustic vigour enabled him to produce in close proximity to Lippo during his brief career.

\* \* \*

Barna is commonly regarded as the chief follower of Simone Martini. This is to say too little, for Barna's nature was far more complex. Up to about the year 1350 he kept to the Ducciesque iconography, as is shown by his type of Christ in scenes like the *Call of St. Peter* (plate CXXXIX) and the *Raising of Lazarus* (plate CXLI), where the transverse rhythm of the hands of Christ, of the disciple, and of Martha, as they point to the tomb, is a further reminiscence of Duccio; and by the scenes of *Judas with the Priests* (plate CXLIV), where the arrangement is a blending of Duccio's *Judas* and *Mitte manum*, and the *Sleeping Apostles* (plate CXLV). This was, in fact, the conventional iconography for similar subjects at the time, and we find it employed almost contemporaneously in Pietro Lorenzetti's frescoes of the Passion painted upon the vault of the Lower Basilica at Assisi.

Further derivatives may be observed in other paintings belonging to the same cycle in the Collegiate Church of San Gimignano – the scenes upon which Barna's fame is chiefly founded – though it is not always easy to decide which of them should be ascribed to Barna and which to Giovanni of Asciano, who continued to work upon the frescoes after his

uncle's death. In Barna's *Annunciation* the Angel follows
Simone's style in a simplified adaptation, and the Virgin
bends her head with a gesture not unlike that we have already seen in Simone's *Annunciation* (followed also by Lippo),
but Barna has introduced the new episode of the handmaid-
en interrupting her work at the loom in order to listen to
the Angel's words (Alinari, 37260). The scene takes place in
a small lofty chamber, entrance to which is obtained by a
staircase with a diagonal profile that enhances the impetus of
the Angel's flight. The Eternal Father with the accompanying
cherubs forms a group strangely akin to the corresponding
figures poised above "Ugolino Lorenzetti's" *Nativity* (plate
LXVIII). The fictitious architecture of the last-named painting suggested to Berenson a comparison with the scenery of
mystery-plays: no more apt term of comparison could be
found for this *Annunciation* by Barna; it seems to be really
acted upon the improvised stage of a convent-theatre.

In Barna's *Crucifixion* the angels repeat the despairing
gestures of Giotto's fresco at Padua and Pietro Lorenzetti's
*Crucifixion* at Assisi (cf. plate CLXVII), but the composition
of the episode follows a movement altogether new. It is a
pageant of great dapple-grey horses, of women swooning and
weeping, of soldiers dicing on their hands and knees, and with
the three crosses in the midst; but whether owing to the intervention of Giovanni of Asciano or for other reasons which
we will not stay to consider, the work is so charged with incident and grotesque detail that, taken as a whole, it does not
reach the level of Barna at his best. Besides the influence of
Simone, we may detect in it a certain dependence upon Duccio, upon the Lorenzetti and the Florentines; the traits borrowed from the last being explained by the circumstance related by Ghiberti and Vasari that Barna worked in Florence,
Arezzo, and Cortona. Barna's design, however, is more summary, and his colour tends to be coarse, with violent contrasts
of light and shade. The incident of the handmaiden in the
*Annunciation* inevitably recalls the woman spinning in the

little room next to the chamber in which the Angel appears to St. Anne in Giotto's fresco at Padua.

According to his contemporaries and their immediate successors, Barna's popularity rested upon two gifts: the keenness of his sense for nature and his dramatic power. To the first of these qualities his epitaph, cited by Della Valle, bears witness: *Naturam diligentius imitatur.* In the same way Vasari informs us that Barna was "the first who began to draw animals well, as we see by some sheets by his hand in our book, covered with wild beasts of various parts of the world." It must be admitted, however, that a capacity of this kind has little in common with the spirit of Simone, even though Barna may have copied his types and drawn hints for composition from him.

The truth of Vasari's description of Barna's lost fresco in Sant'Agostino at Siena, where, in the episode of the young man led to execution while a friar offers him consolation, the "representation of pallor and of the fear of dea this so realistic ... and in fine the entire scene is executed with such vigour as to leave no doubt that Barna had penetrated deeply into the horror of that situation," is admirably borne out by the frescoes at San Gimignano. The anatomy of his Christ in the *Baptism* (plate CXXXVIII), where the figure is immersed in the transparent stream filled with fish, forms the most naturalistic nude painted by the Sienese school. The *Raising of Lazarus* (plate CXLI), the *Entry into Jerusalem* (plate CXLII) and the *Seizure of Christ* require no long examination for us to perceive their search after telling attitudes and expressions, and what a mingling of horrible and grotesque touches we find in the *Crucifixion!* The devils in wait for the soul of the impenitent thief; Longinus, who, as Della Valle observes, resembles an ape on horseback as he gives the lance-thrust; the scorpion painted on the draperies; the soldiers breaking the legs of the two thieves with their iron maces. Similar traits abound in other compositions still left to us or of which we possess written memorials: the devil disputing with St. James –

a motive repeated, according to Vasari, by Barna at Cortona and in the Chapel of St. Nicholas in Santo Spirito at Florence – and devils yet again in the panel now in the Fine Arts Museum at Boston and reproduced by Van Marle (vol. II, fig. 193).

This studious quest of novel moods and movements appears in Barna's rendering of even the most traditional subjects. Take, for example, the *Madonna between St. Paul and St. John the Baptist* in San Pietro at San Gimignano (Van Marle, vol. II, fig. 195). The Madonna leads the Child, a boy of three or four years, by the hand, and He walks beside her, holding two fruits in His right hand. A somewhat similar arrangement will be found in Simone's panel at Liverpool; but while Simone probably intended to represent the Child returning from His disputation with the doctors of the law, or, at all events, a scene in keeping with His age at that time and with the traditional handling of the episode, Barna shows us a child of tender years and altogether innocent of theology. He just portrays an everyday, domestic incident – that of a mother accompanying her little boy to the infant-school. Turn to the panel of *Judas with the Priests* (plate CXLIV). Who would not think that that conversation by glances represented a scene between moneylenders or a bargain amongst " shady " characters well-known on that market-square ?

This feeling for life, his insistence upon vehement gesture, and his taste for the *macabre* are indications of a forthright, " democratic " nature in Barna, which is attested in many other ways. Vasari remarks that "he was a very facile draughts-man, " – a form of praise not without an unconscious hint at Barna's limitations. For his impetuous, fluent design betrays not so much the follower of Simone as the artist who initiated the decline from the supreme tradition handed down by Duccio and Simone to the more uncouth but instinctive art forms that appeared in Bartolo di Fredi and his son Andrea (through whom they influenced Lorenzo Monaco), in Cola di Petrucciolo–whether he is to be identified or not with the " Master of the Assumption of Bettona " is immaterial here – and in Taddeo Bartoli. In the formation of this new current two streams combined: the art of Simone as it had been simplified and popularised by Lippo Memmi, and the art of the Lorenzetti – especially that of Pietro – in a " rustic " version. The products to which this combination gave rise bear the same relation to the work of the greater artists as, towards the close of the fifteenth century, the art of Benozzo and the Ghirlandaio to the creations of the chief representatives of the Florentine school. Barna was the most ardent and creative spirit of a movement the first indications of which are to be found in the Fogg *Nativity*. Indeed, when we consider it in the light of Barna's work, the Fogg *Nativity* will appear as a surprisingly early canon of these new modes in style and feeling.

*  *  *

Our account of the last works of Simone and the art of Barna has occasioned too frequent a reference to the Lorenzetti for us not to turn our attention directly to them without allowing ourselves either to be detained by painters of lesser note like Naddo Ceccarelli (cf. plate CXLVIII) and Giovanni of Asciano, both of whom stand in close proximity to Barna, or to linger over the influence exercised by Simone in Umbria and Northern Italy and the miniaturists who were trained in his school. There is no need for us to mention how the austere personality of Pietro " Laurati " remained long obscure. Ghiberti and Magliabechi's Anonimo had no notion of his existence; Vasari, who was unaware of his connection with Ambrogio, ascribed Pietro's frescoes at Assisi, together with others, to the honourable but absurd paternity of Giotto, whose pupil he supposed Pietro to have been. Despite the best intentions to honour the " excellent painter of Siena, who was employed and caressed by all Tuscany, " Vasari's biography of Pietro Lorenzetti is one of the most confused and scanty in his whole collection, and it was perhaps in the hope of atoning for its deficiencies that he has described at such length the restorations carried out at his own expense in the Collegiate Church of Arezzo where Pietro worked. " As, " he says, " I have spared neither pains nor expense, since I considered myself bound to do my best to honour God, I may venture to affirm that, so far as my ability would allow, this work lacks nothing in the way of ornament, whether of gold, carving, painting, marble, travertine, porphyry, and other stones. " Even after the researches undertaken by Perkins, De Nicola, Berenson, and Van Marle, the development of Pietro's art is still left fragmentary and contradictory, and it will therefore not be out of place for us to attempt a summary statement of it, placing the single works in their most probable chronological order. The first certainly dated painting by Pietro is the *Polyptych of Arezzo*. This belongs to 1320, but there can be no doubt that it was preceded by other paintings, amongst which must be included the famous *Madonna of Cortona*, (plate CXLIX) in spite of a tradition that would bring it down to 1335. The date proposed by Berenson is somewhere about 1315. This group of works illustrates with varying degrees of certainty Pietro's activity from 1305, when we have the first documentary evidence concerning him (cf. Perkins, *Pietro Lorenzetti*, p. 51), down to 1320 or shortly afterwards. We may list these works in the following order:

1. The *Madonna and Angels* in the Collegiate Church of Casole (cf. *Rassegna d'Arte*, 1919, p. 96). De Nicola's attribution of this painting to Pietro has so far not won general acceptance. It is a fresco more Byzantine than Ducciesque in character, and cannot have been executed after the opening phase of the artist's career.

2. The *Madonna of Cortona* (plate CXLIX). Here the angels are entirely in Duccio's manner, and the architecture of the throne is archaïsing. The widely-spaced geometrical or-

namentation on the hem of the Virgin's mantle occurs, as Berenson (*Essays*, p. 12) has pointed out, in works executed in the " atmosphere " of Duccio: *e. g.* the *Madonna of San Casciano* (plate LXVII), although painted so late as 1335; the Platt *Madonna* (cf. Van Marle, vol. II, fig. 95); and the Loeser *Magdalene* (ibid. fig. 91) where the central decoration has a svastika pattern.

3. The *Madonna of Castiglione d'Orcia* (cf. *Vita d'Arte*, July, 1912, fig. 27). Berenson rightly believes this painting to have been inspired by a Ducciesque model, though he observes that its deteriorated condition limits the deductions that can now be drawn from it. De Nicola, in the above-named article, has shown how the painting attempts and develops the theme of the " colloquy " between the Virgin and Child – a theme which Pietro may have derived from Giovanni Pisano – and he has used the iconographical *data* thus provided to establish the following order for Pietro's first works, according as the intimacy of the " colloquy " is more or less accentuated – Castiglione, Arezzo, Monticchiello, Cortona. Perkins, on the other hand, while admitting the identity of the *motif* of the Castiglione and Monticchiello panels with that of the paintings at Assisi, Arezzo, and Cortona, assigns the former – without adducing any stylistic reasons and, in our view, unacceptably – to the close of Pietro's career, after 1340.

4. The *Polyptych of Arezzo* (Alinari, 9961). The date is proved by Pietro's contract with Guido Tarlati, bishop of Arezzo, signed on April 17, 1320. The certainty of this date and the fact that Pietro, who was almost of the same age as Simone Martini, must have been born shortly after 1280 render the efforts of Van Marle to prove that the Arezzo polyptych was not the work of an immature youth inexplicable. Van Marle (Vol. II, p. 345) accepts the accuracy of both the dates in question, but he avails himself of this strange argument to antedate certain other works by Pietro (plates CLIII to CLIX), which, as we shall see presently, cannot possibly be assigned to the date he advocates. In our view, the three following

works should be assigned to the same period as the Arezzo polyptych, allowing a margin of four or five years:

5. The *Madonna of Monticchiello* (*Vita d'Arte*, July, 1912, fig. 28).

6. The *Triptych* in fresco in the Orsini Chapel of the Lower Basilica at Assisi (plate CLXIII).

7. *The Madonna between St. Francis and St. John the Evangelist*, also at Assisi (plates CLXIV and CLXV).

The affinity between these works and their development from the *Madonna of Cortona* may be seen in the following traits:

(*a.*) The angels in the spandrils of the Orsini triptych are still Ducciesque, like the angels in the *Madonna of Cortona*, and they are exceedingly close to the angels in the spandrils of the Arezzo polyptych. The archaic character of the latter is confirmed by the presence of medallions like those decorating the borders of the *Ruccellai Madonna* (plate IX).

(*b.*) The Baptist in the Arezzo polyptych, as also in the Orsini triptych, is derived from the Baptist in Duccio's *Maestà* and, to some extent, from the Baptist in Simone's *Maestà* painted in 1315. Notice especially the serpentine arrangement of the hair and beard. Again, in the Orsini triptych the Baptist holds a large scroll like those we see unfolded in the hands of Duccio's prophets (cf. plates XVI, XVII, and XXV), and frequently in archaic Sienese paintings and sculptures of Ducciesque style. On the whole, despite signs of influence by Simone, Lorenzetti's Baptist is closer to Duccio's type. The arm of the Orsini Baptist with its large spatula-shaped hand is reproduced identically in the Arezzo polyptych. The gesture with which the Baptist in the Arezzo polyptych points with his thumb to the Madonna and Child is identical with the gesture of the Madonna indicating St. Francis (plate CLXIV), and it recurs ten years later in the compartment of a polyptych (dated 1332) formerly in the Pieve of Crevole (Accademia, Siena, n. 79). A further instance of Pietro's attitudes which seem to link his figures dramatically together will be found in the St. Francis of the Orsini triptych, where the Saint turns towards the Madonna and Child as though in the midst of a discourse which he emphasizes by the action of his hand.

(*c.*) The *St. John the Evangelist* of the Assisi fresco (plate CLXIV) has the same widely-spaced geometrical ornamentation upon the hem of the robe which we noticed as an indication of archaism in the *Madonna of Cortona.*

(*d.*) There is a similarity in the attitude of the Virgin in the Orsini triptych and in the *Madonna of Monticchiello,* and the way in which the hand of the Madonna passes round the Child's leg is identical at Monticchiello and at Assisi (plate CLXIV). The Child at Assisi, notwithstanding a greater movement, is the same as the corresponding figure at Arezzo, at Castiglione d'Orcia, and, above all, at Monticchiello. Notice the treatment of the hair and the prominent eyelid. The Madonna bends towards the Child, as though to speak in confidence.

(*e.*) Owing to being painted in fresco, with the object of making it resemble an altar-piece, the Orsini triptych has been supposed to be of earlier date than the *Madonna between St. Francis and St. John the Evangelist* (plates CLXIV and CLXV). Venturi has, in fact, mistaken the triptych for a panel-painting. As if to counterbalance the breadth and simplicity imposed by the fresco medium, Pietro's handling here is dry and sharp; he has insisted upon linear definition and loaded the framework with insets of colour.

Taken together, then, these various characteristics not only convince us that the works so far passed in review fall into a single group, but they afford an argument for supposing that one part of Pietro's frescoes in the Lower Basilica at Assisi was contemporary with the Orsini triptych and the *Madonna between St. Francis and St. John.* In other words, the frescoes at Assisi were painted after 1320 and before 1329, the date at which we find Pietro employed in the Church of Dofana and then upon the polyptych for the Carmelites of Siena.

\* \* \*

That Pietro imitated Giotto was affrmed by Vasari and other historians of art. The inference is unnecessary, and certain characteristics in his work betray the common influence of Giovanni Pisano far more than dependence upon Giotto, yet there can be no doubt that at Assisi Pietro, no less than Simone, came into contact with an art suggesting a grander style than was to be found in the accepted Sienese canon. When we consider the general development of Pietro's style from the *Madonna between St. Francis and St. John* to the *Crucifixion* in San Francesco at Siena, we cannot fail to notice the presence of this character of "monumentality." To it, even after his return to Siena, Pietro remained constantly faithful, though he gave it a different interpretation.

Sienese imaginativeness and resplendent colour were transported for the first time to the realm of the monumental in the *Crucifixion* at Assisi (plates CLXVI and CLXVII). In the *Deposition* (plate CLXVIII), in the *Entombment* (cf. Venturi, vol. V, fig. 555), and in the *Resurrection* (Anderson, 26946) the artist schematizes and impoverishes his colour in order to obtain an effect of deeper pain and desolation. To the frescoes of *Scenes from the Passion* painted on the vault of the Basilica at Assisi (plates CLXIX to CLXXI, and Venturi, vol. V, figs. 557 and 561), we shall have occasion to return later; here we will merely remark that they presuppose assistance by other artists than those who took part in the four frescoes just mentioned, and that they are to be assigned accordingly to a later stage of Pietro's career. The features which indicate a close connection in style and date between the *Crucifixion*, the *Deposition*, the *Entombment*, and the *Resurrection* are the following:

1. The almost complete absence of landscape, this entering largely into the frescoes of the vault.

2. The use of vast monochrome grounds in the Flo-

rentine manner. In the *Crucifixion* at Assisi the ground is of livid blue; in the *Crucifixion* at Siena, it is blood-red. So, too, in another *Crucifixion*, next to the fresco of *St. Francis, St. Clare, St. Louis, and two other Saints* painted by Simone and Donato. In this last painting we seem to detect the hand of an artist who worked in other parts of the Basilica and then became Pietro's assistant during this first period.

3. The deformation of the facial types with a view to expressing violent emotions. Later on, this will become a characteristic trait and, as it were, a cipher or " rhetoric " with Pietro's followers; but in this group of paintings it appears in the more balanced form which usually accompanies the rise of a new motive in surroundings of genuine poetry. Besides this deformation we notice in almost all the frescoes of the series a pronounced tendency towards an angular design with broken rhythm.

The chronological sequence advocated by Perkins (*Pietro Laurati*, p. 21) for this group of paintings, to which, as he has shown, should be added the *Judas*, the five half-length figures of Saints, the five *Franciscans*, and *St. Francis receiving the Stigmata*, is on the whole convincing, especially if we restrict it more closely than Perkins has done, so that all the frescoes included in the group fall within the first period of Pietro's activity and not beyond it. Hence we may assign the entire group to a date not far removed from that of the *Polyptych of Arezzo*. It may be noted, lastly, that the *St. Francis receiving the Stigmata* is markedly reminiscent of the frescoes in the Upper Basilica.

\* \* \*

In considering the renewed activity of Pietro at Siena and in its neighbourhood we have the assistance of several dates. The *Madonna of Dofana*, a panel painted for the Church of Sant'Ansano with figures of St. Anthony the Abbot and St. Nicholas of Bari (cf. Van Marle, vol. II, fig. 229), was painted in 1328; and in 1329 we find mention of the polyptych painted for the Carmelites of Siena – Van Marle is mistaken when he says the Carmelites of Florence. Of this, two panels, each divided into two parts and forming a portion of the "gradine," have been preserved (plates CLX to CLXII).

De Nicola seems to attach little weight to the above-mentioned date for the *Madonna of Dofana*, which certainly has been much repainted, and attributes a much greater importance to his observation that in this panel no trace of a "colloquy" between the Madonna and Child can be found. From the hieratic character of the painting he infers accordingly that it was painted during Pietro's first period of activity. Now if this were so, the mere absence of the "colloquy" – that is, of tender and dramatic expression – would oblige us to date an entire group of works by Pietro and his pupils – works undoubtedly very close to the *Madonna of Dofana* – even before the *Madonna of Cortona* and the *Madonna of Arezzo;* and this is a conclusion which an examination of the group in question forbids us to accept.

Continuing, then, our summary exposition of the works painted after Pietro's early activity at Assisi, we may arrange them as follows:

1. The *Madonna of Dofana*, painted in 1328.

2. The *Polyptych* for the Carmelite Church. Perhaps slightly earlier than the polyptych are the two panels of *St. Agnes* and *St. Catherine* (plates CLIV and CLV), which Perkins dates roughly between 1325 and 1330.

3. The *Crucifixion* in the Church of San Francesco at Siena. The date generally admitted, 1331, is not improbable, but it has less support for Pietro's fresco than for the frescoes painted by Ambrogio Lorenzetti. The latter, formerly in the cloister, are now inside the Church of San Francesco.

4. Parts of the *Polyptych* formerly in the Pieve of Santa Cecilia at Crevola, with figures of St. John the Baptist, St. Cecilia, and St. Bartholomew (Accademia, Siena, nn. 79, 81, 82). The date of this polyptych is 1332.

5. A group of works by Pietro and assistants in the Accademia at Siena, in San Pietro Ovile near Siena, in the cathedral of Grosseto, and elsewhere. These works, amongst others, were attributed by Berenson to his " Ugolino Lorenzetti;" DeWald would assign them to the " Master of the Madonna of San Pietro Ovile." They include:

(*a.*) An *Assumption* (plate CLI) and the *Throned Madonna* (plate CLII). The *Assumption* repeats the facial type, altogether different from that of the Madonnas of the first period, of the *Madonna of Dofana*. The angels, like those in the last-named painting, show the influence of Simone Martini.

(*b.*) A *Throned Madonna* (cf. Van Marle, vol. II, fig. 218).

(*c.*) The *Madonna of San Pietro Ovile* (*ibid.* fig. 219).

(*d.*) The *Madonna of Grosseto* (cf. Berenson, *Essays*, fig. 13).

(*e.*) *St. Gregory* (plate CL).

Berenson, who carefully analysed three of these Madonnas (b, c, d), dated them between 1330 and 1335, remarking upon the close similarities in the elaborate thrones and in the type and attitude of the Child, represented in two of the paintings as playing with a bird a — motive which we find repeated in Luca di Tommè, Andrea Vanni, Taddeo Bartoli, Fungai, and others. Similar traits, however, are to be met with in other paintings, and their frequency indicates a very elaborate phase of solemn colour and sumptuousness. With regard to the *Assumption*, we may note that Cavalcaselle attributed it to Paolo di Maestro Neri, a follower of the Lorenzetti, who painted at Lecceto and is mentioned in documents between 1343 and 1383. This attribution by so acute a critic would be grotesque if, as De Nicola makes out, the *Assumption* could be ascribed to an earlier date than the *Polyptych of Arezzo*. Lastly, the date proposed by Venturi for the *Madonna of San Pietro Ovile* is in substantial agreement with the grouping outlined above.

The frescoes in the Servite Church at Siena – the *Massacre of the Innocents* (plate CLVI) and *Herod's Feast* (plate CLVII) – and the two small panels of *Christ before Pilate* (plate CLVIII) and *Martyr Saints* (plate CLIX) – the first in the Vatican Gallery and the second in the National Gallery – present certain characteristics indicating an affinity with the group just passed in review.

Various conflicting attributions of these frescoes have, it is true, been proposed by critics – the reader will find them recorded in our " Notes on the Plates," to which we refer him – but in the case of the *Massacre of the Innocents*, at all events, a simple comparison with the lower part of the *Crucifixion* at Assisi should be enough to establish the rightness of its attribution to Pietro, in spite of the fact that the panel is now partly ruined. You have the same rhythm of the crowd shut in by the mounted soldiery, the same use of large monochrome zones serving as a frame for the interplay of diversified tones in the centre of the painting. The shields of the horsemen are in both cases yellow; so, too, the tunics of the men-at-arms brandishing their swords with a horizontal movement at either side of the fresco, and the drapery of the man who bends over the heap of slaughtered children almost in the centre. Typical of Pietro are the half-length figures in the compartments of the frame, especially the one (not given in the reproduction) which is seen with joined hands and turning to look upwards.

For the fresco of *Herod's Feast* (plate CLVII) the stylistic evidence is less convincing. The episode is empty and inconclusive; even the composition appears to halt and stumble. On other grounds also the painting seems to be of later date. Perkins refrains from pronouncing definitely upon its authenticity on the ground of its bad state of preservation, but he limits the authorship in any case to the circle of Pietro's pupils.

We now come to the last certain works by Pietro, and their order is as follows:

1. The *Madonna and Child with Eight Adoring Angels*, painted for the Church of San Francesco at Pistoia, and now, without the predella, in the Uffizi Gallery. Vasari read its date, erroneously, as 1315; the correct date, 1340, has been re-established by Venturi (cf. Venturi, vol. V, fig. 546).

2. The *Polyptych of Beata Umiltà* (plate CLXXVIII). Painted in 1341.

3. The *Nativity of the Virgin* (plates CLXXVI and CLXXVII). Signed and dated, 1342.

4. The *St. Lucy* (plate CLXXIX). Painted after 1342.

5. The frescoes of the *Passion* on the vault of the Lower Basilica at Assisi. These were painted a few years later than the foregoing, and it is possible that the actual execution was not the work of Pietro but was entrusted to pupils and followers.

\* \* \*

That the scenes from the *Passion* – the *Entry into Jerusalem*, the *Last Supper* (plate CLXIX), the *Kiss of Judas*, the *Scourging*, (plate CLXXI). the *Ascent of Calvary*, etc. – belong to Pietro's last years, and that, as we have just said, they were carried out by his pupils, are conclusions justified by numerous considerations. In the first place, we may remark at once that the close following of Ducciesque formulæ, noticeable despite excessive ornamentation in these frescoes of the vault, is too feeble an argument, from the point of chronology, for critics to base seriously upon it a claim that they are contemporary with the first frescoes painted by Pietro at Assisi. This is borne out by the fact that Barna followed the same Ducciesque schemes at San Gimignano as late as 1350 or thereabouts. To find the first symptoms of an architecture so charged with ornament, of refinements so florid and complex as these, we must go to Ambrogio Lorenzetti's *Presentation in the Temple* (plate CXCI). As this must be dated after the frescoes of *Good Government* (plates CXCVI to CCI),

104

painted about 1337-1340, its date cannot be earlier than 1342. Moreover, the *Presentation*, being a panel-painting and not a fresco, naturally afforded a more suitable occasion for indulgence in ornament, while Ambrogio's taste for costliness and splendour was generally more pronounced than that of Pietro, as is shown by a comparison of Ambrogio's *Presentation* with Pietro's *Nativity of the Virgin* (plates CLXXVI and CXCI), which was painted in the same year and with equal care.

It is useless to appeal to Ambrogio's frescoes in San Francesco at Siena (plates CLXXXII and CLXXXIV), for there the simpler character of the architecture and decoration renders all comparison impossible. Even if we follow Berenson in assigning the frescoes of St. Martin's chapel to the last years spent by Simone in Italy, the contrast between their uniform, unadorned architecture and the architecture painted by Pietro in these frescoes of the vault would become still more pronounced, and to account for the difference we should have to allow for the lapse of some eight or ten years between the two.

Without entering into a minute examination of the points of similarity in Pietro's frescoes on the vault at Assisi and in Ambrogio's *Presentation* (plate CXCI), we would draw attention to the following traits. In the first place we have a frequent use of statuettes upon the columns, *e. g.* the winged *amorini* with horns of plenty, the *putto* unleashing a hound, another playing the horn; next, the feature of the traceried arches and festoons; thirdly, the employment of animal motives – lions *couchant*, dragons *rampant*, cranes *passant*, and so forth; and lastly, the inordinately slender shafts of the columns united in groups and with their capitals adorned by a wreath of leafage.

At what date, we may ask, notwithstanding certain hints in Giotto and his followers at Padua and Assisi, do bas-reliefs and frescoes of the complicated type seen in the *Entry into Jerusalem* (Anderson, 15407) first begin to be reproduced for purposes of architectonic decoration? And can instances be found either of vaulted roofs powdered with stars or of representations of the night sky and heavenly bodies, as in the *Kiss of Judas* (Anderson, 26944), until after the second quarter of the century?

Barna in none of his frescoes offers us such subtleties as appear in the windows and walls and decorative spaces of the *Entry into Jerusalem;* and we shall not find them even in Ambrogio's city in the fresco of *Good Government* where the search for accessories and anecdotic detail is carried to the extreme – falcons on their perches, masons at work, curtains lowered to ward off curious gaze and keep out the sun, and the like. In the *Ascent of Calvary*, it is true, Pietro's buildings are more varied, but this may be due in part to a diversity of intention. Ambrogio in planning his city aimed at a representation of civic life that should be recognizable as such, whereas Pietro deliberately let his fancy run upon far away cities and fashions, and upon oriental *bric-à-brac*. If the comparison were not too irreverent, we would say that the architectural designs upon the vault of Assisi were a foretaste of the triumphs won by Sienese industry at a later day in the decoration of gingerbread with sugar comfits; but, rising at once above this profane parallel, the reader should notice, as an instance of frigid and almost fatigued taste, the studious care with which each detail of the gnarled trunk and the foliage of the olive trees has been rendered in the *Kiss of Judas.*

One last observation, and we may end our chronological inquiry. The acanthus leaves of the cornices in the frescoes of the vault are incomparably more rich than those of the *Christ before Pilate* (plate CLVIII) and the *Martyrdom of the Franciscans at Ceuta* (plate CLXXXII), while they are of exactly the same type and technique as those which surround the various compartments of the *Seasons* in Ambrogio's frescoes of *Good and Bad Government* (cf. Anderson, 21322). From all these facts taken together we may draw two conclusions. The first is a confirmation of the view expressed above, that Pietro's frescoes on the vault at Assisi cannot have been painted, at the earliest, before 1340 ; and the second, that among the executants must have been a number of artists who had already worked under Ambrogio's direction upon the frescoes of the Communal Palace at Siena. We may go even farther and say that architecture and ornamentation of this overloaded, tormented type only became common in Sienese painting several decades later. They occur, for instance, in Giovanni di Paolo's *Presentation in the Temple* (Anderson, 21102) – a work which brings us down to a date as late as close upon 1430.

\* \* \*

Turning now to the significance of Pietro as an artist, it is remarkable that, unlike most painters of the Sienese school, it was long before critics came to give him – we will not say, an adequate – but even a seemly recognition. That Berenson in his *Central Italian Painters* should have spoken severely of Pietro's expressionism is, indeed, not surprising. At the time when that book was first published, it was customary to attribute to Pietro the frescoes of the *Passion* in which expressionism is carried to its worst limits, but now, as we have suggested, the part actually taken by Pietro in their execution must be held to have been inconsiderable. Yet even Venturi, a critic by no means indifferent to Pietro's art, could speak of him as a " fluent story-teller, abounding in grim types; an artist who by attempting to express too much fell into crude realism, and whose fundamental vulgarity rendered him incapable of understanding the majestic presentations of Duccio which he broke up with disorderly movement. Pietro was a *genre* painter who found himself forced to produce sacred art; in a word, he represents at Assisi the decline of the great principles enounced by Pietro Cavallini, Giotto, and Duccio. " It must be admitted, however, that

107

to-day Venturi would probably express himself somewhat differently.

The new valuation of Pietro is chiefly due to Perkins (1912), and Van Marle has given it his support. According to Perkins, the art of Pietro finds expression in a pronounced and ever growing naturalism, not, however, divorced from idealism. Pietro, he says, is the painter of the soul and the secret of the heart; the entire Trecento can show no work superior to the *Madonna between St. Francis and St. John the Evangelist* in mystical beauty and deep feeling. The formula of a " subjective naturalism, " elaborated by Antal, is in keeping with this view of Pietro's dramatic lyricism. According to Antal, Pietro was the most rigorous representative of the tendency at Siena. When, however, the same critic goes on to speak of what he terms a Sienese " Gothico-naturalistic current, " which came into being spontaneously, existed side by side with international Gothic, and exercised its influence upon the art heritage left by Giotto, propagating it to the north in a new and " Gothicized " form, we must make some reserves. Antal points, in the course of his review of Pietro's works, to the kitchen-scene in the fresco of the *Last Supper* (plate CLXIX) as an illustration of his hypothesis; but here, if we are not mistaken, the critic's argument rather lacks point. It is much more probable that the scene in question is merely an example of the " frantic " naturalism of the Lorenzetti brothers denounced by Berenson when he said that " to find its parallel you must go to Spain and to certain Germans," and that " at his worst, Ambrogio, the more gifted of the two, hardly surpasses the elder Breughel."

\* \* \*

We have seen that Pietro's style was first shaped by Ducciesque models; later on, he met with Simone Martini (who was in turn influenced by Pietro), with Giovanni Pisano and Giotto, and reached his highest achievement in the first frescoes at Assisi and in the *Crucifixion* at Siena. The subsequent productions of Pietro and his pupils reveal a tendency towards preciousness, unaccompanied, however, by any falling-off in inventive power. It may well be that this new tendency was due to actual competition with the taste created by Simone, particularly in the direction of decorative refinement, though we doubt how far Van Marle is right when he says that during this period, which corresponds roughly to the years 1330-1340, leaving out the fresco of the *Crucifixion*, Pietro's work alternates between a manner distinguished by feeling for swiftness, curves, and movement – this manner being employed in his compositions of a narrative or dramatic character – and a second manner closer to that of his first period despite a greater use of ornament, and exemplified in single figures appearing in his altarpieces, polyptychs, and so forth. Certainly, if the date proposed above for the *Madonnas* of Castiglione and Monticchiello be accepted – that is, between 1320 and 1329, or, in other words, some twenty years before the works which Van Marle has here in mind – the significance of the alleged alternative "manners" is considerably lessened; while it is certain that in Pietro's last works – the *Madonna* of the Uffizi Gallery, the *Polyptych of Beata Umiltà*, and the *Nativity of the Virgin* – we go back once more to an uncompromising " monumentality." (We have purposely omitted to mention in this connection the *St. Lucy*, painted, as we have said, after 1342, as it has been too much rehandled to furnish evidence of any importance, except with regard to questions of composition and arrangement). This monumental character it, is true, is now penetrated by a new spirit which at one time was ascribed to the influence of Ambrogio upon his brother; but, as we shall see, with this aspect of Pietro's last works the younger Lorenzetti had little or nothing to do.

We might almost define Pietro Lorenzetti as the most Florentine of the Sienese artists; and such he was, to a greater extent even than his brother, in whom the influence of Florence predominated. This Florentine quality Pietro owed

109

— not, of course, to imitation, which would only have told against him – but to a need for realizing his conceptions dramatically. He was driven to seek for plastic reality as a means of giving relief and significance to attitudes and for conveying a feeling of resistance to touch. But it is not possible to express passion, or physical and moral impulses dramatically, unless the images by which these things are conveyed to the spectator are entirely credible, that is, recognizable as vehicles of the *real;* and this is precisely what Pietro succeeded in doing in paintings like the *Madonna between St. Francis and St. John the Evangelist*, the *Nativity of the Virgin*, and the group of figures in the *Deposition*. At such times Pietro's feeling for plastic reality and movement is hardly inferior to that of Giotto.

In all that concerns space Pietro differs from Duccio and Simone, approaching most closely to the Florentine conception. He ceases to regard space as merely a background for colour or a means of suggesting the infinite; he does not even use it as a plane upon which to project shapes in arabesque design; he considers space as volume surrounding, sustaining, and giving equilibrium to figures. Hence the diversity between Pietro's treatment of line and that of Duccio and Simone, whose chief interest lay in obtaining effects with silhouettes and arabesques. At times Pietro's understanding of line brings him close to the incisive quality that we find, for example, in Pollaiuolo's drawing, though the latter is certainly more crude and dexterous. Line is thus related to the internal effects of mass in the figures, and to their dynamic significance as bodies; it is " functional line ," serving to convey sensations of volume and not merely to describe a superficial outline. These two contrasting uses of line are well illustrated in Pietro's *Resurrection* at Assisi, a fresco carried out with the help of assistants. The figures of the soldiers, with their complicated architecture of foreshortenings notice, in particular, the sturdy yeoman snoring with his mouth half-open – are constructed in the third dimension and give it modelling; whereas the figure of Christ, emerging with a vague sideways gesture from the box-like tomb, is worthy of a pack of playing-cards.

Meanwhile we must be on our guard lest by exaggerating the Florentine quality in Pietro we should be led to forget the purely Sienese elements that characterize his whole artistic production. Both in his autograph works and in paintings executed by pupils under the artist's supervision, the two strains were intimately bound up together. Typically Sienese are the richness in ornament and the feeling for colour exemplified in the mantle of the *Madonna of Arezzo* with its pattern of chequers and flowers, blue, ivory, and gold; the gorgeous *Assumption* (plate CLI) in gold, red, and black; the vermilion, the white amice and *pallium* of *St. Gregory* (plate CL). With what shall we compare the solemn splendour of the panel in San Pietro Ovile: the deep tone of the Virgin's robe with the hem of the white tunic just appearing above it, her golden bodice, the pomegranate dress of the Child, the embroidered veil of white, gold, and red flowers, upheld by angels, the rust-coloured throne with its hue of ancient cashmere shawls ? Or take the *Throned Madonna* (plate CLII), with the black mantle and the vest of pale red and gold brocade, and the pale red of the Child's drapery, and the *Madonna in Glory* (Van Marle, vol. II, fig. 218), vested in a black mantle edged with dull gold, the Child and the angels dressed in gold, and the throne of gold and red. This almost funereal solemnity of colour with its dominant black and gold notes recalls the mood of Duccio in paintings like the *St. Agnes* (plate LVII), and in magnificence it surpasses him. When we search our memory to find some other instance of colouring equally austere and triumphant, we can only think of Godoshi's great panel in black and dead gold, representing the snake killing the tortoise, in the British Museum.

Still more varied accents of colour, adorning rather than disturbing the dramatic contrast of the figures, will be found in the *Christ before Pilate* (plate CLVIII); in the gleaming smoothness of grey architecture set off with vermilion in the *Monk's Dream* (plate CLX); in the striped cloaks of the hermits drawing water from a well of rosy jade in the panel of the *Carmelite Friars* (plate CLXI); and in the fabulous elegance of the *Madonna* of Assisi (Plate CLXIV), with the gold ground, the light grey of St. Francis's habit, the rose drapery of the Evangelist, and the Virgin arrayed in the royal poverty of a dark green veil and blue tunic. This potency of colour with its characteristic intonations was not entirely lost in the subsequent fortunes of the Sienese school; in all the thronging frescoes of the vault it is chiefly colour – colour charming and vigorous – that survives like an indelible family trait.

\* \* \*

But it is in the *Crucifixion* at Assisi (plates CLXVI and CLXVII) that Pietro's colour reaches its greatest magnificence. This, together with the *Crucifixion* at Siena (plate CLXXII), may deservedly be placed among the greatest conceptions of the subject to be found in painting. And yet, incredible as it may appear, the fresco has been described by one writer as " the closing scene of a stage spectacle." It is true that the mutilated state of the painting prevents us from forming a just appreciation of the lower part, but, serious though this damage is, it has not destroyed the stupendous effect of the three crosses rising up above the line of the dense throng. The angels set against the dark blue ground (plate CLXVII) are encircled by a greenish foam which seems to suggest the lightning speed of their flight; and the tint of the background, unlike the red of the Siena *Crucifixion*, gives the impression of a vision beheld under some halo of the moon, yet a vision in which the colours are still vivid and have not lost their individuality by being reduced, as in the Siena *Crucifixion*, to one indistinct monochrome tone. Nor is this all. The movements of the angels and their gestures

112

of horror and pity are less convulsed than in the later painting, and their gleaming aureoles acquire an added brightness
from the transparency of their faces. So, too, the nudes of the
crucified thieves are penetrated by the light. You would say
they were wrought out of alabaster in their slightly exaggerated modelling. In the body of the Redeemer, again, the division of the ribs from the abdomen is less accentuated than
in the *Crucifixion* at Siena, where the intensificaton of the
artist's striving after realistic effects finds expression in an
anatomical formula already used by Giovanni Pisano. The
thronging crowd in the Assisi fresco is admirably set in relief
on the left by the movement of the mounted troops flanking
the Holy Women, and on the right, at the bottom of the
fresco, by a second group of horsemen watching the scene. The
pawing and stamping of the horses' hoofs, even the motion
of their tails, well conveys the tediousness felt by these representatives of the animal world in waiting through an event
that has no interest for them. And, while the single hue of
the azure sky is reflected in the group of the Holy Women, a
dazzling wealth of varied colour is distributed amongst the
group of soldiery — inventions fantastic and grotesque, from
the monstrous trappings of the horses with their yellow head-
covers and the black openings for the eyes, to the armour
plated like fishes' scales and the draperies with their lingering
traces, as in the *Polyptych of Arezzo*, of a pictorial script
made up of squares and lozenges and floral patterns, bizarre
and oriental.

In the *Deposition* (plate CLXVIII) the colour is less robust, but it is handled with more profound if less ostentatious
understanding. The fresco seems to be encased, as it were,
between the two deep tones of green appearing in the mantle
of one of the Marys on the left and in the robe of the disciple
who is seen removing the nails from the Saviour's feet. This
double note of colour, at once sorrowful and earthen, serves as
a frame enclosing the red mantle of the Magdalene, the tint of
which is perhaps intended to allude to the Precious Blood

shed upon the Cross, and the nude figure of Christ lying upon the rich grave-cloth spread out by Joseph of Arimathea. The Virgin's blue mantle and the narrow red strip of the drapery worn by one of the Holy Women standing behind her seem to lessen the excessive symmetry by a gentle touch of subdued colour.

It is doubtful whether Pietro ever again reached the height attained in these two frescoes, unless in the second *Crucifixion* (plate CLXXII) at Siena, with those angels raining down like livid globes, and ending comet-fashion in tails of incandescent fire, in the midst of a blood-red atmosphere suggesting the Last Judgment and the consummation of the world. Pietro was already well past forty years of age when in these paintings he wedded the linked-up harmony of his style to an instinctive tragic impetuosity, in which there constantly appear a rustic element and, as it were, an uncouth accent that in certain respects take us back to the popular Italian realism of Dugento painting. Nor is the vigour of pose less expressive here than in the *Deposition*. Observe how the body of Mary falls between the arms of the Holy Women, the despairing meditation of the Beloved Disciple, and the gesture of the centurion and the soldier, who seem almost to offer their hearts to the Crucified.

In spite, however, of this return in later life to simple forms like those of the first cycle of frescoes at Assisi, Pietro's art shows no symptom of fatigue, as is proved by the *Nativity of the Virgin* (plates CLXXVI and CLXXVII). Far from being a " tired " work – so one critic has described it – the fresco breathes an epic calm; its spirit is patriarchal and homely, yet eminently life-enhancing and poetical. Notice the austerity of the facial types in the *Nativity*, the measured, sacramental gestures, the sober furniture, the solid treatment of spaces, the dignified and thoughtful domesticity; could the artist who painted them have been responsible for the Assisi frescoes of the *Passion* to which we have so often had occasion to refer, and which Pietro is said to have painted during the very years when he was engaged upon this *Nativity?* What greater contrast can be conceived than that between this crowning calm and that busy preoccupation with culture, archæology, knick-knacks – pursuits fit for a Francesco di Giorgio more than a century later? Think for a moment of the *Kiss of Judas* with its animalesque human faces – the deserter-apostle who turns as he runs away, grimacing like a puss-in-boots in fear of a coming blow, or the dog-like, barking features of the dwarfish servant appearing to the right of Christ: a taste so diabolical could only have arisen indirectly from expressions of grief and certain anatomical deformations noticeable in the *Deposition*, or from the fantastic cruelty appearing in certain parts of the first *Crucifixion*.

* * *

Before closing our account of Pietro Lorenzetti, something must be said with regard to three works which are generally considered to prove his advanced sense for landscape – the *Allegory* (plate CLXXIII) and the two landscape panels (plates CLXXIV and CLXXV). And, first of all, the question of their authenticity requires a brief answer. So far as can be judged from its present state of conservation, the *Allegory* is to be assigned, according to Perkins, to a late date in Pietro's career, that is to say, to some time after 1330. That the two landscapes are of a later date than the *Allegory* is a fact so obvious as to need no proof. Hardly legible now and blurred by blue colour, the *Allegory*, however, presents a landscape of an entirely different character from the other two. Moreover, the attribution of the two landscape panels is not free from doubts. Thus, while Berenson, Perkins, and Van Marle have assigned them to Pietro, and Dami and Antal to Ambrogio Lorenzetti, the old catalogue of the Sienese Picture Gallery refers them, together with the *Allegory*, to the " manner of Ambrogio." It is not impossible that this last attribution may reflect one of those local and traditional beliefs which are not always to be regarded as unfounded. In any case, this variety of opinion invites reflection. Not only so, but landscape passages, with the exception of the frescoes of the vault at Assisi, do not as a rule occur in Pietro's work. The Assisi frescoes, again, as we have seen, have little or nothing of Pietro, and, besides this, the landscapes in them have not one feature in common with the castle standing on the shores of the lake or with the city in the panels. On referring to the polyptych of the *Carmelites* and that of *Beata Umiltà*, we notice at once that there, too, the landscapes are of an entirely different style, although from its form and date we should have expected the second to show a marked similarity in landscape to the panels. What we actually find, however, is a landscape of much more massive type: far from having a transparency as of glass, the greys and pinks of the walls barred by black shadows cast by the doors and windows, are thick and solid, suggesting a landscape borrowed from Taddeo Gaddi, only more refined in colouring. Another hypothesis, probably suggested by Ghiberti's description of the frescoes in the cloister of San Francesco at Siena and by the fact that Ambrogio painted landscapes in the *Legends of St. Nicholas of Bari*, in his *Deposition*, and, still more extensively, in his frescoes of *Good Government*, would assign the panels to Ambrogio Lorenzetti; but the country landscapes of Ambrogio show a rudeness and immediacy of conception that admit of no comparison with our two panels, and hence this hypothesis also fails to be convincing.

Some writers have identified the slender tower rising above the others in the sleeping city (plate CLXXV) with the tower of the Communal Palace of Siena. This argument, if such it be, appears to us somewhat inconclusive. The design for facing the tower of Siena with stone belongs to 1341, and the tower itself was finished either after 1345 or after 1348 — historians vary between these two dates. Now the two panels clearly formed parts or, rather, are fragments of one and

116

the same work, now mutilated and dispersed, this being proved by the identical measurements of the panels and by their similarity in style, while if is further inconceivable that two independent works of the kind could have come into being at a period when paintings of exclusively natural or profane subjects were unknown. It follows, therefore, that the panels must either be attributed to the last years of Pietro and Ambrogio, since both artists died in 1348, or fall entirely outside the period of their activity. Without dwelling however, on considerations into which so many doubtful elements enter, we prefer to direct attention to the evidence offered by style. The very architecture of the city (plate CLXXV) – vertical and sharp like needles of crystal or the stems of reeds, with its pearly colour and its roofs rose-tinted as if seen by moonlight or illumined by a greenish frost – seems to point to the art of a later period. We may recall Giovanni di Paolo's white and pale green landscapes, the chill elegance of similar scenes in early Quattrocento painting, or, if particular instances have meaning amidst so large a choice, we would point to the little city in Giovanni's *Flight into Egypt* (plate CCLIV), where the wavelets of the stream on whose bank the city lies are painted with exactly the same suggestion of rippling hair, and to the city in the *Deposition* in the Vatican Gallery (Anderson, 23956) where the planning of the streets is almost identical. Another significant trait is the treatment of the leaves in the two panels. In Pietro and Ambrogio the drawing of foliage is more free, not stylized and " clotted, " as here, where the triangle of the trees is rendered by slight dabs of colour, giving the surface an effect of being punctured or stabbed as in embroidery. Trees painted in exactly the same way will be found in Sassetta's *St. Anthony scourged by Demons* – part of an *ancona* painted between 1423-1426 for the Guild of Wool-workers (Accademia, Siena, nn. 166-169). A further point is that the boats in Ambrogio's *Legend of St. Nicholas* (plate CLXXXIX) are entirely unlike the boat in the first panel (plate CLXXIV),

Ambrogio's boats being less sinuous and pointed. A parallel to the boat in the panel occurs, however, in the predella of the *Legends of the Virgin and San Galgano* (Accademia, Siena, n. 198), in the scene where the saint, vested in a chasuble, gives the Communion to a hirsute anchoress, the figures appearing in a wilderness of rocks with a river in the background. Again, the rocks and the ground in the two panels are painted in a faint grey colour laid on with strokes of the brush backwards and forwards. This was the practice of Giovanni di Paolo, in whom we also find frequent examples of landscapes composed with a gradual rise towards a horizon of pale blue-an arrangement which Giovanni derived from Sassetta. Lastly, Giovanni and Sassetta not infrequently give a suggestion of transverse movement upon the line of the horizon by introducing flights of migrant birds; and in the panel of the city (plate CLXXV) a similar effect is conveyed by the ship sailing with the wind.

But enough of these comparisons and contrasts: the question is not one of deep interest, nor can we hope to arrive at a final solution. To sum up, we will re-state it thus: is it likely that either Pietro with his pronouncedly dramatic inspiration, or Ambrogio with his constant insistence upon the relation of human activity to its natural surroundings, could ever have had a feeling of nature in the absence of man so remote and so dead as here? Even man's own creations seem in their abandonment to have become almost natural objects, and appear crystallized in a barren expectation. A conception of this kind strikes us as already tinged with decadence and far too "precious" for the first half of the fourteenth century.

\* \* \*

It is fortunate that the paintings of Ambrogio Lorenzetti, to whom critics of former days almost exclusively dedicated the interest now equally divided between him and his brother, give rise to very few of those intricate questions about authenticity and dates that have occupied us so painfully in the preceding pages with their lists and minute comparisons. The chief stages in Ambrogio's career are illustrated by the following works, of which the dates are either certain or probable:

1. The *Madonna of Vico L'Abate* (Van Marle, vol. II, fig. 250). Dated (*ibid.*) 1319. Despite the " monumental " character of the Virgin and the lively movement of the Child, there are indications of a want of facility in the artist, which suggest that he was still learning his craft. On the whole, the painting shows what a Sienese painter might have learned, *e. g.*, from Giotto's *Madonna* in the Uffizi Gallery.

2. The *Madonna del Latte* (plate CLXXX). Painted before 1330. Here the violent modelling, the pose of the Child — very close to that in the preceding painting — and the pointed cut of the panel at the top indicate that the work is of relatively early date.

3. The *Madonna of Roccalbegna* (plate CLXXXI). Painted about 1330, the date to which Berenson, in his *Essays* (p. 23), assigns it, together with the *Madonna and Saints* (plate CXC). With these two paintings we must clearly group the *Madonna and Saints* at Massa Marittima (plates CCVI and CCVII), as a simple comparison is enough to prove.

4. The frescoes of the *Franciscans* (plates CLXXXII to CLXXXIII), formerly in the cloister and now in the Church of San Francesco at Siena.

5. The *Legends of St. Nicholas of Bari* (plates CLXXXVIII and CLXXXIX), and the panels with *St. Proculus and St. Nicholas* in the Bandini Collection at Fiesole (Van Marle, Vol. II, fig. 258).

6. The frescoes of *Good and Bad Government* (plates CXCII to CCV).

7. The *Polyptych of St. Petronilla* (plates CCXI to CCXIII), and the *Triptych of Badia a Rofèno* (*Vita d'Arte*, July, 1912, figs. 29 to 31), identified by De Nicola with the painting which Vasari affirms to have been executed by Am-

brogio " at the very end of his life for Monte Oliveto of Chiu-suri."

      8. The *Presentation in the Temple* (plate CXCI). Dated 1342.

      9. The *Annunciation* (plates CCVIII to CCX). Dated 1344.

It is a commonplace of criticism that not long after the careers of the artists whom we have so far passed in review were ended, if not actually during their life-time, Ambrogio began to introduce a new spirit into painting. This was the open spirit, at once versatile and eloquent, of Humanism and the Renaissance. Vasari's estimate of Ambrogio's character as that of a " gentleman and a philosopher rather than a craftsman " bears this out, and a reference in Tizio's *Sienese Chronicle*, cited by Della Valle (Vol. II, p. 213), gives further support to Vasari's words. "*Mappamundum volubilem rotundumque*," Tizio informs us, " *in aula secunda balistarum publici palatii fecit* " – a fact which, taken together with the episodes from Roman history painted on the front of the Communal Palace in 1337 and with Ambrogio's alleged authorship of the verses commenting upon the frescoes of *Good and Bad Government*, points to considerable attainments in science and culture. Vasari speaks also of the "portrait of Ambrogio by his own hand in San Procolo at Florence in the predella of his picture, where he is wearing a hood on his head," and many of the leading figures in the fresco of *Good Government* (plate CXCVI) and in parts of the frescoes in San Francesco (plates CLXXXVI and CLXXXVII) are undoubtedly portraits of contemporaries. In this way painting began slowly to come down from the mediæval Paradise and to cast a glance upon the world below.

* * *

Although the distinctions drawn by critics between the various phases and styles noticeable in an artist's development need always to be interpreted in a broad sense, and a return to an earlier manner is a frequent occurrence – none more so

120

than that exemplified in Ambrogio, of a return in advanced
maturity towards the forms of youth – yet the *Madonna of
Vico l'Abate*, the *Madonna del Latte*, and the *Madonna of Roccalbegna* represent what may rightly be described as Ambrogio's first manner. He was then perceptibly influenced by
Giotto's plastic sense and feeling for volume. The first of the
above-named Madonnas, a painting of about the same date
as Pietro's *Polyptych of Arezzo*, introduces us to an artist full
of energy, but unable as yet to express himself with perfect
freedom; and hence this painting lends a certain measure of
support to the belief that Ambrogio was the younger of the
two brothers. However this may be, Ambrogio's link with tradition must be sought, not, as in the case of Pietro, in the
art of Duccio, but in that of Giotto. And it was this relationship between Giotto and Ambrogio, which, mingling later on
with elements more intrinsically and traditionally Sienese,
gave to Ambrogio's productions a character entirely their own.
Thus it is much less important for us to decide how far
Ambrogio influenced Pietro or the reverse – a question stated
in a variety of ways and one which has received a variety of
answers – than to determine their personal relations and reactions to Giotto. Ambrogio studied Giotto's last works in
Florence; and Pietro, when he was already past middle life
and had formed himself upon the models of the Byzantines
and of Duccio, made acquaintance with Giotto's frescoes at
Assisi. And just as about the year 1328, and particularly
after 1331, we find Pietro on his return from Assisi to Siena
following Sienese formulæ for graceful ornament and pattern
more closely, so, too, the plastic quality of Ambrogio shows
signs of modification towards the year 1330, when it became
acclimatized to the Sienese taste for narrative and decoration.
De Nicola has remarked how Ambrogio, who had devoted
himself to the study of the Florentines in 1319, returned in
1332 to Florence with a complete affirmation of the Sienese
manner in his *Legends of St. Nicholas*. The extent of his success
will be realized when we remember that Sirén, speaking

recently of Bernardo Daddi, Maso-Giottino, and other Florentine artists of the second generation, affirms that " Ambrogio had far more importance for them than Giotto and his immediate successors, who could show nothing comparable to the originality and creative force of the great Sienese painters."

In the frescoes of *Good and Bad Government*, which are to be reckoned among the most typical manifestations of Sienese art, Ambrogio paid tribute to local taste by abandoning his early " Florentinism," or, rather, by making it more complicated; he even made sacrifices in order to comply with the demands of its programme, though he never lost the advantages which it had placed in his power. In the works of his last period – the *Presentation* and the *Annunciation* – a solemnity of modelling in no way inferior to that of his first years is combined with the intense movement that we noticed in his figures of the Child in the early *Madonnas*. And, taking his work as a whole, we may say that feeling for volume at no time obscured its unmistakably Sienese character. Pietro Lorenzetti has the seriousness of the Florentines; he has their abstract energy, their virile idealism; but in Ambrogio, however great we may reckon the contribution of Florence, Sienese delight in decoration and sumptuous colour is never absent, and the traditional feeling for expressive beauty is rendered with a splendid and triumphant sensuousness no less in keeping with prevalent taste. It was, indeed, about this time that the discovery of a statue of Aphrodite Anadyomene at Siena set the whole city in a ferment of joy and wonder; and we read that honours amounting almost to religious veneration were paid to the figure of the goddess until, upon the occasion of certain political mischances, the Sienese destroyed it as devilish and buried it in Florentine soil. Can we wonder, then, that while Pietro was soon forgotten, even in Siena, Ambrogio was reckoned by Ghiberti – the writer who most faithfully represents the early traditions of the city – as one of her greatest painters, and, to judge from

the interest shown by Ghiberti for his work, almost worthy
of a place above Simone ?

\* \* \*

As we have seen, no long time passed before Ambrogio
began to modify the lessons he had learned from Giotto. Not
only did the expression of his Madonnas grow more tender, so
that they seem like mothers surprised in some act of loving
care, but the attitudes of the Child are changed. We now
see Him greedily sucking the breast with wide-open eyes as
if He would defend His possession of it, or He turns with
vigorous gestures towards the spectator like a diminutive
Hercules strangling snakes. In the *Madonna of Roccalbegna*
(plate CLXXXI), while the Virgin's countenance reflects the
characteristically Sienese melancholy even more markedly
than Ambrogio's earlier *Madonnas*, the Child seems to ad-
dress the spectators like an inspired prophet, assuming a
pose similar to that of the Child in the *Madonna and Saints*
(plate CXC) – a pose which Pietro Lorenzetti never dared
to attempt, although in the *Madonna of Dofana* and the *Madonna of San Pietro Ovile*, painted about the same time as
the Roccalbegna picture, we may perhaps discern a distant
resemblance to it. Notice, too, how characteristically Ambrogio tempers the wistful sadness of the Virgin's expression
as she seems to ponder Simeon's prophecy by the refulgent
beauty of her form and its subtle suggestion of femininity.

And now we come to a work of slender dimensions, yet
one of the greatest masterpieces of the Sienese school – the
*Madonna and Saints* (plate CXC). For, if it is possible
that Sienese colouring found in Simone and even in Pietro
Lorenzetti harmonies more rare and austere, it never surpassed the festal joy communicated by this small picture. Words
being almost always doomed to failure as a means of conveying even dexterity in composition and line, it may well seem

123

childish to attempt to suggest the effect of colour, and a colour like this, by mere description. Still, let the reader imagine the Virgin apparelled in a mantle of deep ultramarine and a vest of red, and the Child clad in a tunic of blue and gold. St. Catherine, whose left hand rests upon her wheel, is vested in a blue tunic powdered with flowers and a rose-coloured mantle. St. Dorothy, facing her and holding in her lap her gift of red and white roses, wears a mantle of blue. The first two Doctors of the Church are robed in red, against which stands out the gleaming white of their tippets and their oriental mitres. All the accessories are of oriental splendour — the blue, white, and red carpet; the pavement with its tiles and insets of the same colours; the precious vase of finely chased gold; the blue cushions; and the throne upon which the Virgin sits in state, likewise white, red, and blue.

With regard to the relation between the grouping of the figures and the Florentine treatment of space and volumes, Sirén has observed that in this painting Ambrogio clearly aimed at conveying a sense of the various planes. Thus the four kneeling Doctors serve as " wings " to a perspective carried farther backwards by the steps of the throne, while the double line of saints and angels on either side of the Madonna — a new version of the old motive of the angels leaning against the throne — creates a sense of increasing distance, as if the figures disappeared at last into the gold horizon. The sense of depth is further increased and a new interval of distance between the spectator and the figures is introduced by the vase of flowers in the extreme foreground — a motive used timidly also by Giotto — and the perspective effect is heightened by the variegated interplay of colour in the chequered pavement and the patterned carpet.

Though not, perhaps, in certain details inferior to this august *Madonna*, the panel of the *Madonna and Saints* at Massa Marittima (plates CCVI and CCVII) falls far short of it as a whole. Perkins, indeed, has called it Ambrogio's masterpiece, but this enthusiastic praise is perhaps to be explained by his having been the first to publish the painting. The very arrangement of the composition with its crowded figures disposed horizontally, while the apostles and prophets are packed away under the arches like spectators in the gallery of a theatre, hinders the effect of the third dimension. Ambrogio has nevertheless endeavoured to draw attention to it by exaggerating the steps of the throne, and by introducing the spatial – and theological – relations of the three Virtues who appear gesticulating and are seated upon them. Other artifices, like the violin held almost perpendicular to the observer by the angel on the right, and the tower balanced sideways on the knees of Hope, were no doubt intended to help in the same way. Meanwhile Charity, like the ineffectual conductor of an orchestra, sits holding up her slender bâton, manifestly powerless to dominate the tumult which is increased by the billowy draperies of the angels above scattering flowers and by the swinging censers. Yet, as we said, there are details in the picture not unworthy of the panel at Siena : angels that would have obsessed the mind of Goethe's Mephistopheles ; and the figure of Faith with a delightfully hysterical air that seems to anticipate Sassetta.

Ambrogio, as is well known, had a fondness for symbolical adjuncts. A striking instance may be noticed in the frescoes painted during this period at Monte Siepi near San Galgano but now hopelessly damaged, where Eve, holding in one hand a leaf plucked from the tree of knowledge of good and evil, and with the Serpent twined about her arm, lies stretched on the ground before the Madonna. Admixtures of this kind do not so far disturb the plastic sense; but we have only to contrast the slight inflection of line, hardly perceptible and only just hinting at beauty, in Simone's *St. Catherine* (plate C) with the modelling of St. Dorothy in Ambrogio's *Madonna and Saints* (plate CXC), or with the ample forms of this *Madonna and Saints* at Massa Marittima, to perceive that Sienese taste has already begun to develop a double character of symbology and sensuality. Full of life and charm as such traits may be, it is certain that the theological Virtues will never again weave their dances at the feet of a Madonna so comely and loving as the Madonna of Massa Marittima.

\* \* \*

It is probable that the frescoes painted by Ambrogio in the cloister of San Francesco at Siena would have marked his crowning achievement, if they had all been preserved to us even in the poor condition of the two that remain – the *Martyrdom of the Franciscans at Ceuta* (plates CLXXXII and CLXXXIII) and *Boniface VIII receiving St. Louis as a Novice* (plates CLXXXIV to CLXXXVII). Such, at least, is the impression conveyed by Ghiberti's unqualified praise. Moreover, although the frescoes confirm the divided taste of which we have just spoken, it is certain that up to the year 1331 or thereabouts – the period at which they were painted – symbolism applied to the representation of life in society, of theology and culture, had not yet taken hold of Ambrogio to the extent manifested in the later frescoes of *Good and Bad Government*. Indeed, from Ghiberti's description we should have expected nothing except fine painting in these Franciscan scenes.

The episode of the *Martyrdom* need not long detain us. Its colour, or, rather, the vestige of its colour, is of a greenish hue. Some of the figures – the executioner and the priest on the right, for instance – betray a partial derivation from Pietro, while the exhibition of exotic types and, particularly, the figure of the fat mandarin in a plumed conical hat, are strikingly naive, and recall the figures one sees at a masquerade during Carnival. Notice, besides, how the arrangement of all these personages bending like reeds in the wind over the heap of slaughtered bodies seriously compromises the stability of the whole composition. In the fresco of

*Boniface VIII receiving St. Louis*, on the other hand, the structure of the painting is carried, as if by a deep breath, right up to the vaulted ceiling by four parallel lines marking the third dimension. The first is formed by the crowd of bystanders in the background (cf. plate CLXXXV); the second, by King Robert and the seated cardinals (plates CLXXXIV and CLXXXV); the third, by the Saint on his knees with the friars standing in front of the papal throne; and the fourth, by the cardinals in the foreground with their backs turned towards the spectator. (In our reproductions the lower part of the fresco – now half perished – has been sacrificed in order to give a more ample view of the painting as a whole; this part merely represents in its full length the desk against which the cardinals are represented leaning). In order to realize the effect of this perspective to the full, however, we must mentally supply the original colour from the scanty traces that remain. Had the red hats of the cardinals and the other tints of the first three planes been better preserved, the less damaged colour of the row of young men looking on would cause them to fall into their proper place in the perspective plan. Beginning from the left (plate CLXXXVI), the tunics are red or green; and the youth wearing a cap and placing his hand on his neighbour's shoulder is in blue with white stripes. The whites in the linings of the hoods, in the high lights of the faces, and in the gloves of the Pope – seated on a red throne with a gold back – are extremely bright, and may be due to restoration.

And now just a glance at the portraiture of the youthful figures. In the works of earlier, archaïsing painters, for whom faces, types, and expressions represented no more than a mere iconographical element transportable at will, portraiture was a feature of slight importance; here, however, there is evidence of deliberate research and choice, so that we have what we may call the artist's personal comment upon his plastic inventions. We have alluded elsewhere to the group of personages in the fresco of *Good Government* (plate CXCVI),

where Ambrogio has clearly portrayed the prosperous magis-
trate, the long-nosed doctor, and the pretentious *hobereau;*
here he introduces us to the world of young exquisites, the
*jeunesse dorée* of Siena, encircling the humble saint upon his
knees and the almost finical gallantry of King Robert. You
can imagine them watching Ambrogio as he painted their
likenesses, just as nowadays people visit the studio of some
fashionable artist. With their complicated hoods and caps, their
turned-back linings and hair-nets, and with all the modishness
of a well-to-do middle-class of no long standing, these young
men are pretty much the heroes of Folgore's rhymes: open
countenances, thoughtless, sensual, and with perhaps a faint
odour of the peasant still lingering about their smart clothes.
Observe, too, the famous gesture of the thumb – the Lorenzetti trade-mark as familiar as Whistler's – and the other
thumb thrust into the opening of the tunic, as the provincial
*beau* of a later age stuck his between waistcoat and shirt,
with the other fingers spread out (plate CLXXXV). To
complete the group, we have that ecstatic youth – unfor-
tunately he has come out too dark in our reproduction
(plate CLXXXVII) – with the " killing " eyes, the *accroche-
cœur* glued to his cheek, and the high, stiff collar. How he
abstracts himself from the scene in order to strike the pose
that will best show off his beauty! He is, we may be sure, a
sonnet-writer, and let us hope that he is no worse. The friars,
with their hands joined, have a vague look of regimental cor-
porals that seems not altogether out of place; in any case they
are defended from the irony of the exquisites by the good-
natured cardinals comfortably seated on the bench – figures
strangely colloquial and massive. On the other hand, what
feminine, conventual poesy in the last relic of these frescoes –
the profiles of the *Four Nuns*, published by Hutton! Perhaps
the most seductive image of religion considered as an instru-
ment of social dignity, the nobility of the good and beautiful, has been given us – in Italian painting – by Ambrogio
Lorenzetti. He could do no more, for, virtuous though he

was, he was too much the man of letters to concern himself
with religion under the form of asceticism or as the source
of " immortal longings." If ever the two brothers conversed
upon such subjects, their discussions must have been deeply
interesting: Pietro viewed the world, religion included, in the
black and gold of the funeral pall ; Ambrogio saw it arrayed
in azure and rose.

* * *

As the frescoes painted in the Church of San Procolo at
Florence have perished and its altar-piece has been mutilated and dispersed, the only paintings left to testify to Ambrogio's activity from 1332 to 1334 are the four small *Legends
of St. Nicholas of Bari* in the Uffizi Gallery, which seem originally to have belonged to a series of panels now incomplete
(plates CLXXXVIII and CLXXXIX). Here Ambrogio appears with the most marked Sienese characteristics, though
the material is not so rich as in the small *Madonna and Saints.*

In these panels the architecture has grown more slender
and the types of the figures are longer and thinner − evidence, according to Van Marle, of Ambrogio's return, after
his early Giottism, to forms used by Pietro Lorenzetti. In
colour, too, Ambrogio has now abandoned the prevalent red
and blue tones of his other panels for a graduated harmony
of complementary tints. Of the four panels, the best are the
*Consecration of St. Nicholas in the Cathedral of Myra* − with
the golden triptych upon the altar and the staircase down
which the white figures of monks are seen descending − and
the gloomy sea-shore enclosed by rocks and a horizon peopled
with sails. Especially notable are the effect of atmospheric
depth secured by gradations of chiaroscuro − an effect rendered still more subtly, however, in the *Presentation*, painted
some ten years later − and the sense of distance obtained by
the play of lights and shadows. It is for this reason that
Ambrogio seems to have kept the colouring subdued and

delicate. Van Marle has detected signs of Pietro's influence in the *St. Proculus* and *St. Nicholas* of the Bandini Collection, where a marked tendency towards angularity and other uncouth traits is in contrast with Ambrogio's habitual manner.

And now at last we come to the frescoes of *Good and Bad Government* (plates CXCII to CCIII). As their allegorical meaning is either so obvious as to render comment unnecessary, or, in other parts, so conjectural and disputable as rather to belong to the literature of charades, we will not spend time in discussing their interpretation from this point of view. At a first glance, the frescoes, like some others painted by the Sienese school, convey the impression of a certain limitation in their laying-out or, rather, of an imperfect correspondence between it and the vastness of the composition. This defect is to some extent noticeable in Ambrogio's frescoes in San Francesco at Siena, though it is entirely absent from Simone's frescoes in the Chapel of San Martino at Assisi. In the latter you have a perfect balance — the conception is grandiose and yet at the same time there is something which softens and tempers it. The frescoes of *Good Government*, on the other hand, not only cover a more extensive surface, but the number and the crowding together of buildings and figures of widely different dimensions, from the diminutive to the monumental, constantly breaks up the rhythm and introduces confusion into the visual effect. For this reason figures like that of *Peace*, draped in olive-colour against a red background and reclining upon pale violet and black cushions (plate CXCII), and those of *Fortitude, Prudence, Concord*, and *Justice* (plates CXCIII to CXCV) are probably more effective when viewed singly than in the tightly packed composition where Ambrogio and his assistants were led by allegorical rather than artistic considerations to crowd them together. Nor is the result any different when we turn to the wall frescoed with the *Effects of Good Government in the City* (plate CXCVII). Here, again, the group of maidens dancing and playing cymbals and the monastic escort following the

130

bride need to be viewed as they appear in our reproductions
(plates CXCVIII and CXCIX), as the oppressive weight of the
architecture allows the eye no rest in its search for a point
at which it may take in the whole scene and yet enjoy the
various details one by one. Moreover, this feeling of breath-
lessness is increased by the chemical action of centuries upon
the colour; the sky has been changed into a heavy roof of
lead, and the other tints have assumed a general tone of red
and black or of *terra verde,* like that of excavated pottery.
Such language may sound harsh; yet the rhetorical exegesis in
which some critics have indulged would only be justified if
the single episodes could be reconstructed from a radiance of
colouring equal to that of Ambrogio's Madonnas and the Saints
in his panel paintings, and this is impossible. Unless we are
prepared to give full rein to fantastical conjectures, we must
affirm that, notwithstanding a wealth of marvellous incidents –
and these incidents, it should be remembered, scattered and
sometimes wasted over an ill-constructed arrangement, must
from the very first have stood out in too vivid relief – the
frescoes, the most celebrated of all Ambrogio's works, belong
less to the domain of æsthetics than to that of conundrums
and the history of costume. The truth is that Ambrogio has
here allowed himself to become entangled in a kind of chart
or planisphere, designed to present a panoramic view of the
social life of his day. To a far greater degree than is wil-
lingly admitted, he had the spirit of those early painters of
maps who took delight in depicting figures of Æolus and Fa-
vonius blowing with puffed-out cheeks upon a coastline of
ultramarine blue, while galleys are seen making for port or
in danger of shipwreck. Thus in the midst of these frescoes
we find him suspending winged allegorical figures holding up
great scrolls of writing, or introducing that symbol of the
hanged man (plate CC) which speaks for itself, reminding
you of Pulcinella setting the swing in motion to amuse the
children. Thus, if Pietro Lorenzetti exceeded in his search for
the dramatic, Ambrogio sank into a habit of professorial

131

dissertations; he has planned the frescoes in the same spirit with which he constructed his " *mappamundus volubilis.*" We find a parallel proceeding in the Romanesque sculptors with their friezes and capitals illustrating human " works and days," and in the small representations of arts and crafts unearthed from Egyptian tombs – soldiers marching with lances on their shoulders, sailors trimming their sails, bakers on their knees kneading bread, and the like – subjects more interesting as " documents " for the history of manners and customs than as artistic creations.

The most important fresco is the one illustrating the *Effects of Good Government in the Country* (plates CC and CCI). Like the others, it is now much deteriorated, with harsh contrasts of colour in the black spots of the trees and fences and the red patches of the houses standing out against the faded green of the landscape. Critical fancy has not been idle with regard to this fresco, which certainly gives scope for untrammelled exercise of imagination now that the unfelt hand of time has worked upon it no less dexterously than human intelligence and the brush. Has not Leonardo spoken of the hidden meanings conveyed by damp and lichens staining the wall? Thus in the allegory of *Bad Government* there is nothing to prevent our finding correspondences between the mysterious fragment of the three soldiers (plate CCIII) and the most widely differing modes of painting, from that of ancient pottery to the encaustic tiles of Pompeii. Some critics have seen traces of Impressionism, of Post-Impressionism, and even of Cézanne, in Ambrogio's country scene; others, again, have found a parallel between the landscape of his city and the patterns invented by Florentine *tesseristi* of the Quattrocento, and have caught a glimpse – no less – of certain tricks belonging to the *macchiaioli.*

That the problem in these frescoes was one of conveying the sense of gradually increasing distance towards the horizon must have been clear to the artist whose rendering of spatial depth within the limited surface of the *Madonna and Saints*

132

(plate CXC) was so perfect in its telling rhythm. But the actual state of the frescoes makes it impossible for us to determine now whether or not Ambrogio endeavoured to obtain effects of atmospheric transparence by introducing differences of tone and passages of light and shade. However this may be, the number and variety of the incidents taken from country life which the artist insisted upon crowding into the fresco – lords and ladies riding out with their falcons, the two peasants driving a laden ass and a fat pig, the blind man cautiously feeling his way with his face turned upwards as if in a hopeless effort to see (plate CCII), the caravan of merchants nearing the bridge, the warehouses by the shore, men ploughing and beating out the grain, animals feeding or chased by huntsmen, and all the other incidents which together form a kind of rural almanac – compelled him to raise the composition as far as possible towards the ceiling, with the result that the realization of the horizon and the sky has been either seriously diminished or, in places, entirely lost. Later on, Sienese artists went back to the old use of mere surface-projections and snippets of arabesque against an undefined background; here, in order to give the sense of distance, Ambrogio has had recourse to a painstaking modelling of hilly protuberances and undulating ground – an forced and almost microscopic application of Giotto's treatment of volume to a theme so little in harmony with it. We should, however, be better able to judge of the results of these combinations and contrasts from the point of view of space-composition, if the scenes and figures in the foreground had not been so terribly disembodied and almost consumed by time.

Before leaving the frescoes of the Communal Palace, a word must be said about the *Seasons* – the most singular of the many figures adorning their leafy borders. *Autumn* presents the type of a middle-aged man familiar to ancient sculpture – he is either a Hellenistic Neptune or a pugilist. *Winter* (plate CCV), a good-humoured old man, seems just about to throw the snowball held in his right hand. *Summer* (plate

133

CCIV) has his head engarlanded with leaves, a vivid figure thrilling with the life of a painting from Pompeii. Let us, however, be on our guard against stylistic inferences founded solely upon fragmentary relics and marginal annotations: a deft research can delude itself into finding Futurism in Shakespeare and anticipations of Mallarmé in Homer.

\* \* \*

The close of Ambrogio's career is marked by a group of works in which the artist's characteristics are summed up with greater precision, though we feel some hesitation in following the date proposed by De Nicola for the *Polyptych of St. Petronilla* and the *Triptych of Badia a Rofèno*. To assign these paintings, as he does, to the period immediately following the frescoes, implies that they were practically contemporary with the *Presentation in the Temple* (plate CXCI), painted in 1342, and with the *Annunciation* (plates CCVIII to CCX), painted in 1344, whereas the presence of certain archaïsing traits, particularly in the saints in the two extreme panels (plate CCXI, and *Vita d'Arte*, July, 1912, fig. 29), would seem to indicate an earlier date. On the other hand, the insertion in the very centre of an altar-piece of an episode so striking and rich in movement as the *Deposition* (plate CCXII), and the plastic quality of the flaming St. Michael in the *Triptych*, combined with the narrative element of conflict with the Dragon, were evidently recent artistic inventions, or they would have been more widely imitated. This transference of narrative upon a grand scale from a humble place in the predella to the centre of the painting marks an advance of Sienese practice upon the Florentine school.

The way in which Ambrogio has treated the *Deposition* recalls Angelico a century later. The colour has all the glamour of the artist's most ornate moods, bright with tender shades of green and with the white of the grave-clothes and the alabaster vase of ointment borne by the faithful Nicodemus. The women wear striped *mazzocchi* on their heads like those which Sassetta delighted to give to his figures. St. Dorothy (plate CCXIII), with her veil of pale violet bordered with gold, her flowers of blue and white and red, and the red ribbon edged with black twined through her golden hair, is, in the restrained modelling of her form, one of Ambrogio's best creations; and only a little inferior in charm is the figure of the Magdalene, clad in a purple mantle, and with her hair, not less golden, bound by a blue ribbon, while in her right hand she holds a vase of green-hued jade, and a golden star inset with the image of Christ adorns her breast. Other instances at this period of the artist's joy in painting similar ornaments will be found in the shield with which he has decorated thes St. John the Evangelist in this polyptych, and the heavily embossed armour of the St. Michael in the Rofèno triptych, where the Archangel's hair is threaded by a ribbon, as though in a woman's *mazzocchio*.

We have already more than once had occasion to refer to the *Presentation in the Temple* (plate CXCI), drawing attention to the over-elaborate character of its slender architecture, which recalls Francesco di Giorgio, and to Ambrogio's attempt to communicate a sense of perspective by lessening or deepening effects of light and shade. The figures in this painting repeat the artist's grandiose types, with an exquisite symmetry of colour in the Child and the white cloth held by the Madonna; but the tone is kept low and its vibrations seem to lack vitality. *The Annunciation* (plates CCVIII to CCX) possesses greater plastic solidity, and its colour is treated with the earlier classical simplicity of red and blue tints – red in the angel's gold-hemmed tunic, dark blue in the Virgin's mantle, and red again in the lining of the mantle and in the Virgin's robe. Ambrogio ends upon his most brilliant note of colour in the angel of the *Annunciation*, in the *Deposition*, and the small *Crucifixion* of the Fogg Museum (Van Marle, Vol. II, fig. 276), which in turn influenced

Lippo Memmi's *Crucifixion*, now in the Vatican Gallery. The increased sumptuousness of these last paintings was handed on to Ambrogio's followers, reappearing in the *Legends of St. Stephen and St. Nicodemus* (plates CCXIV to CCXVII) likewise in the Vatican Gallery. The authorship of these panels has given rise to much discussion, but their material splendour admits no question.

\* \* \*

To trace the developments that took place in the Sienese school after the middle of the fourteenth century would require a separate study; here we can do no more than give an extremely limited selection from the vast production of its minor artists (plates CCXVIII to CCXLI). Among the executants whose work most clearly recalls the painting of the great epoch from 1285 to 1348 we may name Andrea Vanni, Lippo Vanni, Luca di Tommè, Paolo di Maestro Neri, Bartolo di Fredi, the Master of the *Scenes of Wedded Life* in the Communal Palace of San Gimignano, Giacomo di Mino del Pellicciaio, Niccolò di Buonaccorso, Paolo di Giovanni Fei, Cola di Petrucciolo, Taddeo Bartoli, and Andrea di Bartolo. No wonder that in a page of his *Essays* Berenson pleaded the cause of these lesser painters of the late Trecento and lamented their excessive neglect. Each of them is capable of giving us, in one aspect or another, a genuine æsthetic pleasure – and this in especially true of Bartolo, of Taddeo Bartoli – a far more harsh and vigorous artist – of Andrea and Lippo Vanni. Besides this, they all provide opportunities for instructive soundings and exercises in criticism, helping us towards a better division amongst them of the artistic patrimony left by the past and enabling us in addition to trace the course of the stylistic forms which, created during the first decades of the century, lasted right up to the appearance of Sassetta and Giovanni di Paolo, whose art blossomed about the close of the first quarter of the fifteenth century. Neither of these artists ever reached the level of the great painters with whom we have been chiefly concerned, but they nevertheless expressed themselves with a new accent and created a new poetry (plates CCXLII to CCLIV).

It was characteristic of Sassetta and Giovanni di Paolo, the former of whom was born in 1392 and the latter in 1403, that they were both free from the mannerism which had marked Sienese art in the second half of the fourteenth century. For it was mannerism of one form or another that betrayed itself in Bartolo di Fredi's diversified yet somewhat strident colour, in the harsh contortions of Taddeo Bartoli's design, and in the frank but clumsy gaiety of Paolo di Giovanni, who rendered as best he could the elegance of Simone (transmitted to him through Andrea Vanni) and the schemes of Pietro Lorenzetti's closing phase, by a naive ostentation of flowers and marbles and carpets and vivid contrasts of strips of black embroidery against white dresses (cf. plate CCXXVIII). Even in the noblest productions of this half century and the opening Quattrocento – in paintings like Andrea Vanni's *Madonna and Child* (plate CCXX), and Taddeo's *Throned Madonnas* and his *Crucified Christ* (plates CCXXX ff.) you feel that the school continues but that its inspiration is changed. The breach between religious tradition and the natural tendency of the individual artists was, indeed, now past healing, as any reconciliation of the claims of tradition with those of naturalistic taste, such as had been accomplished by the Lorenzetti brothers, implied the existence of artists endowed with a temperament no less exceptional than theirs. The resulting discrepancy is well illustrated by Taddeo's *Burial of the Virgin* (plate CCXXXVI). There you have an interpretation of a landscape in a composition of ritual character. What could be more wooden, more huddled, more German? It is architecture of the chess-board – a structure of queens, castles, knights, and pawns.

But there were other causes contributory to this decline. The materials for painting were now less rich, and the level of technique consequently fell. Furthermore, art production extended increasingly into the provinces and to towns of less importance where painters were able to obtain materials and commissions on more favourable terms than at Siena, saturated as the city already was with the incomparable masterpieces of her golden age of art. On the whole, the most vital and successful painting of the period came from artists who made no effort to react against the decadence of the school by vain attempts at renewing its early splendour: we allude to the " prose narrative " of Bartolo di Fredi and his unknown follower in the frescoes of San Gimignano (plates CCXXVI and CCXXVII; Alinari, 37241), to the work of Andrea di Bartolo and one or two more – all of them artists who took up and continued the popular vein of " Ugolino Lorenzetti " and Barna.

\* \* \*

With Sassetta and Giovanni di Paolo the situation is different. While they retained whatever was genuinely Sienese in the provincialism of Bartolo and Paolo di Giovanni Fei, their special gift lay in the silver-clear *timbre* of their painting, which seems to have been created in an atmosphere wherein expression is re-born with perfect docility and with inward charm. Thus they became the *genre* painters of devout inspiration, or, rather, of so much of it as still survived. Besides this, they invented – Sassetta, especially – a new landscape and a new type of countenance. Simone's knightly faces, Ambrogio's fleshly matrons and classicizing angels, have now become memories of the past. The figures that now come before us belong, if we may use the expression, to a neurasthenic generation; they are figures exquisitely jaded and sickly, their heads bald in front and their eyes wide with dread, figures of an hydrocephalic aristocracy whose progeny is obese and flabby (cf. the *Polyptych of Cortona*, reproduced by Alinari, 9295). They move in surroundings full of the poetry of fragile things, viewed in sadness and decay and overflowing

138

with curious decoration. Strange costumes-black-striped, fretted with silver, or bordered with fur; pavements set in squares minute and vertiginous like lozenges of Persian carpets or cells of a honeycomb; everywhere fashions and modes in which the plastic intention is mingled with a reflex pleasure, as if commenting upon itself with ornaments and artifices no longer the result of creation but the choice of personal taste. Look at Sassetta's *Nativity of the Virgin* (plate CCXLII). This weariness in riches, as we may call it, sets in high relief the morning activities in the rooms of St. Anne, where the logs crackle on the hearth and a flood of light pours in from the open horizon, against which the woman wearing the brocaded dress appears so suddenly. Or turn to the *St. Thomas Aquinas* at Budapest (plate CCXLIV), and notice the mystery of the deserted study with the books left lying open on the desk, and, in the orchard beyond, the spaces and espaliers set in ordered lines like the premises of a syllogism. The same spirit shows itself again in *The Magi and the Star* (plate CCXLVI), with the gates of the sleeping city, the flight of cranes beating the metallic sky, the ostriches standing on the summit of the hill, the plodding hound, the star moving like a lantern almost level with the way, the trees shaped like coral spikes and knobs. Where the artist's inspiration is more fervent, as in the *Temptation of St. Anthony* (plate CCL), the celestial sphere spins and describes its circle about the rounded mass of the forest, the inverse flight of birds like arrows seeming to accompany its whirling movement. Or you have the desolation of land-locked ships, and wandering beasts trembling in the bitter cold of an icy landscape in the *Legend of St. Anthony* (plate CCLI). Space has no more the golden nudity and mysteriousness that characterized the space of Duccio's legends, nor yet the fixity of a gleaming abyss as in Simone; it is tenanted by visual images springing from an all-subtle pictorial Romanticism. Line, composition, and arrangement lose their former exaltation, their symmetry, their summariness, and adapt themselves to purposes of illustration. This function

139

was discharged with imaginative charm and versatile invention by even lesser artists than Sassetta. Take, for instance, Giovanni di Paolo, Sassetta's younger contemporary. His chequered fields and miniature Paradises, conceived like Gardens of the Hesperides. anticipate the devotion of Angelico, complicated, however, by the gambols of hares amongst the lilies for the delight of the Holy Innocents (cf. plates CCLII to CCLIV; Alinari, 2326A and 36673). Even an artist usually so commonplace as Sano di Pietro is not without his moments of grace – the freshness of the morning before daybreak in *The Angel and the Shepherds* (plate CCLV) ; the dark trees against the sky in the *St. Bernardine Preaching* (Plate CCLVI). Here, though there is an excessive use of vermilion in the rest of the scene, the upper part is entirely true and yet transfigured like a Japanese water-colour. In the *St. Jerome* of the Siena Academy, again — a painting which brings us to art in its minutest form — you have such details as the tiny red altar covered with black embroidered linen and set up in the desert, while a lion no bigger than a domestic cat mounts guard over the cardinalitial hat hanging from the tree and a thin snake glides across the sand.

When we leave these exquisite *minutiae,* we find the old Sienese tradition continuing its work in the form which Sassetta had given it, just as towards the middle of the Trecento it had been modified by the activity of a far greater master Ambrogio Lorenzetti. Henceforwards Sienese tradition irrigates a wider field, the field in which some of the most fruitful harvests of the Renaissance were destined later to ripen. Of these the roseate Mediævalism of Masolini may be reckoned the first. As a return to archaïsing, legendary colour, the influence of that Mediævalism upon painting, which Florentine influence tended all too rapidly and brusquely to restrict and " classicize " can scarcely be exaggerated. We have said that the discussion of these developments would require a separate study; and, indeed, the interest of the subject would handsomely reward the toil.

# SHORT BIBLIOGRAPHY.

F. Antal. Gedanken zur Entwicklung der Trecento und Quattrocentomalerei in Siena und Florenz, 1926.

Arte antica Senese. Published by the " Commissione di Storia Patria, " on occasion of the Exhibition of Early Sienese Art, 2 vols. Siena, 1904-5.

P. Bacci. Il Barna o Berna e mai esistito ? In *Balzana*, VI, 1927.

B. Berenson. The Central Italian Painters of the Renaissance. New York, 1897.

B. Berenson. A Sienese Painter of the Franciscan Legend (Sassetta). London, 1909.

B. Berenson. Essays in the Study of Sienese Painting. New York, 1918.

B. Berenson. Due dipinti del decimosecondo secolo venuti da Costantinopoli. In *Dedalo*, 1921, p. 285.

B. Berenson. Due illustratori italiani dello " Speculum Humanae Salvationis. " In *Boll. d'Arte del Min. P. I.*, Jan. and Feb., 1926.

(B. Berenson). *The Golden Urn.* N. 3. List of Sacred Pictures. Fiesole, 1898.

E. Bertaux. Santa Maria di Donna Regina e l'arte senese a Napoli nel sec. xiv. Naples, 1899.

E. Bertaux. Les saints Louis dans l'art italien. In *Revue des Deux Mondes*, April, 1900.

F. Bonaini. Memorie inedite intorno alla vita e ai dipinti di Francesco Traini. Pisa, 1846.

S. Borghesi and L. Banchi. Nuovi documenti per la storia dell'arte senese. Siena, 1898.

C. Brandi. Barna e G. d'Asciano. In *Balzana*, vol. 11, 1928.

J. Carlyle Graham. Una scuola d'arte a San Gimignano nel Trecento. *Rass. d'Arte Sen.*, 1909, p. 39.

E. Cecchi. Intorno al Barna. In *Fiera Letteraria*, October 14, 1928.

E. Cecchi. Un pannello di Paolo di G. Fei. In *Vita Artistica*, 1927, p. 70.

E. Cecchi. D'una arcaica scultura policroma senese. In *Vita Artistica*, 1927, p. 234.

A. Colasanti. L'Arte bizantina in Italia. Milan, 1912.

L. Coletti. Arte senese. Treviso, 1906.

G. Cristofani. Dipinti inediti di S. Martini nella Basilica inferiore di Assisi. *Arte*, 1913, p. 131.

G. Cristofani. Le vetrate del Trecento nella Basilica inferiore di Assisi. *Rass. d'Arte*, 1909, p. 153.

Crowe and Cavalcaselle. History of Painting in Italy (Ed. R. Langton Douglas). London, 1903.

P. D'Achiardi. Guida della Galleria Vaticana. Rome, 1914.

L. Dami. Siena e le sue opere d'arte. Florence, 1915.

L. Dami. Simone Martini. Florence, 1921.

L. Dami. La Galleria di Siena. Florence, 1924.

L. Dami. Il polittico pisano di S. Martini. In *Dedalo*, 1922, p. 5.

L. Dami. Giovanni di Paolo miniatore e i paesisti senesi. In *Dedalo*, 1923, p. 269.

141

W. DE GRüNEISEN. On oriental Byzantine tradition, local influences, and individual inspiration in the scenes from the life of Christ in Duccio's " Maestà. " In the volume published under the title " In onore di Duccio di B. e della sua scuola. " Siena, 1913.

W. DE GRüNEISEN. On the portraits of Monna Muccia and an unknown donor in the Exhibition of Duccio's works at Siena. *Ibid.* Siena, 1913.

G. DELLA VALLE. Lettere senesi di un socio della Accademia di Fossano sopra le Belle Arti. Venice and Rome, 1782-1786.

P. DEL ZANNA. Le " crete " di Certaldo. Rome, 1915.

G. DE NICOLA. L'affresco di S. Martini ad Avignone. In *Arte*, 1906, p. 336.

G. DE NICOLA. The Masterpiece of Giovanni di Paolo. In *Burlington Magazine*, XXXIII, 1918.

G. DE NICOLA. Review of C. H. Weigelt's " Duccio. " In *Bull. Sen. Storia Patria*, 1911, p. 431.

G. DE NICOLA. Duccio di B. and his School in the Exhibition of Duccio's works at Siena. In *Burlington Magazine*, 1912, p. 138.

G. DE NICOLA. Arte inedita in Siena e nel suo antico territorio. In *Vita d'Arte*, March and July, 1912.

G. DE NICOLA. Sassetta between 1423 and 1433. In *Burlington Magazine*, 1913, p. 276.

G. DE NICOLA. Ugolino e Simone a San Casciano Val di Pesa. In *Arte*, 1916, p. 13.

G. DE NICOLA. Review of Berenson's " Essays in the Study of Sienese Painting. " In *Rass. d'Arte*, 1919, p. 95.

G. DE NICOLA. Due dipinti senesi della collezione Liechtenstein. In *Boll. d'Arte del Min. P. I.*, 1921, p. 243.

G. DE NICOLA. Andrea di Bartolo. In *Rass. d'Arte Sen.*, 1921, p. 12.

G. DE NICOLA. Il soggiorno fiorentino di Ambrogio Lorenzetti. In *Boll. d'arte del Min. P. I.*, 1922, p. 49.

E. T. DEWALD. The Master of the Ovile Madonna. In *Art Studies* (Harvard and Princeton Univ. U. S. A.), 1923, p. 45.

E. DOLBERT. Die Sienischer Malerschule. Leipzig, 1878.

R. LANGTON DOUGLAS. A History of Siena. London, 1902.

R. LANGTON DOUGLAS. Illustrated Catalogue of Sienese Paintings (Burlington Fine Arts Club). London, 1905.

R. LANGTON DOUGLAS. A Forgotten Painter (Sassetta). In *Burlington Magazine*, 1903, p. 306.

C. FEA. Descrizione ragionata della Basilica di San Francesco d'Assisi. Rome, 1820.

G. FRIZZONI. Esp. di Arte senese al Burlington Fine Arts Club. In *Arte*, 1904, p. 256.

R. FRY. A Note on Giovanni di Paolo. In *Burlington Magazine*, 1904, p. 312.

R. FRY. " The Journey of the Three Kings " by Sassetta. In *Burlington Magazine*, vol. 22, p. 131.

L. GHIBERTI. Commentarii, t. II. Berlin, 1912.

L. GIELLY. Les Primitifs siennois. Paris, 1926.

O. H. GIGLIOLI. On the " St. Lucy " of Pietro Lorenzetti. In *Rivista d'Arte*, 1906, p. 184.

O. H. GIGLIOLI. L'allegoria politica negli affreschi di A. Lorenzetti. In *Emporium*, April, 1904.

142

U. GNOLI. Review of R. Van Marle's " Simone Martini. " In *Rass. d'Arte Umbra*, 1921, p. 5.

U. GNOLI. Il tesoro di S. Francesco d'Assisi. In *Dedalo*, 1922, p. 555.

A. GOSCHE. Simone Martini. Leipzig, 1899.

F. HERMANIN. Il miniatore del codice di San Giorgio. In " Scritti vari di filologia a E. Monaci. " Rome, 1901.

W. HEYWOOD, L. OLCOTT, F. MASON PERKINS. Guide to Siena. Siena, 1924.

E. HUTTON. The Sienese School in the National Gallery. London, 1925.

Inventories of the Sacristy of the Convent of Assisi, compiled in 1338 and preserved in cod. 337 of the Communal Library of Assisi. Edited by L. ALESSANDRI and F. PENNACCHI. Quaracchi, 1920.

E. JACOBSEN. Sienesische Meister d. Trecento, etc. Strassburg, 1907.

L. LANZI. Storia pittorica dell'Italia. Bassano, 1809.

A. LISINI. Notizie di Duccio pittore e della sua celebre ancona. In *Bull. Sen. di Storia Patria*, 1898, p. 20.

A. LISINI. Le tavolette dipinti di Biccherna (1258-1689); con 103 tavole. Siena, 1904.

R. LONGHI. Review of L. Dami's " Siena e le sue opere d'arte. " In *Arte*, 1916, p. 360.

R. LONGHI. Piero della Francesca. Rome, 1927.

V. LUSINI. On Duccio, with the catalogue and an account of the Exhibition at Siena (1912). In the volume " In onore di Duccio di B. e della sua scuola. " Siena, 1913.

V. LUSINI. Storia della Basilica di San Francesco in Siena. Siena, 1894.

V. LUSINI. Il duomo di Siena. Siena, 1911.

R. VAN MARLE. The Development of the Italian Schools of Painting. The Hague, 1924.

R. VAN MARLE. Simone Martini. Strassburg, 1920.

R. VAN MARLE. Recherches sur l'iconographie de Giotto et de Duccio. Strassburg, 1920.

R. VAN MARLE. Dipinti del Barna. In *Balzana*, vol. VI, 1927.

R. VAN MARLE. Memmo di Filippuccio. In *Rass. d'Arte Sen.* 1920, p. 50.

E. VON MEYENBURG. Ambrogio Lorenzetti. Zürich, 1903.

R. ANDRÉ MICHEL. Avignon, les fresques du palais des Papes. In *Mélanges d'histoire et d'archéologie*. Paris, 1920.

G. MILANESI. Della vera età di Guido, pittore senese. In *Giornale storico degli archivi toscani*. Florence, 1859.

G. MILANESI. Documenti per la storia dell'arte senese, vol. I. Siena, 1854.

G. MILLET. Recherches sur l'iconographie de l'Évangile d'après les monuments de Mistra, de Macedoine, et du Mont Athos. Paris, 1904.

P. MISCIATTELLI. Mistici Senesi. Siena, 1913.

E. MÜNTZ. Les peintures de Simone Martini à Avignon. In *Mémoires de la Soc. Nation. des Antiquaires de France*. Paris, 1884.

U. OJETTI and L. DAMI. Atlante di storia dell'Arte italiana, vol. I. Milan, 1925.

L. OZZOLA. Lippo Memmi collaboratore del padre Memmo e di Simone Martini. In *Rass. d'Arte*, 1921, p. 117.

W. PATER. The Renaissance. London, 1873.

L. PATINI. San Gimignano. Bergamo, 1908.

A. PÉRATÉ. Duccio di B. In *Gazette des B. A.* 1893, p. 89.

A. PÉRATÉ. Peinture ital. au XIV$^e$ siècle. In " Hist. de l'art publ. sous la direction de A. Michel, " vol. II, part II. Paris, 1906.

F. MASON PERKINS. Andrea Vanni. In *Burlington Magazine*, 1903, p. 309.

F. MASON PERKINS. The Forgotten Masterpiece of A. Lorenzetti (Altarpiece of Massa Marittima). In *Burlington Magazine*, 1904, p. 81.

F. MASON PERKINS. Alcune opere poco note di A. Lorenzetti. In *Rass. d'Arte*, 1904, p. 186.

F. MASON PERKINS. Pitture senesi agli Stati Uniti. In *Rass. d'Arte Sen.*, 1905, p. 74.

F. MASON PERKINS. Intorno al Santo Giacomo del Museo di Pisa e ai Santi Pietro e Paolo della raccolta Chiaramonte Bordonaro di Palermo. In *Rass. d'Arte*, 1906, p. 31.

F. MASON PERKINS. Dipinti sconosciuti della scuola senese. In *Rass. d'Arte Sen.*, 1907, p. 73; 1908, p. 3.

F. MASON PERKINS. Gli affreschi di Simone Martini ad Avignone. In *Rass. d'Arte Sen.*, 1908, p. 87.

F. MASON PERKINS. Vita di Pietro " Laurati, " di G. Vasari. With Introduction, Notes, and a Bibliography. Florence, 1912.

F. MASON PERKINS. Alcuni dipinti senesi sconosciuti o inediti. In *Rass. d'Arte*, 1913, p. 121.

F. MASON PERKINS. Illustrazione della " Madonna di Mosciano. " In *Rass. d'Arte*, June, 1916.

F. MASON PERKINS. Alcune opere d'arte ignorate (Altarpiece of San Procolo by A. Lorenzetti). In *Rass. d'Arte*, 1918, p. 106.

F. MASON PERKINS. Alcuni appunti sulla galleria di Siena. In *Rass. d'Arte Sen.*, 1908, p. 46.

F. MASON PERKINS. Some Sienese Paintings in American Collections. In *Art in America*, 1920.

F. MASON PERKINS. Opere d'arte senese. In *Rass. d'Arte Sen.*, 1920, p. 110.

R. OFFNER. Italian Primitives at Yale University. New Haven, U. S. A., 1927.

L. PETROCCHI. Massa Marittima. Florence, 1900.

*Rassegna d'Arte Senese* (Boll. della Società Senese " Amici dei Monumenti "). Siena, 1905 to 1925.

C. RICCI. Il Palazzo pubblico di Siena e la Mostra d'Antica Arte Senese. 1904.

W. ROTHES. Die Blütezeit der Sienesischen Malerei. Strassburg, 1904.

G. ROWLEY. Ambrogio Lorenzetti, il pensatore. In *Balzana*, vol. V, 1927.

L. DE SCHLEGEL. " L'Annunciazione " del Barna. In *Arte*, 1909, p. 204.

C. SCHNAASE. Geschichte der bildenden Künste im Mittelalter, Band VII. Düsseldorf, 1876.

M. SALMI. Catalogo della pinacoteca communale di Arezzo. Città di Castello, 1921.

P. SCHUBRING. Ein Passionsaltärchen von Simone Martini. In *Jahrbuch der K. P. Kunslsammlungen*, 1902.

P. SCHUBRING. Die Fresken der Incoronata in Neapel. In *Repertorium für Kunstwissenschaft*, XXIII, 1900.

P. SELVATICO. Storia estetico-critica delle arti del disegno. Venice, 1852.

O. SIRÉN. Toskanische Maler im XIII Jahrb. Berlin, 1922.

O. SIRÉN. Il problema Maso-Giottino. In *Dedalo*. 1927, p. 395.

O. SIRÉN. A Picture by Pietro Cavallini (The " Kahn Madonna "). In *Burlington Magazine*. Feb., 1918.

O. SIRÉN. A Descriptive Catalogue of the Paintings in the Jarves Collection. New Haven, 1916.

144

O. SIRÉN. Don Lorenzo Monaco. Strassburg, 1905.

O. SIRÉN. Quadri sconosciuti del Museo Cristiano Vaticano. In *Arte*, 1906, p. 321.

Sonetti burleschi e realistici dei primi due secoli, a cura di A. F. MASSERA. Bari, 1920.

G. SOULIER. Les influences orientales dans la peinture toscane. Paris, 1924.

B. SPAVENTA. La filosofia italiana nelle sue relazioni con la filosofia europea. Bari, 1926.

W. SUIDA. Einige Maler aus der Uebergangszeit vom 200 in 300. In *Jahrb. der K. Preuss. Kunstsammlungen*, 1905.

U. THIEME and F. BECKER. Künstler Lexikon. Leipzig, 1907.

H. THODE. Franz von Assisi und die Anfänge der Kunst der Renaissance. Berlin, 1885.

P. TOESCA. Storia dell'Arte italiana, I. Dalle origini cristiane alla fine del secolo XIII. Turin, 1927.

G. VASARI. Vite. Florence, 1846.

A. VENTURI. Storia dell'Arte italiana, vol. V. La pittura del Trecento. Milan, 1907.

A. VENTURI. La quadreria Sterbini in Roma. In *Arte*, 1905, p. 422.

A. VENTURI. Attraverso le raccolte artistiche d'Europa. Milan, 1927.

L. VENTURI. La collezione Gualino. Rome, 1926.

L. VENTURI. Il gusto dei primitivi. Bologna, 1926.

C. H. WEIGELT. Duccio di B. Leipzig, 1911.

F. WICKHOFF. Article on " The Rucellai Madonna. " In *Mittheilungen d. Inst. f. Oesterrich. Geschichte*, 1899, p. 244.

# NOTES ON THE PLATES

PLATE I. – The HAMILTON MADONNA. – The Hamilton Madonna, with another panel showing the Madonna seated on a quadrangular instead of a round throne, was found at Calahorra (Spain). Sirén (*Burlington Magazine*, February, 1918) attributed the second panel to Cavallini. Berenson (*Dedalo*, II, fasc. 5), on the other hand, believes both panels to be the work of a painter of Constantinople and assigns them, roughly, to 1200. This is also the view of Toesca (*Storia*, I, p. 1035, n. 39). The Hamilton Madonna is reproduced here as an example of noble Byzantine or Italo-Byzantine art, painted during the first years of the thirteenth century.

PLATE II. – " PALIOTTO. " – De Nicola (*Vita d'Arte*, July, 1912) considers that these so-called " paliotti " were " destined for finer employment than the common, rudely decorated small frontals." The " paliotto " here reproduced comes from the Abbey of Berardenga and bears the inscription, " *Anno Dñi Millesimo CCXV mense novembris haec tabula facta est.*" A Venturi (*Storia*, V, p. 82) has traced a correspondence between the three scenes to the left and a passage in the Golden Legend of Jacobus de Voragine relating to the Exaltation of the Cross; De Nicola (*loc. cit.*) recognized similar allusions to the Invention and Proof of the Cross in the scenes to the right.

PLATE III. – "PALIOTTO." – This "paliotto" was originally in the suppressed church of San Pietro in Banchi, Siena. The scenes on the right represent the Nativity of Christ, the Imprisonment and the Crucifixion of St. Peter; those on the left, the Annunciation, the Call of St. Peter, and the Fall of Simon Magus. The tints are clear and luminous; the architecture is rose and yellow touched with blue. A derivation from miniatures is suggested, particularly by the gleaming brightness of the colour.

PLATE IV. – MADONNA. – The face, veil, and hands of the Madonna, besides other parts of the painting, were rehandled during the period of Duccio. As is well known, Milanesi thought that the date of the dedicatory inscription should be changed from 1221 to 1271. A Venturi (*Storia*, V, p. 50) rejected both dates; Wickhoff, Thode, Langton Douglas, Weigelt, De Nicola, Van Marle, and, more recently, Toesca (*Storia*, I, pp. 993, 1038), hold the earlier date of 1221 indisputable. The red robe with the blue and green mantle of the Madonna, the white draperies, and the vermilion back to the throne form a whole of singular chromatic vividness. This, making allowance for later rehandling, os perhaps the best result of Guido's new manner.

PLATE V. – MADONNA. – Toesca (*Storia*, I, p. 994) attributes this Madonna with some hesitation to Guido or to one of his followers, and supposes it to derive from a Byzantine example of the thirteenth century, modified by more

146

subtle facial expression and by greater plastic liveliness. The painting was given to the Sienese Gallery by Marcello Galli-Dunn in 1906. The *Madonnas* at Arezzo and Florence are to be assigned to imitators (Venturi, Salmi, Toesca).

PLATES VI & VII. – DIPTYCH. – These are probably the wings of two triptychs of which the central panels have been lost. The panels of plate VI show incidents from the lives of St. Francis, St. Bartholomew, St. Clare, and St. Catherine of Alexandria; those of plate VII, from the lives of St. Francis and the Blessed Andrea Gallerani.

PLATE VIII. – The GUALINO MADONNA. – About the year 1910 this Madonna was in the possession of the antiquary Pavi of Florence. It was then concealed by a Cinquecento repainting, which Paoletti, its next owner, removed. After becoming the property of Verzocchi, the painting entered the Gualino Collection. Lionello Venturi (Catalogue of *La Collezione Gualino*, 1926, plate I) attributes it with the *Rucellai Madonna* to Cimabue. Cf. Sirén, *Toskanische Maler*, p. 293; Van Marle, I, p. 302; and Toesca, *Storia*, I, p. 1012.

PLATES IX & X. – The RUCELLAI MADONNA. – Roger Fry and Lionello Venturi are perhaps the only modern critics who follow Cavalcaselle in accepting Vasari's attribution and assigning the *Rucellai Madonna* to Cimabue. Sirén supposes that the painting was begun by Cimabue and finished by Duccio – a somewhat complicated theory. Wickhoff, Strzygowsky, Richter, Langton Douglas, Adolfo Venturi, and Van Marle assign it, with varying degrees of certainty, to the beginning of Duccio's career. Suida formed the hypothesis of a so-called " Master of the *Rucellai Madonna* ; " and, following him, Perkins, Berenson, De Nicola, and Toesca (*Storia*, I, p. 1011) have drawn up a list of the works of this artist. At present, besides the *Rucellai Madonna* and the *Gualino Madonna*, this list appears to include – though there are some differences ot opinion upon the point – the *Madonna of St. Cecilia* at Crevole, the *Madonna of Mosciano*, and another *Madonna* in the Servite Church at Orvieto. For De Nicola's view ot the whole question, singularly valuable as his judgments always are, see *Boll. Senese di Storia Patria*, 1911, p. 431.

PLATE XI. – MADONNA WITH ADORING FRANCISCANS. – This, in order ot time, is perhaps the earliest certain work by Duccio (about 1278). For the characteristics of miniature painting in the hanging with its stamped pattern and for similar backgrounds in illuminated French Gothic MSS., see Toesca, *Storia*, I, p. 996, and for " Gothic " curves in the Madonna's robe, of which we have one of the earliest Sienese examples in this panel, cf. Toesca. *loc. cit.*, and Van Marle, II, p. 12.

PLATE XII. – The STROGANOFF MADONNA. – Formerly at Rome in the Stroganoff Collection, and now in the Stoclet Collection at Brussels. The date is about 1295 and hence the painting belongs to Duccio's early maturity (Van Marle, II, p. 15).

PLATE XIII. – The MADONNA OF PERUGIA. – Formerly in the Church of S. Domenico at Perugia. The two chief figures were repainted in the fifteenth century – a deturpation which has recently been removed. Between the *Stroganoff Madonna* (plate XII) and this *Madonna of Perugia* should be placed the triptych of the London National Gallery (Van Marle, II, fig. 5), in which a close affinity to the *Stroganoff Madonna* is noticeable in the central group of the Madonna and Child.

PLATES XIV to LVI. – The MAESTÀ. – The " Majesty " was ordered from Duccio by Jacomo Mariscotti, workman of Siena Cathedral, on October 9, 1308, and on November 28, 1310, the artist was urged to hasten on the completion of the work. For the contract relative to the commission, the celebrations when the Maestà was being borne to its place in the Cathedral on June 9, 1311, and an account of its subsequent dispersion, see Della Valle, *Lettere Senesi*, II, pp. 63 ff.

A reconstruction of the *Maestà* has been attempted by Lisini, by Langton Douglas, by Lusini, and by Weigelt (*Duccio di B.*, plates 45 and 46). Weigelt, who succeeded in tracing the *Temptation* reproduced in plate XXX, attempted to reconstruct it, and added to it the compartments preserved in the Museum of the Opera of the Cathedral. The compartments reproduced in plates XXIX and XXXI, together with two others representing the *Call of St. Peter* and the *Raising of Lazarus*, passed in June, 1927, from the Benson Collection to that of Duveen in London; and the compartment with the *Temptation* (plate XXXI) from the latter to the Frick Collection in New York. The *Annunciation* (plate XXIV) and the compartments with the *Transfiguration* and the *Healing of the Blind Man* (Weigelt, *Duccio*, plates 18, 20, 21, 22), are in the London National Gallery; the *Nativity* (plate XXV) is in the Kaiser Friedrich Museum in Berlin.

To the numerous iconographical parallels to the *Nativity* mentioned in the text should be added the illuminated initial letter in the Corale 25 belonging to the Museum of the Opera of Siena Cathedral (Toesca, *Storia*, I, p. 1065, fig. 754). This initial is clearly the work of a craftsman who worked in close proximity to Duccio. Weigelt believes that, beginning with the compartment *Mitte manum* (following the order of episodes from the life of Christ) and continuing through the scenes from the life of the Madonna – with the exception, however, of the *Announcement to Mary of her Death* – the intervention of pupils can be detected; Van Marle, on the other hand, without adopting the view expressed by Weigelt, confines himself to the remark that from the *Mitte manum* onwards the artistic level is not so high as in the remaining parts of the *Maestà*.

PLATE LVII. – TWO PANELS OF A POLYTYCH. – These two panels form part of a polyptych which belonged formerly to the Hospital of S. Maria della Scala. The central part and the two saints in the right-hand panels are much damaged. The polyptych, like the fragment at Santa Maria dei Servi at Montepulciano (De Nicola, *Burlington Magazine*, XXII, 1912), appears to be only very little later in date than the *Maestà*. According to G. Frizzoni (*Arte*, 1904, p. 256), the triptych at Buckingham Palace is to be assigned to Duccio's " Roman " period, owing, as he says, to " the absence from it of any Gothic element whatever." For the attribution to Duccio of the triptych at Buckingham Palace, see, however, W. G. Constable, *Dedalo*, 1930, p. 724.

148

PLATE LVIII. – POLYPTYCH. – Lusini (*Rassegna d'Arte Senese*, 1912, p. 118) holds that this polyptych was painted for the Monastery of San Paolo, founded in 1342, but the date in that case seems too late. Cf. Van Marle, II, p. 70.

PLATE LIX. – MAESTÀ. – Formerly in the Church of San Domenico at Città di Castello. Much restored. The figure of the Child is the part least repainted.

PLATE LX. – MADONNA. – The painting, which belonged to the heirs of bishop Alessandro Toti of Colle d'Elsa, passed to the Accademia of Siena in 1906 as a work by Duccio. V. Lusini and F. Mason Perkins recognized it to be a school work. The frame-work is modern.

PLATE LXI. – MADONNA. – Attributed to Duccio by P. d'Achiardi, A. Venturi, and Langton Douglas. Lusini and Weigelt consider it a workshop product; Perkins and Van Marle assign it to a follower of Duccio.

PLATE LXII. – MADONNA. – Attributed, without foundation or likelihood, to a Maestro Gilio who is mentioned in a document of 1250. A. Venturi (*Storia*, V, p. 586) assigns it to Pietro Lorenzetti. The painting comes from the suppressed Church of San Pellegrino. There is a painting by the same hand, with six half-figures of angels praying around the Madonna throned, in the London National Gallery.

PLATE LXIII. – CRUCIFIX. – Dated 1305 and attributed, though without proof, to Massarello di Gilio.

PLATE LXIV. – The PREACHING OF ST. JOHN THE BAPTIST. – Lusini and (with some hesitation) Berenson assign this painting to Duccio. A. Venturi (*Storia*, V, p. 287) believes that it formed part of the predella of the polyptych of Santa Croce; but the seven small panels which apparently formed the predella in question have all been traced, and hence Venturi's hypothesis falls to the ground. It is, however, true that the *Preaching of the Baptist* is much closer to Duccio than the *Ascent of Mount Calvary*; and hence the panel would seem to belong to a different period of Ugolino's career. The attribution to Ugolino is due to Perkins.

PLATE LXV. – The ASCENT OF MOUNT CALVARY. – One of the compartments of the polyptych painted for the Church of Santa Croce at Florence. Della Valle read the inscription " *Ugolinus de Senis me pinxit* " upon this polyptych - the only work known to have been signed by the master. Its central panel has been lost, but the left-hand small panels with the half-figures of SS. Peter, Paul, and John are in the Kaiser Friedrich Museum at Berlin, while the seven compartments of the predella together with various fragments are divided between the Kaiser Friedrich Museum, the London National Gallery, and the Collections of Meyers, Wagner, White, Crawford, Butler, and some others. An attempt at reconstructing the polyptych was made by E. Hutton in *The Sienese School in the National Gallery*, 1925, p. 20.

PLATE LXVI. – ST. FRANCIS OF ASSISI. – De Nicola supposes that this St. Francis and a St. Peter of the same size, also belonging to the Confraternity of the

149

Misericordia at San Casciano, came originally from the Dominican Convent of Santa Maria Novella at Florence (De Nicola, *Arte*, 1916, p. 13).

PLATE LXVII. – MADONNA. – Differences in measurement and pictorial structure preclude the possibility that this panel and the preceding smaller panels with St. Francis and St. Peter, which are to be reckoned amongst the least spoiled paintings of this period, formed originally one work. Their critical valuation and the attribution to Ugolino are due to De Nicola (*Burlington Magazine*, 1912, p. 138). There is a large-size reproduction of the detail of the " *dantino* " with a tunic and hood of purple and a white cap, together with the small portrait of Monna Muccia from the panel in the ex-Convent of San Francesco at Lucignano, in the work entitled *In onore di Duccio di B.*, Siena, 1913, fig. 15. The latter panel is attributed to the school of Ugolino.

PLATE LXVIII. – The NATIVITY. – For this painting and " Ugolino Lorenzetti " see Berenson, *Essays in the Study of Sienese Painting*; and E. T. Dewald, " The Master of the Ovile Madonna " in *Art Studies* (Harvard). With regard to the possible identification of " Ugolino Lorenzetti " with Biagio da Siena cf. De Nicola, *Rassegna d'Arte*, 1919, p. 95. Berenson proposes to date the Fogg *Nativity* at about 1335.

PLATE LXIX. – S. ANSANO AND S. GALGANO. – At one time attributed to Segna; later, to Ugolino of Siena. The date, according to Berenson, is, approximately, 1335. The two figures formed the side-panels of a triptych, of which the central part, reproduced by Berenson (*Essays*, fig. 7), is still in the church at Fogliano.

PLATE LXX. – The CRUCIFIXION. – This *Crucifixion* together with the *Crucifixion* in the Louvre is typical of the transition from Duccio to Pietro Lorenzetti, or, rather, it represents the blending together of the two styles (Berenson, *Essays*, p. 26).

PLATE LXXI. – The CRUCIFIXION. – At one time assigned to Duccio, from whom it is most closely derived, this *Crucifixion* has been correctly attributed by A. Venturi, Lusini, and Perkins to Segna di Buonaventura.

PLATE LXXII. – FOUR PANELS OF A POLYPTYCH. – Formerly in the Abbey of Berardenga, these panels formed part of a triptych, of which the central part has been lost. Segna's signature is upon the sword of St. Paul.

PLATE LXXIII. – MADONNA. – Akin to the *Madonna* in the Servite Church at Siena (Van Marle, II, fig. 89), though the latter is perhaps slightly nearer to Duccio, and to the *Madonna* of the Lehman Collection in New York (*ibid.* fig. 92). The attitude of the Child in the last-named painting is similar to that of the corresponding figure in the *Madonna with Adoring Franciscans.* (plate XI).

PLATE LXXIV. – MAESTÀ. – The four figures at the extreme sides of the painting – St. Louis of France and St. Anthony of Padua on the right, and St. Anthony the Abbot and St. Fina (?) on the left – were probably added or repainted by Benozzo Gozzoli when he restored the *Maestà* in 1467. In repainting the inscription, only the name of Lippo Memmi was left; but that Memmo di Filippuccio had a share in this free copy of the *Maestà*, which had been painted in fresco by Simone two years previously, is established beyond all doubt by a document quoted by Davidsohn and by Van Marle (*Rassegna d'Arte*, 1920, p. 50), and also by archaïsing features in the painting itself. With regard to what was said in the text in reference to the persistence of mediæval grotesques, it is interesting to note that J. Carlyle Graham (*Rassegna d'Arte Senese*, 1909, p. 39) has even gone so far as to attribute to Memmo di Filippuccio the *Last Judgment* painted by Taddeo Bartoli at San Gimignano in 1393.

PLATES LXXV TO LXXX. – MAESTÀ. – A mistaken reading of the last verse in a strophe, which also indicates the date 1315, gave rise to a belief that the author of the *Maestà* was one Ser Mino di Simone. For the two strophes, each containing seven verses, which are inscribed on the steps of the throne – *Li angelichi fiorecti, rose e gigli*, and *Diletti mei, ponete nelle menti* – cf. A. Venturi, *Storia*, V, p. 591. The fresco has been much damaged and repainted. It was retouched for the first time by Simone himself in 1321.

PLATE LXXXI. – The SAVIOUR. – Attributed to Simone by Berenson and, doubtfully, by Venturi. The left hand appears to rest upon a globe; the gold ground has recently been crudely restored. A greater nearness in type to Duccio seems to indicate that this was one of the works painted by Simone previously to the *Maestà*. These works must have been both numerous and distinguished, as Simone would not have been commissioned to paint in the Communal Palace, if his fame had not already been secure. The painting comes from the Museo Cristiano.

PLATES LXXXII TO LXXXV. – ST. LOUIS OF TOULOUSE CROWNING ROBERT OF ANJOU. – Formerly in Santa Chiara, later in San Lorenzo Maggiore, and now in the National Museum at Naples. Signed: *Symon de Senis pinxit*. The central panel has greatly deteriorated, and the five scenes forming the predella are still more seriously damaged. The subjects of the " histories " of the predella are as follows:

1. *St. Louis of Anjou, kneeling before the Pope, refuses the episcopal mitre, and, pointing tho the friars standing behind him, makes known his desire to enter the Franciscan Order.*

2. *St. Louis enters the Franciscan Order and is raised to the episcopal dignity.*

3. *St. Louis humbles himself to serve the poor.*

4. *St. Louis upon his death-bed.*

5. *St. Louis appears miraculously and raises a child to life.*

For the political significance of the figure of St. Louis crowning his brother Robert of Anjou cf. E. Bertaux, *Revue des Deux Mondes*, April, 1900.

PLATE LXXXVI. – MADONNA. – Formerly in the Borghese Gallery, later in the Corsini Gallery, and now in the Palazzo Venezia in Rome. The painting was bought by A. Venturi at Naples in 1903. The place of purchase and considerations based upon style – but especially the latter – lead us to assign the painting to Simone's Neapolitan period.

PLATES LXXXVII to XCVIII. – POLYPTYCH OF PISA. – The parts of this polyptych which are now in Santa Caterina were until a few years ago in the Episcopal Seminary at Pisa. Proceeding from the left, the figures of the saints in the principal panels (plates LXXXVII to XC) are: St. Dominic, St. Mary Magdalene, St. John the Evangelist, St. John the Baptist, St. Catherine, and St. Peter Martyr; and, in the predella (plates XCII to XCVIII), besides the Pietà with the Madonna and St. Mark, are the following saints: Gregory, Thomas Aquinas, Ambrose, Augustine, Agnes, Apollonia, Ursula, the Magdalene, etc. For the contract drawn up between Simone and Fra Pietro of the Convent of Santa Caterina, cf. E. Bonaini, *Memorie inedite*, 1846, p. 38.

PLATE XCIX. – PANELS OF A POLYPTYCH. – Formerly at Orvieto, the property of the Mazzocchi family. Perkins (*Rassegna d'Arte Senese*, 1905, p. 74) described the polyptych after it had passed to the Gardner Collection at Boston, U.S.A., and believes that Lippo Memmi had a predominating part in the collaboration. Berenson dates the polyptych about 1325. Jacobsen (*Sienesiche Meister d. Trecento*, 1907, p. 32) unhesitatingly assigns to Memmi the other and larger polyptych with Simone's signature at Orvieto, in the Opera of the Cathedral. The Gardner polyptych has been completely reproduced by L. Dami, *Simone Martini*, 1921, figs. 14-16. Van Marle now appears inclined to consider Memmi's collaboration in the works painted at Orvieto as more extensive than he at one time supposed. Particularly noticeable in the Orvieto polyptych is the iconographical detail of St. Paul carrying his Epistles divided up into separate tomes, upon one of which can be read the words *Ad Romanos* (Alinari, 25978). This is a feature found in other Sienese representations of St. Paul. See plate LXXXIX (the Pisa polyptych), and Lippo Memmi's *St. Paul* (Metropolitan Museum, New York) in Van Marle, II, fig. 178.

PLATE C. – ST. CATHERINE (?). – Van Marle (II, p. 197) traces signs of Lippo's collaboration in this panel, which was published contemporaneously by De Nicola (*Boll. Min. Pubbl. Istr.*, 1921, p. 243) and by A. Venturi (*Arte*, 1921, p. 198). Berenson (*Central Italian Painters*, p. 202) attributed it to Memmi, and believed that it represented St. Justina. Against the attribution to Memmi and for the identification of the figure with St. Catherine, cf. A. Venturi, *Attraverso le raccolte artistiche di Europa*, 1927, p. 78.

PLATES CI to CXV. – SCENES FROM THE LEGEND OF ST. MARTIN. – Fea (*Descrizione della Basilica di San Francesco*, 1820) denied Vasari's attribution of the frescoes in the Chapel of St. Martin to Puccio Capanna, and rightly named Simone Martini as their author. It is strange that Schnaase, who wrote fifty years afterwards, makes no mention of these frescoes in his pages on Martini although, considering the time at which he wrote, Schnaase has much to say (as usual) that is by no means without interest. Cavalcaselle believed that the frescoes were painted at about the same date as the *St. Louis* (1317). A date between 1322 and 1326 was admitted by Venturi and Van Marle, while Langton Douglas referred the frescoes to Simone's last years in Italy – that is, to not long before 1339. This is also the view of Berenson (*Essays*, p. 21). It is difficult to accept Van Marle's opinion (II, p. 230) that from the point of view of style, the fresco of *Guidoriccio*, the date of which (1328) is certain, presupposes the frescoes at Assisi; for, on the contrary, the former seems to hint at a greater archaism. The features of the *Annunciation* (1333), which show an accentuation of French Gothic in the sense of calligraphic refinement, might very well have been modified and corrected at Assisi through the influence of Giotto — if we accept the date proposed by Langton Douglas and by Berenson. For the commission to paint the frescoes given to Simone by the heirs of the Franciscan Cardinal, Gentile Partino da Montefiore, cf. A. Venturi, *Storia*, V, p. 604, and Van Marle, II, p. 202. Van Marle believes that Simone also painted another chapel, facing that of St. Martin, with scenes from the life of St. Louis of France, but of this work nothing now is left attributable to Simone except the windows. Simone also designed the windows for St. Martin's Chapel (A. Venturi, *Storia*, V, fig. 816). The execution of these windows is assigned by Lusini to Sienese glass-painters; Van Marle (II, p. 222), on the other hand, believes that the work was done by Bonino of Assisi.

The subjects of the frescoes in the Chapel of St. Martin are the following. Above the entrance arch: Cardinal Gentile kneeling before his patron saint; on the inside of the entrance-arch: eight figures of saints (L. Dami, *Simone Martini*, figs. 31-33); and in the embrasure of the window: eight half-figures of saints alternating with emblems of the Cardinalate (plates CXIII to CXV). According to the sequence of events in the life of St. Martin, the order of the frescoes upon the walls should be as follows:

1. *St. Martin gives half of his cloak to a poor man* (plate CI).
2. *The Redeemer, wearing the cloak given to the poor man, appears in a dream to St. Martin* (plates CII and CIII).
3. *The Emperor Constantius confers the dignity of knighthood upon St. Martin* (plates CIV and CV).
4. *St. Martin leaves the army of the Emperor Julian* (plates CVI and CVII).
5. *St. Martin in meditation* (plate CVIII). Venturi (*Storia*, V, p. 611) believes that this scene represents St. Martin bidding farewell to St. Hilary, bishop of Poitiers.
6. *The miracle of the Mass at Albenga* (plate CIX).
7. *St. Martin raises a child to life.*
8. *St. Martin meets the Emperor Valentinian and converts him.* These last two frescoes are much deteriorated.

9 and 10. *The Death and Obsequies of St. Martin* (plates CX to CXII). Venturi believes that the fresco reproduced in plate CXI represents St. Martin taking part in the funeral ceremonies performed at the death of Liborius, bishop of Tours.

Van Marle (*Martini*, pp. 48, 89) has suggested that the figure of St. Mary Magdalene, painted with seven other saints above the entrance-arch, may possibly betray the influence of French ivories belonging to the Treasury of the Basilica, and especially of the statuette of the *Madonna and Child* (Anderson, 26963). The first regular Inventory of the Treasury of San Francesco was compiled in 1338 at the order of Pope John XXII; the second is dated 1370; the third, 1430; and the fourth, 1473. No mention of the statuette is to be found in the first two of these; it is, however, entered in the third (1430), but without any indication of the donor.

PLATES CXVI to CXVIII. — ST. FRANCIS, ST. CLARE, AND ST. LOUIS. — The first half - figures frescoed in the lower Church — St. Francis, St. Louis of Toulouse,

St. Elizabeth, St. Clare, and a youthful saint, who may be St. Louis IX of France – have been variously assigned. Vasari attributed them to Lippo Memmi; Fea assigned the two female figures to Simone; A. Gosche admitted the collaboration of Lippi; Berenson and Gielly attributed all five compartments to Simone. Gnoli (*Rassegna d'Arte Umbra*, 1921, p. 5) put forward the unlikely hypothesis that in these paintings Simone intended to give a sort of proof of his skill before the decoration of the chapel was entrusted to him. Venturi and Van Marle more definitely favour the attribution to Donato Martini, the brother of Simone, and find still clearer traces of Donato's handiwork in the upper parts of the *Dream of St. Martin* (plate CIII), and the *Death of St. Martin* (plate CX). For Donato, cf. Van Marle, II, p. 225.

PLATE CXIX. – GUIDORICCIO RICCI DEI FOGLIANI. – This painting commemorates Guidoriccio's victory over Castruccio Castracani and the conquest of the citadels of Montemassi and Sassoforte. The date, 1328, of these exploits and of the painting is recorded in the frescoed frame below the image of the knight.

PLATES CXX to CXXIV. – POLYPTYCH OF BEATO AGOSTINO NOVELLO. – Cavalcaselle attributes the design of this polyptych to Simone and its execution to Memmi. Berenson refers it to the last years spent by Simone in Italy. Venturi, Pératé, and Gielly attribute it to Memmi; Langton Douglas and Dami assign it to Simone, working, however, with the help of assistants. According to Van Marle (II, p. 232), the polyptych is the work of Simone, although he recognizes its great diversity from all Simone's other paintings, not only in its vehemence of movement, but also because two or more episodes of the same " history " are represented contemporaneously in some of the lateral panels – a proceeding in contrast, he thinks, with Simone's usual practice. This observation, however, is contradicted by the fresco of the Emperor Valentinian in the Chapel of St. Martin – where we have the scene of the Emperor compelled by the fire to stand up and do reverence, and the second scene of the Conversion – and also by the second compartment in the predella of the *St. Louis*.

PLATES CXXV to CXXVIII. – The ANNUNCIATION. – At one time in the Cathedral, and later in Sant'Ansano at Siena (Della Valle, *Lettere Senesi*, p. 83), this painting is now in the Uffizi Gallery, Florence. The collaboration of Lippo Memmi is proved, not only by the inscribed signature, but also by the type of the S. Julitta and S. Ansano, and by the style of the medallions. Cavalcaselle, however, attributed to Memmi only the ornaments and gilding of one lateral panel; Venturi would allow him a larger share in the painting, but does not define its extent. Ozzola (*Rassegna d'Arte*, 1921, p. 117) supposes that the Angel and the S. Ansano are the work of Lippo, and attributes the rest of the painting to Simone, thereby robbing him of one of his most singular creations and cancelling a peculiarly important piece of evidence for his stylistic development. The frame is modern.

PLATE CXXIX. – THE VIRGIN OF THE STROGANOFF ANNUNCIATION. – A. Venturi (*Storia*, V, p. 629) ascribes this fragment of a diptych to the last period of Simone's career although the so-called " Northern Gothic " characteristics are still more strongly marked in the Antwerp *Annunciation* and in the other panels of the polyptych whereof that *Annunciation* formed a part. The *Madonna* formerly in the Stroganoff Collection may be regarded as practically contemporary with the small panel at Liverpool, which is signed and dated 1342, and apparently represents the unusual subject of the Divine Child returning from His disputation with the Doctors.

For the remains of Simone's frescoes at Avignon, see De Nicola, *Arte*, 1906, p. 336; and Perkins, *Rassegna d'Arte Senese*, 1908, p. 87. For the illuminated miniature in Petrarch's codex of Virgil, cf. Van Marle, II, p. 235. Müntz, Berenson, Venturi, and Van Marle ascribe the latter to Simone, and believe that, like the ex-Stroganoff panel, the small Liverpool panel, and the Antwerp polyptych, the miniature belongs to the period of the frescoes at Avignon.

PLATES CXXX and CXXXI. – The ANTWERP POLYPTYCH. – These panels together with four others formed part of a polyptych now mutilated and dispersed. The parts of it still in existence are the following:

1-2. Two panels with the *Angel* and the *Madonna Annunciate* in the Antwerp Gallery (A. Venturi, *Storia*, V, figs. 512 and 513).

3-4. The *Crucifixion* and the *Deposition* (plates CXXX and CXXXI). These bear, respectively, the words *Pinxit* and *Simon*, whence we may conclude that the *Deposition* – with the name of the painter – was on the left side of the polyptych.

5. The *Way to Calvary* in the Louvre.

6. The *Entombment*, formerly in the Pacully Collection at Paris, and now in the Kaiser Friedrich Museum at Berlin.

The fact that the four Antwerp panels were purchased (1828) at Dijon supports the view, on other grounds extremely probable, that the polyptych was painted during Simone's stay at Avignon. There is a copy of the Christ of the Antwerp *Crucifixion* without the other figures in the Fogg Art Museum, Cambridge, U.S.A. This *Christ* was formerly in the Bonnat Collection (Van Marle, II, fig. 164).

PLATE CXXXII. – THE MADONNA OF MISERICORDIA. – Formerly in the Chapel of the Holy Corporal in Orvieto Cathedral. Berenson differs from Van Marle in assigning this panel to a very late date in Lippo's career – between 1350 and 1355. So, too, Venturi (*Storia*, V, p. 663).

PLATE CXXXIII. – MADONNA. – This panel has affinities with the *Madonna* (plate LXXXVI) painted during Simone's Neapolitan period; and so also has the more clumsy *Madonna* painted by Naddo Ceccarelli (1347) and now in the Cook Collection, Richmond (Van Marle, II, fig. 200).

PLATE CXXXIV. – MADONNA. – The so-called *Madonna del Popolo*, also strongly influenced by Simone and painted probably not long after the *Maestà* of San Gimignano. The ears of the Child with their broken outline and in the same perspective recur in Bartolo di Fredi, who was a follower of Lippo, and in Paolo di Giovanni Fei.

PLATE CXXXV. – ST. JAMES. – The throne is ornamented with lion's heads and an hexagonal platform, as in two panels with St. Peter and St. Paul in the

Chiaramonte Bordonaro Collection at Palermo (cf. Van Marle, II, fig. 170?
and Perkins, *Rassegna d'Arte*, 1906, p. 31).

PLATE CXXXVI. – S. ANSANO AND S. JULITTA OF THE ANNUNCIATION. – Anno
1333. See notes on plates CXXV and CXXVIII.

PLATE CXXXVII. – The CRUCIFIXION. – Attributed to Lippo Memmi by Berenson, Sirén, Perkins, Langton Douglas, d'Achiardi, and Van Marle. Van Marle
considers it a very late work painted somewhere about 1350; he rightly traces
in it the influence of Lorenzetti. In the gable, below the pelican, are the figures
of St. John the Evangelist and St. Luke; in the predella – beginning from
the left – St. John the Baptist, St. John the Evangelist (?), St. Francis, St.
Louis of Toulouse (?), St. Catherine, and St. Dorothy. The panel comes from
the Museo Cristiano, and perhaps formed the central part of a small triptych.

PLATES CXXXVIII to CXLV. – THE SAN GIMIGNANO FRESCOES. – Vasari assigns
the death of Barna, which occurred during the execution of the frescoes at
San Gimignano, to the year 1381. Tradition, however, is unanimous in as-
serting that Barna died young and was an immediate follower of Simone
Martini. Simone left Siena for good at the beginning of 1339. Moreover, even
according to Vasari, Barna was the master of Luca Tommè, who was already inscribed in the artists' guild in 1355 and painted the Pisan *Crucifixion* in 1366 with his familiar brusque vivacity and chiaroscuro effects – an
indication that by that time his artistic formation was complete (Van Marle,
II, fig. 304). On these grounds alone, therefore, and apart from the documentary evidence adduced by Milanesi (*Documenti Senesi*, I, p. 245), Barna's
untimely death and his frescoes at San Gimignano would seem to belong to
the middle years of the fourteenth century (De Nicola, *Thieme-Becker Künstler
Lexikon*, II, p. 506). C. Brandi (*Barna e G. d'Asciano, Balzana*, 1928, p. 20),
insists upon Vasari's date.

The frescoes at San Gimignano were repainted in 1745 by Bartolomeo
Lupinari, but in 1891 a good deal of this repainting was removed. Parts of
the frescoes are to be attributed to Giovanni d'Asciano, the pupil (Vasari)
and nephew of Barna, who continued the work after his uncle's death.

Della Valle has divided up the compositions between the two artists,
but in such a way as to do violence to all æsthetic reason. The *Massacre of
the Innocents* and the group of animals in the *Adoration of the Magi* are no
doubt poor, but I cannot agree with Van Marle's depreciation of a composition like that of the *Raising of Lazarus* (plate CXLI). Following Byzantine
usage, the *Entry into Jerusalem* (plates CXLII and CXLIII) occupies twice
the space of each of the other scenes, and the *Crucifixion* (Alinari, 9564) occupies it four times. For iconographic relations to Duccio, cf. Van Marle,
*Martini*, p. 123; and for the motive of the man extricating his head from
the cloak (plate CXLIII), cf. Berenson, *Estratto dal Boll. d'Arte P. I.*, 1926,
p. 42. Barna's romantic taste for violent movements and situations, *e. g.*
in compositions like that of the *Seizure of Christ* (Alinari, 37278), has been
related to Gothic expressionism by F. Antal in *Gedanken zur Entwicklung
der Trecento– und Quattrocentomalerei in Siena und Florenz* (1926).

PLATE CXLVI. – CHRIST CARRYING HIS CROSS. – The silhouette, which is turned
here towards the right instead of to the left, corresponds in almost every other

detail to that of the *Way to Calvary* at San Gimignano. Cf. Van Marle, II, plate facing p. 290. Frizzoni (*Arte*, 1904, p. 256), following an opinion expressed by R. Fry, finds the work so far superior to Barna's style that he thinks the design may be by Simone Martini.

PLATE CXLVII. – DETAIL OF MADONNA. – Cavalcaselle attributed the panel to Giovanni d'Asciano; others – Langton Douglas, Jacobsen, Berenson – to Lippo Memmi. It is completed by a small figure of the donor kneeling. The attribution to Barna is due to Perkins, but is not considered decisive by Van Marle. The panel should be compared with what is left of the figure of the Virgin and Child in the *Adoration of the Magi* at San Gimignano (Alinari, 37262). According to Perkins, the panel is a good deal earlier than the San Gimignano frescoes.

PLATE CXLVIII. – The NATIVITY. – Berenson attributed this *Nativity* and the *Annunciation* in the same Museum to the earliest phase of Bartolo di Fredi. Van Marle thought of Naddo Ceccarelli, in whose work the present panel would then form the "rustic gem." It is probable that Berenson's judgment was influenced by analogies in the small Vatican panel, which both he and Sirén likewise attributed to Bartolo's youth, but which has been assigned with greater exactness by De Nicola to Andrea di Bartolo (plate CCXLI). If the two paintings had been by the same hand, the date of the Aix-en-Provence panel would be shortly before 1400. In spite of such similarities as the small trees behind the player on the pipes here and behind the player on the cornemuse (plate CCXLI), the shape of the dogs, and the modelling of the landscape with its rounded, smooth outlines like those of a pudding just poured out of a mould, the *Nativity* seems to me to have a more archaic quality than the *Annunciation* – notice also the pose and proportions of the Madonna, the large aureoles, etc. – and to be attributable to some other painter than Bartolo, or at best to Andrea di Bartolo.

PLATE CXLIX. – MADONNA OF CORTONA. – After Berenson (*Essays*, p. 11) had touched upon the chronological order of Pietro Lorenzetti's first works, De Nicola (*Rassegna d'Arte*, 1919, p. 95) contributed some further and more precise details upon the same subject in his review of Berenson's volume. It is curious, however, to observe that De Nicola, like Gielly still more recently, still continues to assign the polyptych of *Beata Humiltà* to 1316, whereas the real date is 1341. Van Marle confirms Berenson's view that the Ducciesque elements in the *Madonna of Cortona* entirely rule out the date of 1335, which has frequently been proposed for this second panel. It was the younger Lorenzetti – Ambrogio, not Pietro – who painted for degli Ubertini, bishop of Cortona, in 1335.

PLATE CL. – ST. GREGORY. – The reproduction slightly cuts off the lower part of the panel. Cavalcaselle, Berenson, Van Marle, and others attribute it, with the works mentioned in the next paragraph, to Pietro. This was formerly the view of Perkins, but at present he seems rather to agree with the view expressed by DeWald (*Art Studies*, 1923, p. 45), who attributes the works cited in this and the following paragraph to "the Master of the Ovile Madonna" – an artist who painted in close proximity to Pietro and yet is clearly distinguished from him. According to DeWald, this " Master of S. Pietro Ovile " must in the last resort be identified with Berenson's " Ugolino Lorenzetti."

PLATES CLI and CLII. – THE ASSUMPTION and MADONNA. – Formerly in the Hospital della Scala, now in the Accademia at Siena. St. Thomas, kneeling, receives the Holy Girdle (plate CLI). Two other paintings, derived from the above-mentioned Hospital and now in the Accademia (plate CLII, and Van Marle, II, fig. 218), the panel in San Pietro Ovile, Siena (Van Marle, II, fig. 219), the *Madonna of Grosseto*, and the polyptych in the Chiaramonti Bordonaro Collection at Palermo, show affinities with this work.

PLATE CLIII. – MADONNA. – One of the works which best illustrate the relation between Pietro Lorenzetti and Giovanni Pisano – *e. g.*, the poise of the Madonna upon her right hip (cf. the *Madonna* in Prato Cathedral, and the ivory statuette of the *Madonna* in the Cathedral of Pisa, reproduced by R. Papini in *Catalogo delle cose d'arte*, etc., at Pisa, fig. 159) – although in the coiffure and in the summary character of the folds of the drapery Lorenzetti has modified some of Giovanni Pisano's Gothicisms.

PLATES CLIV and CLV. – ST. AGNES and ST. CATHERINE. – Parts of a polyptych originally in the (suppressed) Convent of Sant'Egidio at Siena (1325-1330).

PLATES CLVI and CLVII. – THE MASSACRE OF THE INNOCENTS and HEROD'S FEAST. – Perkins judged it imprudent to attribute the fresco representing the *Beheading of St. John the Baptist* and a second fresco, now much spoiled, of the *Vision of St. John the Evangelist* to Pietro Lorenzetti, as he rightly considered them inferior to the *Massacre of the Innocents*. On the other hand, Berenson, Van Marle, and Antal assigned all these paintings to Pietro; while Venturi (*Storia*, V, p. 695) who regards as them of slight value, seems disposed to attribute to Pietro merely the scenes representing the Baptist and the Evangelist. The motive of the prison-window which occurs in a small panel by Giovanni di Paolo, now in the Lehman Collection, New York, is apparently taken from the fresco of the Baptist; some of the bars of the window have been removed in preparation for the beheading. The man playing the lute, in the same fresco, is an obvious reminiscence of Giotto's figure in Santa Croce.

PLATE CLVIII. – CHRIST BEFORE PILATE. – This small panel, which came from the Museo Cristiano, has been published by Sirén (*Arte*, 1906, p. 325). It is approximately of the same date as the frescoes in the Servite Church.

PLATE CLIX. – MARTYR SAINTS. – Formerly in the Collection of Charles Fairfax Murray, who presented it to the National Gallery in 1882. The painting, though somewhat inferior, shows great similarity to the preceding small Vatican panel – compare the figure of the Pharisee accusing Christ in the latter with the figure of the priest carrying the statuette of the idol. Cavalcaselle referred it to an *ancona* representing scenes from the life of St. Savinus. If this view be correct, the date will be somewhere about 1335 (Milanesi, *Documenti*, I, p. 194).

PLATES CLX to CLXII. – THE POLYPTYCH OF THE CARMELITES. – According to Cavalcaselle, these three scenes, together with a fourth in the Gallery of Siena, in which Pope Honorius again appears with Carmelite friars, formed part of a polyptych with the Madonna, St. Nicholas, Apostles, etc., ordered for the Carmelite convent in 1329 and sold in England in 1818. E. T. DeWald (*Art Studies*, 1929) identifies this altar-piece with the *Madonna enthroned* at St. Ansano di Dofana. For a document relating to this work, cf. Della Valle, *Lettere Senesi*, II, p. 209. Van Marle and Venturi ascribe Pietro's frescoes at Assisi to much the same period of time.

PLATE CLXIII. – THE MADONNA WITH ST. FRANCIS AND ST. JOHN THE BAPTIST – Venturi assigns this fresco to Pietro Lorenzetti with some reserve, noticing as features alien from his style the small heads of the saints, the complicated folds in the drapery, and the angels with their close affinity to the Ducciesque type modified by Simone Martini.

PLATES CLXIV to CLXXI. – THE FRESCOES OF THE LOWER BASILICA, SAN FRANCESCO. – Vasari attributed the frescoes of the Lower Church to Pietro Cavallini, Giotto, and Puccio Capanna. Cavalcaselle, once again with entire rightness, restored them to Pietro Lorenzetti. Thode formed the hypothesis of a special master, to whom he also assigned the *Crucifixion* and the *Martyrdom of Ceuta* in San Francesco at Siena. According to Dobbert, the author of the frescoes was Ambrogio Lorenzetti. Schubring named Pietro, working with the help of assistants; but, in defiance of all likelihood, he maintained that the frescoes were painted between 1307 and 1320, previously to the Arezzo polyptych, in which we see Pietro still under the influence of Duccio. Affinities with the *Crucifixion* at Siena would seem to point to a date close upon 1329, as has been proposed by Venturi and Van Marle. Perkins, however, is content with a wider margin of time and suggests that the frescoes were painted between 1320 and 1330. With Van Marle and Perkins I consider the following scenes in the Lower Church to be the work of Pietro – the *Crucifixion*, the *Deposition*, the *Entombment*, the *Stigmata of St. Francis*, part of the *Resurrection*, part of the *Descent into Limbo*, and *Judas*. Beginning with the *Entry into Jerusalem*, the execution of the frescoes passes into the hands of followers. Venturi (*Storia*, V., p. 688) considers that Pietro's assistant was the painter " of the great Crucifixion attributed to Cavallini. " This artist is probably the so-called assistant B of Giotto (Berenson, *Florent. Paint.*, p. 142). With regard to the iconography of the *Deposition from the Cross* (plate CLXVIII), notice Lorenzetti's preference for archaïsing models affording scope for dramatic effect – the body of Christ turned on its back is a good example of this. Similar models are to be found in the *Deposition* by the " Master of St. Francis " in the Perugia Gallery, and in a second *Deposition* by the same painter in the Basilica of San Francesco at Assisi (Sirén, figs. 73 and 75). Other works by Pietro are five busts of saints in the frieze running below the *Crucifixion* and the *Deposition*, and five half-figures of Franciscans below the *Madonna* of Cimabue (Perkins, *Pietro Lorenzetti*, pp. 15, 20).

PLATE CLXXII. – THE CRUCIFIXION. – Della Valle (*Lettere Senesi*, II, p. 213), relying upon a notice in Tizio's *Historiae Senenses*, MS. in the Communal Library of Siena, assigns the frescoes painted by Ambrogio Lorenzetti in

San Francesco at Assisi and described by Ghiberti (plates CLXXXII to CLXXXVII) to the year 1331. We may conclude from this that Pietro's painting of the *Crucifixion* was executed at about the same time. It is known that on several occasions the two brothers undertook works together (Venturi, *Storia*, V, p. 686). There is no need to point out the obvious affinities of style in the *Crucifixion* and the *Deposition* at Assisi. At the time of its removal from the Chapter House to the Bandinelli Chapel in San Francesco, the lower part of the fresco was somewhat shortened. Berenson on two occasions has alluded to his own opinion that Pietro's hand can be detected in the frescoes in San Francesco at Siena, which commonly go under the name of Ambrogio (cf. his *Sassetta*, p. 19; and *Essays*, p. 31); but hitherto he has offered no proof in support of this singular proposition.

PLATE CLXXIII. – ALLEGORY. – Attributed to Pietro by Berenson and Van Marle. In spite of the ruinous state of the panel, which was originally in the Convent of Monna Agnese, there can still be made out – the Killing of Abel, Christ upon the Cross set up in the midst of a heap of corpses over which a number of monks are unfolding large inscribed labels, and Christ in Glory with the Madonna kneeling beside Him – a kind of allegory of Sin, Death, and Redemption.

PLATES CLXXIV and CLXXV. – LANDSCAPES. – Berenson attributed (1908) these two landscapes to Pietro – a view upheld by Van Marle (II, p. 360). Other students have ascribed them to Ambrogio, without adducing any explicit reason, and, in some instances, without even being aware (it would seem) of the attributions previously made. (Cf. L. Dami, *Dedalo*, IV, p. 292; F. Antal, *Gedanken zur Entwicklung*, etc.).

PLATES CLXXVI and CLXXVII. – THE NATIVITY OF THE VIRGIN. – Together with the *Throned Madonna*, painted in 1340 for the Church of San Francesco at Pistoia, and now, without the predella, in the Uffizi Gallery (Venturi, *Storia*, V., fig. 546), the polyptych of *Beata Umiltà* (1341), and the *St. Lucy*, this *Nativity of the Virgin* belongs to Pietro Lorenzetti's last period, and forms one of its most sublime examples. To this group of works, Van Marle, quoting the opinion of Perkins, would add the *Madonnas* of Castiglione d'Orcia and Monticchiello; but, as was said above, his chronology does not at this point appear convincing. The *Nativity of the Virgin* (plate CLXXVI) is signed and dated 1342. In later Sienese painting the same subject was treated, with evidence of dependence upon the present panel, by Paolo di Giovanni Fei (plate CCXXVIII) and by Sassetta (plate CCXLII). (Cf. Perkins, " Andrea Vanni," in *Burlington Magazine*, August, 1903; and Berenson, *Sassetta*, p. 57).

PLATE CLXXVIII. – THE POLYPTYCH OF BEATA UMILTÀ. – " The inscription, although renewed, is undoubtedly genuine at least as regards the date, which is 1341." (Berenson, *Essays*, p. 9). As is well known, owing to the fact that in the above-mentioned inscription V was persistently read instead of L, the date of the polyptych was long held to be MCCCXVI instead of MCCCXLJ, and hence the polyptych came to be assigned by Venturi, by Berenson in his first lists of Pietro's paintings (1908), and, still more recently, by Gielly and De Nicola, to the first period of Pietro's career, and prior to the Arezzo polyptych. The central panel of the predella, representing *B. Umiltà healing a Nun,* and now substituted by the dedicatory inscription, together with the other small left-hand panel, representing the *Death of B. Umiltà,* now missing from the polyptych, are in the Kaiser Friedrich Museum at Berlin. Thieme-Becker questions the attribution of the polyptych to Pietro, but assigns no motive.

PLATE CLXXIX. – ST. LUCY. – Much restored by Jacopo del Sellaio. (Cf. O. H. Giglioli, *Rassegna d'Arte,* 1906, p. 184).

PLATES CLXXX and CLXXXI. – THE MADONNA DEL LATTE and MADONNA OF ROCCALBEGNA. – The following paintings (amongst others) illustrate the development of Ambrogio Lorenzetti at the beginning of his career:

    1. The *Madonna of Sant'Angelo* at Vico l'Abate, near Florence, dated 1319, and betraying strong influence by Giotto (De Nicola, *Boll. Minist. Pubbl. Istr.,* 1922, p. 49).

    2. Four panels, showing *St. Francis, St. Catherine, St. Mary Magdalene,* and *St. Romuald* (?), in the Opera of Siena Cathedral (Van Marle, II, fig. 251).

    3. The *Madonna del Latte* (plate CLXXX).

    4. The *Madonna of Roccalbegna* (plate CLXXXI). Berenson (*Essays,* p. 23) attributes this painting to Ambrogio.

    We omit all reference to less convincing works, such as the *Madonna* at Budapest (Van Marle, II, fig. 253).

PLATES CLXXXII to CLXXXVII. – THE SAN FRANCESCO FRESCOES. – See the note to plate CLXXII. For the view that instead of the incidents here assigned to plates CLXXXIV and CLXXXII in accordance with Langton Douglas and Lusini, these frescoes represent (1) St. Francis of Siena asking leave of Pope Boniface VIII to go as a missionary, and (2) the Martyrdom of the Four Friars at Ceuta, cf. Gielly, *Primitifs Siennois,* p. 83 n. The date 1331, which is commonly received and not improbable, is founded, as we have said, solely upon Della Valle's extension of the information given by Tizio in his *Historiae Senenses,* III, p. 140. (Cf. E. von Meyenburg – persistently called " Marienburg " by Gielly – *Ambrogio Lorenzetti*). The frescoes originally decorated a cloister pulled down in 1517. To the same series belongs the National Gallery fragment – acquired at Siena in 1878 – representing the profile of four nuns. A detailed description of the frescoes will be found in Ghiberti. The subjects were: St. Francis of Siena clothed with the Franciscan habit, St. Francis starting on his mission, the Beheading of his companions, the Storm at sea, etc. Vasari made use of Ghiberti's description and praises especially the representation of the storm. For the extent to which Giovanni di Paolo may have derived inspiration from this storm for a small panel in the Johnson Collection at Philadelphia, and Lorenzo Monaco for his *Shipwreck of St. Nicholas* in the Uffizi Gallery, cf. L. Dami, *Dedalo,* IV, pp. 291, 294.

PLATES CLXXXVIII and CLXXXIX. – EPISODES FROM THE LEGEND OF ST. NICHOLAS OF BARI. – The paintings – according to Ghiberti " frescoes and an altar-piece " – executed by Ambrogio for the Church of San Procolo would seem to belong, together with these "Histories" of St. Nicholas of Bari, to the year 1332. In that year Ambrogio was at Florence and became a member of the painters' guild – an indication that his stay there was of some duration. The *pala* of San Procolo was partly traced and reconstituted by Perkins (*Rassegna d'Arte*, 1918, p. 106) and by De Nicola (*Boll. Min. Pubbl. Istr.*, 1922, p. 53). The four scenes from the life of St. Nicholas (plates CLXXXVIII and CLXXXIX) must have formed part of another work. It is difficult to follow A. Venturi when he traces their stylistic and chronological derivation from Pietro's *Polyptych of B. Umiltà*, as the latter appears to have been painted some ten years later.

PLATE CXC. – MADONNA AND SAINTS. – Even Van Marle considers that this work belongs to no very late date (about 1330). Strangely enough, however, he sees eight female saints on either side of the Madonna, whereas it is clear that the figures represent – St. Catherine of Alexandria, with her wheel of martyrdom; St. Dorothy, with the flowers in her lap; three angels on either side; and four bishop saints in the foreground.

PLATE CXCI. – The PRESENTATION IN THE TEMPLE. – Originally in the Convent of Monna Agnese. Venturi (*Storia*, V, p. 172) mentions that this *Presentation in the Temple* formed the central part of an altar-piece known as the *pala* of St. Crescentius, painted by Ambrogio for Siena Cathedral between 1339 and 1342 – that is, during the period immediately following the frescoes of *Good and Bad Government*. The *Presentation* is signed and dated 1342. The same figuration in a no less rich architectonic setting is repeated in a *Presentation* belonging to the Louvre, which Venturi (*Storia*, V, fig. 600) attributes to Barna, but which is more probably by Bartolo di Fredi; and again, in a painting by Giovanni di Paolo, originally in the Hospital della Scala and now in the Accademia (n. 211) at Siena; and, for a third time, by Sano di Pietro in the Cathedral at Massa Marittima (C. Ricci, *Il Palazzo pubblico di Siena*, fig. 93).

PLATES CXCII to CCV. – The FRESCOES OF GOOD AND BAD GOVERNMENT. – The date of the frescoes of *Good and Bad Government* is variously given. Della Valle suggests the period between 1343 and 1348; Meyenburg and Gielly, between 1337 and 1339; Berenson, between 1338 and 1340. Milanesi refers to these frescoes a payment made in June, 1340. Venturi places them after 1337, and assigns to 1340 the *Madonna*, now almost entirely destroyed, in the loggia of the Communal Palace at Siena. That assistants collaborated in the painting is clearly shown by the unequal merit of the various parts. This feature becomes only too clear as soon as we compare the three figures representing the *Virtues* seated at the right hand of the figure of *Good Government* with the other figures representing *Peace, Fortitude, Justice*, etc. The frescoes bear the signature " *Ambrosius Laurentii hic pinxit utrinque.*" As Ambrogio Lorenzetti enjoyed the fame of being a man of letters, he has been held to be the author of the Italian verses inscribed in the ornamental borders below the paintings, and transcribed in full by Della Valle in his description (*Lettere Senesi*, II, p. 217). With regard to the interpretation of the allegories, cf. O. H. Giglioli, *Emporium*, April, 1904. The frames surrounding the frescoes are filled up with decorative subjects – figures representing the *Seasons* (plates CCIV and CCV), the sciences, effigies of tyrants, signs of the zodiac, planets, and so forth – set in medallions amidst acanthus foliage.

162

PLATES CCVI and CCVII. – MADONNA AND SAINTS. – Perkins (*Burlington Magazine*, April, 1904) considers this panel a fairly youthful work. It is, in fact, of about the same period as the painting reproduced in plate CXC. Petrocchi (*Massa Marittima*, 1909) definitely states that its date in 1316, but this is absurdly early. Van Marle assigns the fresco in the chapel of Monte Siepi, near San Galgano, representing the *Madonna between Angels, with Saints and Eve*, to the same period as the present panel, the date of which, according to him, is later than that of the frescoes of *Good Government* (Perkins, *Rassegna d'Arte*, 1904, p. 186). The motive of Eve occurs in a number of paintings by artists more or less directly influenced by the Lorenzetti – for instance, in the triptych by Lippo Vanni in the Monastery of SS. Domenico and Sisto in Rome, and in the *Madonna and Saints* by Paolo di Giovanni Fei in the Chigi Saracini Collection at Siena (Van Marle, II, figs. 298, 340).

PLATES CCVIII to CCX. – THE ANNUNCIATION. – This is the last dated work by Ambrogio Lorenzetti – December 17, 1344. To the same year belongs a small allegory of *Good Government* on the cover of a register of receipts and expenses (Anderson, 21597). The *Annunciation* was formerly in the Communal Palace. Van Marle has drawn attention to the gesture of the angel's hand, similar to that found in the *Madonna* by Pietro at Assisi; and hence we may conclude that the panel originally formed part of a polyptych.

PLATES CCXI to CCXIII. – POLYPTYCH OF S. PETRONILLA. – Formerly in the Monastery of Santa Petronilla. Van Marle is of opinion that notwithstanding a certain affinity to the *Madonna* in the Platt Collection, Englewood, U.S.A. – a painting very similar to the *Madonna* reproduced in plate CXC – the present polyptych should be assigned to the last years of Ambrogio's activity, and he associates with it the cusps with the figures of St. Maximinus and St. Anthony in the Gallery of Siena (nn. 89, 91).

PLATES CCXIV to CCXVII. – PANELS FROM THE VATICAN GALLERY. – These " histories " were attributed by Cavalcaselle to Pietro Lorenzetti. Suida assigns them to Bernardo Daddi; Meyenburg, to Ambrogio Lorenzetti. Sirén (*Arte*, 1906, p. 325) and Perkins attribute them to an artist " between " Ambrogio Lorenzetti and Bernardo Daddi, though Sirén considers the influence of Daddi to be the more pronounced of the two, whereas Perkins affirms this of Ambrogio. In the *Golden Urn* (1898) Berenson supported the attribution to Ambrogio, but he has presumably modified his opinion since. Analogies with the predella in the Museum at Prato (Alinari, 30787-8) do not decide the question of the attribution of these panels to Daddi, as authorship of the predella is itself a matter of doubt. Some of these panels, which were originally in the Museo Cristiano and are now in the Vatican Gallery, have been reproduced here, as memorable examples of the influence exercised by the Lorenzetti in Florence, particularly in the beauty of their colour.

PLATES CCXVIII to CCXXI. – ANDREA VANNI. – Van Marle considers the *Madonna* (plate CCXVIII) one of the works of Vanni's early maturity, and dates it earlier than the *Madonna of Santo Spirito* (plate CCXIX), which, so far as one can judge, has been much repainted. Della Valle (*Lettere Senesi*, p. 143) quotes a reference by Tizio to a painting executed by Vanni in 1398 for the principal altar in the Church of San Francesco at Siena – a painting which must not, however, be confused with the *Madonna* reproduced in plate CCXX. The latter – a panel in San Francesco, showing the Virgin in a dark blue mantle edged with gold, and the Child in a tunic of gold – is one of the most remarkable works painted during the second half of the fourteenth century. The lower part of the panel is slightly shortened in the reproduction. The fresco of *St. Catherine*, which Van Marle dates before 1396, has been much restored. Della Valle (*Lettere Senesi*, p. 142) informs us that the " likeness of his Teacher was painted by Vanni on the wall of the Church of San Domenico during her lifetime. " This indicates a date previous to 1380.

PLATE CCXXII. – LIPPO VANNI. – This triptych, attributed in the catalogue of the Vatican Gallery to the " manner of Lippo Memmi, " has been restored to Lippo Vanni by Berenson (*Rassegna d'Arte*, 1917, p. 41). Berenson discovers affinities in colour and technique with the *Madonna* of the Perugia Gallery and with the triptych in the Walters Collection, Baltimore, U.S.A. The painting was previously in the Museo Cristiano. The frame is modern.

PLATE CCXXIII. – LUCA DI TOMMÈ. – At one time attributed to Bartolo di Fredi. Van Marle assigns this *ancona* to the last period of Luca's career, when the near influence of Barna and the Lorenzetti had been partly superseded by a return to the influence of Simone, as in the *Madonna of Montalcino*.

PLATES CCXXIV to CCXXVII. – BARTOLO DI FREDI. – These *Scenes from the Life of the Virgin* with other panels representing the *Passion of Christ* formed part of a *Coronation of the Virgin* (1388), of which the central part (Van Marle, II, fig. 321) is in the Gallery at Montalcino. Of the *Scenes from the Life of the Virgin*, painted in the Church of Sant'Agostino at San Gimignano, only a few fragments remain – the *Nativity* (plate CCXXVI) and the *Death*. The frescoes in the tower of the Communal Palace at San Gimignano, representing *Scenes of Married Life*, are the work of an artist akin to Bartolo. Van Marle considers that this artist betrays, even more than Bartolo, a very close dependence on Lippo Memmi.

PLATES CCXXVIII and CCXXIX. – PAOLO DI GIOVANNI FEI. – For the *Nativity of the Virgin*, see note on plate CLXXVI. The relation to Simone Martini, most marked in the expression of the Madonna (plate CCXXIX) and in the arabesques of the drapery, has induced Van Marle to assign the painting to a comparatively early date in Paolo's career.

PLATES CCXXX to CCXXXIX. – TADDEO DI BARTOLO. – Plate CCXXX reproduces the central part of the polyptych in the Gallery of Perugia. To the left of this central panel are *St. Mary Magdalene* and *St. John the Baptist;* to the right *St. John the Evangelist* and *St. Catherine of Alexandria*. On the reverse of the polyptych, which was at one time above the high altar in San Francesco at Perugia, is the scene of *St. Francis receiving the Stigmata*; and at the sides, *St. Anthony of Padua, St. Louis of Toulouse*, and *St. Herculanus*, the patron saint of Perugia. A label at the feet of the Virgin bears the signature of the painter and the date 1403. There is a mutilated copy of this central panel in the Museum at Nancy. The painting of the *Madonna between*

*St. James and St. Dominic* (plate CCXXXI) is considered by Lionello Venturi (*Catalogo della Raccolta Gualino*, plate 9) to be not a late work; he detects affinities between the Virgin and Child and the corresponding figures in the polyptychs of Perugia and Volterra (1411). The decorative paintings in the chapel of the Communal Palace of Siena (plates CCXXXV and CCXXXVI) belong to the year 1406. The allegory of Jupiter and Mars, flanked by a second allegory representing other pagan divinities, is painted on the vault. In the *Resurrection of the Virgin* (plate CCXXXVII), now in the Vatican Gallery and formerly in the Museo Cristiano, the figure of Christ descending from heaven with seraph's wings in order to bear His mother away with Him, is worthy of remark. The frescoes in the Collegiate Church of San Gimignano, signed and dated 1393 (plates CCXXXVIII and CCXXXIX), are the earliest work by Taddeo of which the date is certain. Cf. the note on plate LXXIV.

PLATE CCXL. – GREGORIO DI CECCO. – Signed and dated 1423. At one time in the Cathedral, now in the Opera of the Cathedral at Siena.

PLATE CCXLI. – ANDREA DI BARTOLO. – The painting was formerly in the Museo Cristiano, and is attributed by Berenson and Sirén (*Arte*, 1906, p. 333) to the youth of Bartolo di Fredi. De Nicola (*Rassegna d'Arte Senese*, 1921, p. 12) has transferred the authorship to Andrea di Bartolo. Cf. note on plate CXLVIII.

PLATES CCXLII to CCLI. – SASSETTA. – The polyptych at Asciano (plates CCXLII and CCXLIII) is considered by Berenson to be earlier than the altar-piece of Sansepolcro and the triptych at the Osservanza, dated 1436. Cavalcaselle was the first to attribute the polyptych to Sassetta. According to Berenson, the Asciano triptych is not only the first important work by Sassetta which has come down to us, but the work which best illustrates the artist's formation. The date, he thinks, is, presumably, 1430. The small panel with the *Vision of St. Thomas* (plate CCXLV) comes from the Museo Cristiano. Roger Fry discovered the small panel of the *Magi and the Star* (plate CCXLVI), formerly attributed to Paolo Uccello, in the Crewe Collection, and gave an account of it in the *Burlington Magazine*, XXII (1912), p. 131. For the *St. Martin and the Beggar* (plate CCXLVII) see the article by De Nicola, " Sassetta between 1423 and 1443," in the same review, XXIII, (1913), p. 335. The Sansepolcro altar-piece has been fully described by Berenson in his work on Sassetta. The contract for this painting, which originally adorned the principal altar in the Church of San Francesco at Sansepolcro, was signed on September 5, 1437, but the work was only finished seven years later. In 1752 it was taken down and dispersed. The paintings reproduced in plates CCL and CCLI, together with a third not shown here, formed part of a predella representing episodes in the *Temptation of St. Anthony*; Berenson (*Sassetta*, p. 64) attributes them to the artist's maturity, yet at a time when he was still mindful of Paolo di Giovanni and Lippo Vanni.

PLATES CCLII to CCLVI. – GIOVANNI DI PAOLO AND SANO DI PIETRO. – This detail of the *Flight into Egypt* (plate CCLIV) is taken from a panel in the Accademia of Siena, formerly in the Ciaccheri group of paintings. The ground is painted in gold, and the shadows of the trees and of the ass near the river with its driver, are outlined upon it. Maurice Denis (*Théories*, 1912) has based upon this painting a number of interesting observations concerning the feeling for landscape in the painting of the period. It is worthy of remark, however, that not even this landscape and the landscapes of the *" Histories " of the Virgin and S. Galgano* (Accademia of Siena, n. 198), not even figures like that of the *Madonna* (plate CCLII) nor imaginative paintings like *The Retirement of John the Baptist into the Wilderness* in the Ryerson Collection at Chicago (Berenson, *Central Italian Painters* (German trans.) plate 16) have succeeded in disarming one student of Sienese painting: Gielly has quite recently deplored *" ce Giovanni di Paolo, qui commit bien les pires horreurs de l'école italienne tout entière."* For Giovanni di Paolo and the primitive landscape painters the reader may consult the following – L. Dami, *Dedalo*, 1923, p. 269; E. Baes, " Histoire de la peinture de paysage " in *Annales de la Soc. Roy. de Bibl. et de Littér.*, Gand, 1873, tom. VII; W. Kallab, " Die Toskanische Landschaftmalerei, XIV and XV, Jahr." in *Oesterr. Jahrbücher*, 1900; I. Guthmann, *Die Landschaftmalerei der Toschanischen und Umbrischen Kunst*, Leipzig, 1902; and H. Bouchot, " Le paysage chez les primitifs " in *Gazette des Beaux Arts*, 1907, II, p. 456. For the *Angel and the Shepherds* (plate CCLV) by Sano di Pietro, see the article by Dami quoted above.

# LIST OF PLATES

169

170

171

CVIII. – SIMONE MARTINI. ST. MARTIN IN MEDITATION. Assisi, S. Francesco, Lower Basilica. (*Photo. Anderson*).

CIX. – SIMONE MARTINI. THE MIRACLE OF THE MASS. Assisi, S. Francesco, Lower Basilica. (*Photo. Anderson*).

CX. – SIMONE MARTINI (and DONATO ?). THE DEATH OF ST. MARTIN. Assisi, S. Francesco, Lower Basilica. (*Photo. Anderson*).

CXI. – SIMONE MARTINI. THE OBSEQUIES OF ST. MARTIN. Assisi, S. Francesco, Lower Basilica. (*Photo. Anderson*).

CXII. – SIMONE MARTINI. DETAIL OF THE OBSEQUIES. Assisi, S. Francesco, Lower Basilica. (*Photo. Anderson*).

CXIII. – SIMONE MARTINI. A SAINT. Assisi, S. Francesco, Lower Basilica. (*Photo. Anderson*).

CXIV. – SIMONE MARTINI. ST. BENEDICT (?). Assisi, S. Francesco, Lower Basilica. (*Photo Anderson*).

CXV. – SIMONE MARTINI. ST. ANTHONY (?). Assisi, S. Francesco, Lower Basilica. (*Photo. Anderson*).

CXVI. – DONATO (?). ST. FRANCIS. Assisi, S. Francesco, Lower Basilica. (*Photo. Anderson*).

CXVII. – DONATO (?). ST. CLARE. Assisi, S. Francesco, Lower Basilica. (*Photo. Anderson*).

CXVIII. – DONATO (?). ST. LOUIS OF TOULOUSE. Assisi, S. Francesco, Lower Basilica. (*Photo. Anderson*).

CXIX. – SIMONE MARTINI. GUIDORICCIO RICCI DEI FOGLIANI (1328). Siena, Communal Palace. (*Photo. Anderson*).

CXX. – SIMONE MARTINI (?). BEATO AGOSTINO NOVELLO. Central Panel. Siena, S. Agostino. (*Photo. Anderson*).

CXXI. – SIMONE MARTINI (?). BEATO AGOSTINO. The Second Left-Hand Panel of the Pala. Siena, S. Agostino. (*Photo. Anderson*).

CXXII. – SIMONE MARTINI (?). BEATO AGOSTINO. The First Left-Hand Panel of the Pala. Siena, S. Agostino. (*Photo. Anderson*).

CXXIII. – SIMONE MARTINI (?). BEATO AGOSTINO. The First Right-Hand Panel of the Pala. Siena, S. Agostino. (*Photo. Anderson*).

CXXIV. – SIMONE MARTINI (?). BEATO AGOSTINO. Detail of the Second Right-Hand Panel of the *Pala*. Siena, S. Agostino. (*Photo. Anderson*).

CXXV. – SIMONE MARTINI AND LIPPO MEMMI. THE ANNUNCIATION (1333). Florence, Uffizi Gallery. (*Photo. Anderson*).

CXXVI. – SIMONE MARTINI. THE ANGEL AND THE VIRGIN OF THE ANNUNCIATION. Florence, Uffizi Gallery. (*Photo. Anderson*).

CXXVII. – SIMONE MARTINI. DETAIL OF THE ANGEL OF THE ANNUNCIATION. Florence, Uffizi Gallery. (*Photo. Anderson*).

CXXVIII. – SIMONE MARTINI. Another DETAIL OF THE ANNUNCIATION. Florence, Uffizi Gallery. (*Photo. Anderson*).

CXXIX. – SIMONE MARTINI. THE VIRGIN OF THE STROGANOFF ANNUNCIATION. Formerly in the Stroganoff Collection, Rome. (*Photo. Lombardi*).

CXXX. – SIMONE MARTINI. THE CRUCIFIXION. Antwerp, Museum. (*Photo. Braun*).

CXXXI. – SIMONE MARTINI. THE DEPOSITION. Antwerp, Museum. (*Photo. Braun*).

174

175

176

THOMAS AQUINAS. Città del Vaticano, Vatican Gallery. (*Photo. Anderson*).

# REPRODUCTIONS

I               THE HAMILTON MADONNA (about 1200)

*New York, Collection of Carl Hamilton*

"PALIOTTO." Formerly at the Abbey of Berardenga (1215)

Siena, Accademia

(Photo. Anderson)

II

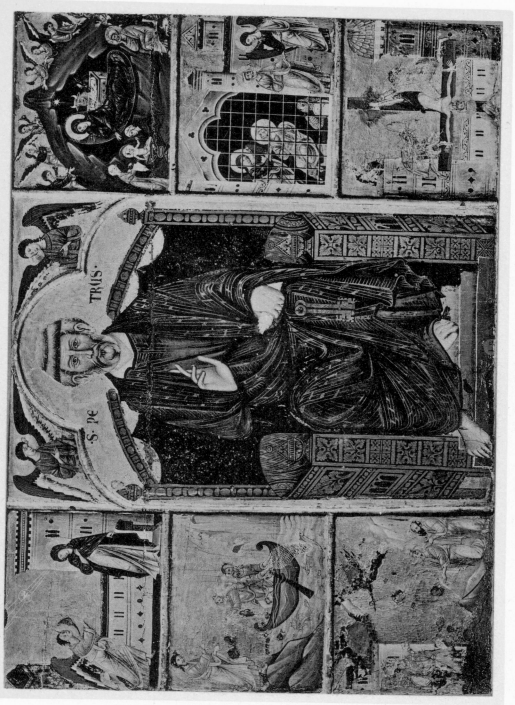

"PALIOTTO." Formerly in the Church of S. Pietro in Banchi, Siena

*Siena, Accademia*

*(Photo. Anderson)*

III

IV            GUIDO OF SIENA - MADONNA       *(Photo. Lombardi)*

*Siena, Communal Palace*

V           GUIDO OF SIENA - MADONNA           *(Photo. Anderson)*

*Siena, Accademia*

VI        UNKNOWN SIENESE ARTIST - DIPTYCH      *(Photo. Lombardi)*

*Siena, Accademia*

VII          Unknown Sienese Artist - DIPTYCH      *(Photo. Lombardi)*
Siena, Accademia

VIII     Master of the Rucellai Madonna - THE GUALINO MADONNA
*Turin, Collection of R. Gualino*

MASTER OF THE RUCELLAI MADONNA - THE RUCELLAI MADONNA (1285) *(Photo. Anderson)*
*Florence, S. Maria Novella*

X       Master of the Rucellai Madonna - DETAIL OF THE RUCELLAI MADONNA *(Photo. Anderson)*
*Florence, S. Maria Novella*

XI      DUCCIO - MADONNA WITH ADORING FRANCISCANS (about 1278)    *(Photo. Anderson)*
*Siena, Accademia*

XII       Duccio - **THE STROGANOFF MADONNA**       *(Photo. Lombardi)*

*Formerly in the Stroganoff Collection, and now in the Stoclet Collection, Brussels*

Duccio - MADONNA OF PERUGIA     *(Photo. Anderson)*
*Perugia, Art Gallery*

XIV

Duccio - "MAESTÀ" (1308-1311)
Siena, Opera del Duomo

(Photo. Anderson)

Duccio - DETAIL of the "MAESTÀ" *(Photo. Anderson)*
*Siena, Opera del Duomo*

Duccio - DETAIL of the "MAESTÀ" *(Photo. Ministry of Public Instruction)*
*Siena, Opera del Duomo*

EX EGI
PTO VO
CAVI
FILIŪ
MEVM

Duccio - DETAIL of the " MAESTÀ " *(Photo. Ministry of Public Instruction)*
*Siena, Opera del Duomo*

XVIII           Duccio - Left part of the " MAESTÀ "        *(Photo. Anderson)*
*Siena, Opera del Duomo*

Duccio - Right part of the " MAESTÀ "
Siena, Opera del Duomo

(Photo. *Anderson*)

XX        Duccio - ANGEL; from the "MAESTÀ"        *(Photo. Anderson)*
*Siena, Opera del Duomo*

XXI     Duccio - ADORING ANGELS; from the " MAESTÀ "
*Siena, Opera del Duomo*

*(Photo. Lombardi)*

Duccio - ST. CATHERINE; from the " MAESTÀ "  *(Photo. Anderson)*
*Siena, Opera del Duomo*

XXIII        Duccio - ST. AGNES; from the "MAESTÀ"        *(Photo. Anderson)*
*Siena, Opera del Duomo*

XXIV     Duccio - THE ANNUNCIATION; from the " MAESTA "

*London, National Gallery*

XXV    Duccio - THE NATIVITY AND PROPHETS; from the "MAESTÀ"

*Berlin, Kaiser Friedrich Museum*

*(Photo Hanfstaengl)*

XXVI · Duccio · THE FLIGHT INTO EGYPT; from the "MAESTÀ"
Siena, Opera del Duomo

(Photo. Ministry of Public Instruction)

XXVII    Duccio - THE MASSACRE OF THE INNOCENTS: from the " MAESTÀ "

*Siena, Opera del Duomo*

XXVIII — DUCCIO - CHRIST DISPUTING WITH THE DOCTORS OF THE LAW; from the "MAESTÀ"

*Siena, Opera del Duomo*

Duccio - CHRIST AND THE WOMAN OF SAMARIA ; from the " MAESTÀ "

*London, Duveen Collection*

*(Photo Artists' Illustrators, Ltd)*

XXX    Duccio - THE TEMPTATION OF CHRIST; from the " MAESTÀ "    (Photo. Anderson)

Siena, Opera del Duomo

Duccio – THE TEMPTATION OF CHRIST; from the "MAESTÀ"

*New York, Frick Collection*

XXXI

XXXII    Duccio - THE ENTRY OF CHRIST INTO JERUSALEM; from the "MAESTÀ" *(Photo. Anderson)*
*Siena, Opera del Duomo*

Duccio - THE LAST SUPPER; from the "MAESTÀ"
Siena, Opera del Duomo

(Photo. Anderson)

Duccio - **CHRIST WASHING THE DISCIPLES' FEET**; from the " MAESTÀ ".    *(Photo. Anderson)*

*Siena, Opera del Duomo*

XXXV

Duccio - THE PRAYER IN THE GARDEN; from the "MAESTÀ"
*Siena, Opera del Duomo*

*(Photo. Anderson)*

Duccio - THE SEIZURE OF CHRIST; from the " MAESTÀ "

*Siena, Opera del Duomo*

(*Photo. Anderson*)

XXXVII

Ducсio - THE DENIAL OF ST. PETER; from the " MAESTÀ "

Siena, Opera del Duomo

(Photo. Anderson)

XXXVIII

Duccio - CHRIST BEFORE PILATE; from the "MAESTÀ"

*Siena, Opera del Duomo*

*(Photo. Anderson)*

XXXIX      Duccio - THE CRUCIFIXION; from the "MAESTÀ"     *(Photo. Anderson)*
*Siena, Opera del Duomo*

XL    Duccio - Left Hand Group of the CRUCIFIXION; from the "MAESTÀ"  *(Photo. Anderson)*
*Siena, Opera del Duomo*

Duccio - Right Hand Group of the CRUCIFIXION; from the "MAESTÀ" *(Photo. Anderson)*
*Siena, Opera del Duomo*

XLII　　　DUCCIO - THE DEPOSITION FROM THE CROSS; from the "MAESTÀ"　　(Photo. Anderson)

Siena, Opera del Duomo

XLIII    Duccio – CHRIST LAID IN THE SEPULCHRE; from the "MAESTÀ"    *(Photo. Anderson)*
*Siena, Opera del Duomo*

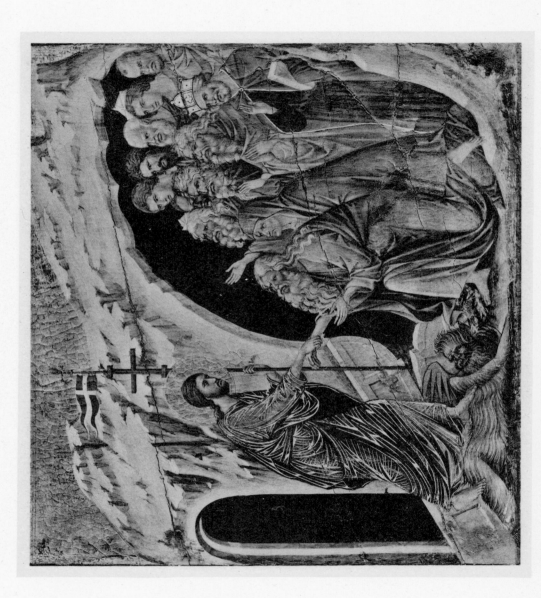

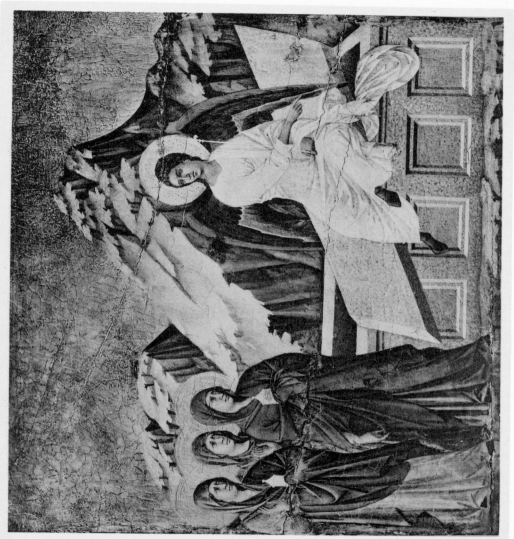

XLV - DUCCIO - THE MARYS AT THE SEPULCHRE; from the " MAESTÀ "

*Siena, Opera del Duomo*

*(Photo. Anderson)*

XLVI     Duccio - DETAIL OF THE MARYS AT THE SEPULCHRE     *(Photo. Anderson)*
*Siena, Opera del Duomo*

XLVII    Duccio - THE ANGEL AT THE SEPULCHRE; from the "MAESTÀ"    (Photo. Anderson)
Siena, *Opera del Duomo*

XLVIII - DUCCIO - "NOLI ME TANGERE"; from the "MAESTÀ"
Siena, Opera del Duomo

XLIX        Duccio - DETAIL OF "NOLI ME TANGERE"      *(Photo. Lombardi)*
*Siena, Opera del Duomo*

L

Duccio - CHRIST ON THE WAY TO EMMAUS; from the " MAESTÀ "    (Photo. Anderson)

Siena, Opera del Duomo

DUCCIO · **DETAIL OF CHRIST ON THE WAY TO EMMAUS**    *(Photo. Anderson)*
*Siena, Opera del Duomo*

Duccio · THE APPEARANCE OF CHRIST ON THE SHORE OF LAKE TIBĒRIAS ; from the "MAESTÀ" (*Photo. Anderson*)

*Siena. Opera del Duomo*

LIII - DUCCIO - THE APPEARANCE OF CHRIST UPON THE MOUNTAIN; from the "MAESTÀ" *(Photo Anderson)*

*Siena, Opera del Duomo*

LIV - THE FAREWELL OF MARY TO THE APOSTLES; from the "MAESTÀ"

DUCCIO

Siena, Opera del Duomo

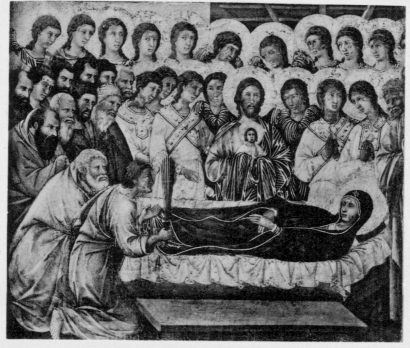

Duccio - **PENTECOST and THE DEATH OF THE VIRGIN**; from the "MAESTÀ" *(Photo. Alinari)*
*Siena, Opera del Duomo*

DUCCIO - THE BURIAL OF THE VIRGIN; from the "MAESTÀ"

*Siena, Opera del Duomo*

*(Photo. Anderson)*

Duccio - TWO PANELS OF A POLYPTYCH
*Siena. Accademia*

*(Photo. Anderson)*

WORKSHOP OF DUCCIO - POLYPTYCH

*Siena, Accademia*

LVIII

SCHOOL OF DUCCIO - "MAESTÀ"

*Città di Castello, Art Gallery*

*(Photo. Alinari)*

LX        School of Duccio - **MADONNA**       *(Photo. Anderson)*
*Siena, Accademia*

LXI          SCHOOL OF DUCCIO - MADONNA

*(Florence, Tadini-Buoninsegni Collection)*

THE PSEUDO MASTER GILIO · MADONNA  *(Photo. Alinari)*
Siena, Accademia

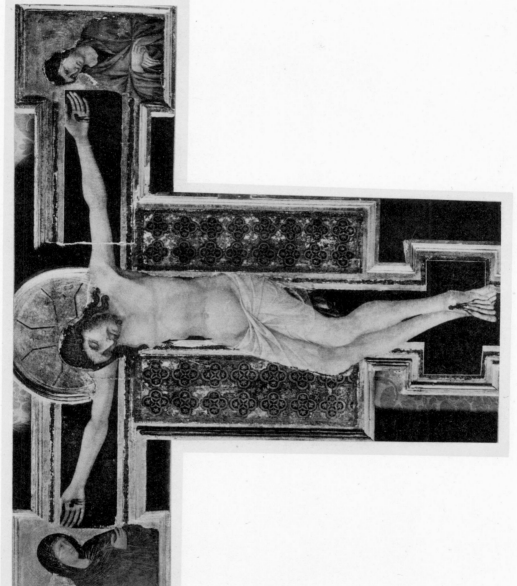

LXIII     The Pseudo Masarello di Gilio - CRUCIFIX (1305)     (Photo. Anderson)

*Siena, Accademia*

UGOLINO OF SIENA · THE PREACHING OF ST. JOHN THE BAPTIST

*Budapest, Art Gallery*

LXIV

UGOLINO OF SIENA - THE ASCENT OF MOUNT CALVARY

*London, National Gallery*

LXV

LXVI      Ugolino of Siena - ST. FRANCIS OF ASSISI    *(Photo. Lombardi)*
*San Casciano, Confraternity of the Misericordia*

UGOLINO OF SIENA (?) - MADONNA     (*Photo. Lombardi*)

*San Casciano, Confraternity of the Misericordia*

LXVIII       " Ugolino Lorenzetti " - NATIVITY (about 1330-40)
Cambridge, U. S. A., Fogg Art Museum

LXIX      "Ugolino Lorenzetti" - S. ANSANO AND S. GALGANO      *(Photo. Lombardi)*

*Siena, Accademia*

LXX      " UGOLINO LORENZETTI " - THE CRUCIFIXION
*Settignano, Collection of Bernard Berenson*

SEGNA DI BUONAVENTURA - THE CRUCIFIXION
*London, Collection of Lord Crawford*

LXXII

SEGNA DI BUONAVENTURA - FOUR PANELS OF A POLYPTYCH

*Siena, Accademia*

(*Photo. Anderson*)

SEGNA DI BUONAVENTURA - MADONNA
*Siena, Seminary*

*(Photo. Anderson)*

LXXIV    MEMMO DI FILIPPUCCIO AND LIPPO MEMMI - "MAESTÀ"    (*Photo. Anderson*)

*San Gimignano, Communal Palace*

(Photo. Anderson)

Simone Martini - "Maestà" (1315)
*Siena, Communal Palace*

LXXV

LXXVI       Simone Martini · DETAIL of the "MAESTÀ"       *(Photo. Anderson)*
*Siena, Communal Palace*

LXXVII      SIMONE MARTINI - MADONNA of the "MAESTÀ"      *(Photo. Anderson)*
*Siena, Communal Palace*

LXXVIII       SIMONE MARTINI - FEMALE SAINT; from the " MAESTÀ "     *(Photo. Anderson)*
*Siena, Communal Palace*

SIMONE MARTINI - FEMALE SAINT; from the " MAESTÀ "     *(Photo. Anderson)*
*Siena, Communal Palace*

LXXX               SIMONE MARTINI - ANGEL; from the "MAESTÀ"        *(Photo. Anderson)*
*Siena, Communal Palace*

LXXXI           Simone Martini - THE SAVIOUR         *(Photo. Anderson)*
                           *Città del Vaticano, Vatican Gallery*

LXXXII          Simone Martini          *(Photo. Anderson)*

ST. LOUIS OF TOULOUSE CROWNING ROBERT OF ANJOU (1317)

*Naples, National Museum*

SIMONE MARTINI - DETAIL OF ST. LOUIS

*(Photo. Anderson)*

*Naples, National Museum*

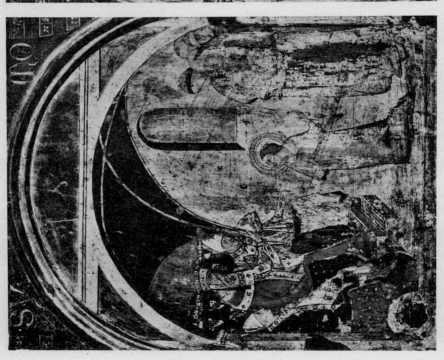

LXXXIV     SIMONE MARTINI · TWO COMPARTMENTS OF THE PREDELLA; from the "St. Louis of Toulouse"     (Photo. Anderson)

Naples, National Museum

LXXXV  SIMONE MARTINI - TWO OTHER COMPARTMENTS OF THE PREDELLA; from the "St. Louis of Toulouse"

*Naples, National Museum*

LXXXVI        SIMONE MARTINI - MADONNA      *(Photo Anderson)*
*Rome, Palazzo Venezia*

LXXXVII

SIMONE MARTINI - POLYPTYCH OF PISA (1320)

Pisa, Church of Santa Caterina. The predella and the fifth panel in the Civic Museum, Pisa

(Photo. Alinari)

Simone Martini - POLYPTYCH OF PISA. Panels 1 and 2    *(Photo. Alinari)*

*Pisa, Santa Caterina*

LXXXIX       Simone Martini - POLYPTYCH OF PISA. Panels 3 and 5      *(Photo. Alinari)*

*Panel 3 in Santa Caterina, Pisa, and panel 5 in the Civic Museum, Pisa*

SIMONE MARTINI · POLYPTYCH OF PISA · Panels 6 and 7    *(Photo. Alinari)*
*Pisa, Santa Caterina*

XCI     SIMONE MARTINI - POLYPTYCH OF PISA. Central panel (4)     *(Photo. Alinari)*
*Pisa, Santa Caterina*

SIMONE MARTINI - POLYPTYCH OF PISA. Centre of the predella

*Pisa, Civic Museum*

*(Photo. Ministry of Public Instruction)*

SIMONE MARTINI          (*Photo. Ministry of Public Instruction*)

PREDELLA OF THE POLYPTYCH OF PISA. Compartments 1 and 2

*Pisa, Civic Museum*

Simone Martini     *(Photo. Ministry of Public Instruction)*

PREDELLA OF THE POLYPTYCH OF PISA. Compartments 3 and 4

*Pisa, Civic Museum*

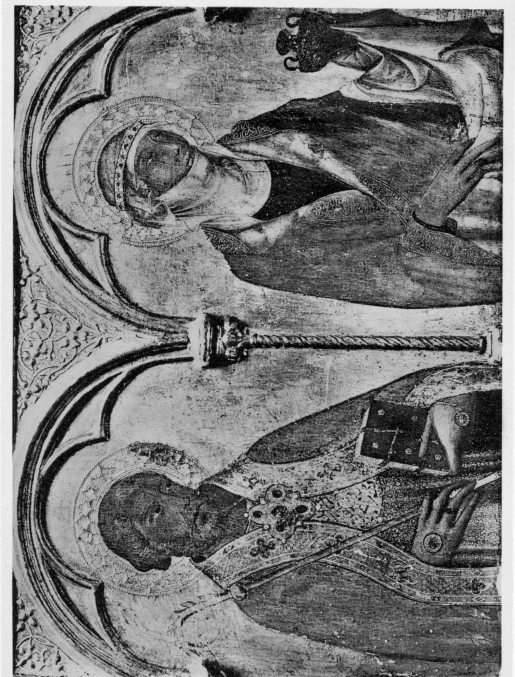

SIMONE MARTINI                              (Photo. Ministry of Public Instruction)
PREDELLA OF THE POLYPTYCH OF PISA. Compartments 5 and 6
Pisa, Civic Museum

XCVI

SIMONE MARTINI                                    (Photo. Ministry of Public Instruction)
PREDELLA OF THE POLYPTYCH OF PISA. Compartments 7 and 8
Pisa, Civic Museum

(Photo. Ministry of Public Instruction)

SIMONE MARTINI
PREDELLA OF THE POLYPTYCH OF PISA. Compartments 9 and 10
*Pisa, Civic Museum*

XCVII

XCVIII

SIMONE MARTINI

PREDELLA OF THE POLYPTYCH OF PISA. Compartments 11 and 12

SIMONE MARTINI · PANELS OF A POLYPTYCH
Boston, U. S. A., Gardner Collection

XCIX

C         SIMONE MARTINI - ST. CATHERINE (?)
*Vienna, Liechtenstein Gallery*

CI          SIMONE MARTINI - ST. MARTIN AND THE BEGGAR      *(Photo. Anderson)*

*Assisi, San Francesco, Lower Basilica*

CII          Simone Martini (and Donato?)          *(Photo. Anderson)*
CHRIST APPEARING TO ST. MARTIN IN A DREAM
*Assisi, S. Francesco, Lower Basilica*

CIII      Donato (?) - DETAIL OF CHRIST APPEARING TO ST. MARTIN      (*Photo. Anderson*)

*Assisi, S. Francesco, Lower Basilica*

SIMONE MARTINI - THE KNIGHTING OF ST. MARTIN    *(Photo. Anderson)*
*Assisi, S. Francesco, Lower Basilica*

CV                SIMONE MARTINI - DETAIL OF THE KNIGHTING OF ST. MARTIN    *(Photo. Anderson)*
Assisi, S. Francesco, Lower Basilica

CVI                     SIMONE MARTINI - ST. MARTIN LEAVING THE ARMY        *(Photo. Anderson)*

*Assisi, S. Francesco, Lower Basilica*

SIMONE MARTINI - DETAIL OF ST. MARTIN LEAVING THE ARMY  *(Photo. Anderson)*
*Assisi, S. Francesco, Lower Basilica*

CVIII        Simone Martini - ST. MARTIN IN MEDITATION       (Photo. Anderson)

Assisi, S. Francesco, Lower Basilica

CIX       SIMONE MARTINI - THE MIRACLE OF THE MASS       *(Photo. Anderson)*

*Assisi, S. Francesco, Lower Basilica*

CX       SIMONE MARTINI (and DONATO ?) - THE DEATH OF ST. MARTIN    *(Photo. Anderson)*
*Assisi, S. Francesco, Lower Basilica*

Simone Martini - THE OBSEQUIES OF ST. MARTIN    *(Photo. Anderson)*
*Assisi, S. Francesco, Lower Basilica*

SIMONE MARTINI - DETAIL OF THE OBSEQUIES
*Assisi, S. Francesco, Lower Basilica*

CXII

SIMONE MARTINI - A SAINT     *(Photo. Anderson)*

*Assisi, S. Francesco, Lower Basilica*

CXIV          SIMONE MARTINI - ST. BENEDICT (?)          *(Photo. Anderson)*
                    *Assisi, S. Francesco, Lower Basilica*

CXV        SIMONE MARTINI - ST. ANTHONY (?)      *(Photo. Anderson)*
*Assisi, S. Francesco, Lower Basilica*

CXVI        DONATO (?) - ST. FRANCIS        *(Photo. Anderson)*
*Assisi, S. Francesco, Lower Basilica*

Donato (?) - ST. CLARE   (Photo. Anderson)

Assisi, S. Francesco, Lower Basilica

CXVIII    Donato (?) - ST. LOUIS OF TOULOUSE   *(Photo. Anderson)*

*Assisi, S. Francesco, Lower Basilica*

CXIX

SIMONE MARTINI - GUIDORICCIO RICCI DEI FOGLIANI (1328)
*Siena, Communal Palace*

*(Photo. Anderson)*

CXX    Simone Martini (?) - BEATO AGOSTINO NOVELLO - Central Panel  *(Photo. Anderson)*
*Siena, S. Agostino*

CXXI              Simone Martini (?)           *(Photo. Anderson)*

BEATO AGOSTINO. The second left-and panel of the *Pala*
Siena, S. Agostino

SIMONE MARTINI (?) *(Photo. Anderson)*
BEATO AGOSTINO. The first left-and panel of the *Pala*
*Siena, S. Agostino*

CXXIII            SIMONE MARTINI (?)            *(Photo. Anderson)*

BEATO AGOSTINO. The first right-and panel of the *Pala*

*Siena, S. Agostino*

CXXIV

Simone Martini (?) - Beato Agostino. DETAIL of the second right-and panel of the *Pala*

*Siena, S. Agostino*

*(Photo. Anderson)*

CXXV        Simone Martini and Lippo Memmi - THE ANNUNCIATION (1339)        (Photo. Anderson)
Florence, Uffizi Gallery

CXXVI    SIMONE MARTINI · THE ANGEL AND THE VIRGIN OF THE ANNUNCIATION    (Photo. Anderson)

Florence, Uffizi Gallery

CXXVII    SIMONE MARTINI · DETAIL OF THE ANGEL OF THE ANNUNCIATION    (*Photo. Anderson*)

*Florence, Uffizi Gallery*

CXXVIII    SIMONE MARTINI - Another DETAIL OF THE ANNUNCIATION    *(Photo. Anderson)*
*Florence, Uffizi Gallery*

CXXIX   SIMONE MARTINI - THE VIRGIN OF THE STROGANOFF ANNUNCIATION  (Photo. Lombardi)
*Formerly in the Stroganoff Collection, Rome*

SIMONE MARTINI - THE CRUCIFIXION *(Photo. Braun)*
*Antwerp, Museum*

Simone Martini - THE DEPOSITION     *(Photo. Braun)*
*Antwerp, Museum*

LIPPO MEMMI - MADONNA

*Settignano, Collection of Bernard Berenson*

CXXXIV        LIPPO MEMMI - MADONNA        *(Photo. Anderson)*
*Siena, Servite Church*

Lippo Memmi - ST. JAMES *(Photo. Ministry of Public Instruction)*
*Pisa, Civic Museum*

LIPPO MEMMI *(Photo. Alinari)*

S. ANSANO AND S. JULITTA OF THE ANNUNCIATION (1333)

*Florence, Uffizi Gallery*

CXXXVII        Lippo Memmi - THE CRUCIFIXION       (Photo. Anderson)
*Città del Vaticano, Vatican Gallery*

CXXXVIII        BARNA - THE BAPTISM OF CHRIST        *(Photo. Alinari)*
*San Gimignano, Collegiate Church*

CXXXIX        BARNA - THE CALL OF ST. PETER        *(Photo. Alinari)*
            *San Gimignano, Collegiate Church*

BARNA - THE MARRIAGE FEAST AT CANA *(Photo. Alinari)*
*San Gimignano, Collegiate Church*

BARNA - THE RAISING OF LAZARUS            *(Photo. Alinari)*
*San Gimignano, Collegiate Church*

CXLII      BARNA - THE ENTRY OF CHRIST INTO JERUSALEM      *(Photo. Alinari)*

*San Gimignano, Collegiate Church*

CXLIII    BARNA - DETAIL OF THE ENTRY INTO JERUSALEM    *(Photo. Alinari)*

*San Gimignano, Collegiate Church*

CXLIV                 Barna - JUDAS WITH THE PRIESTS           *(Photo. Lombardi)*
*San Gimignano, Collegiate Church*

CXLV       BARNA - THE SLEEPING APOSTLES       *(Photo. Lombardi)*
DETAIL OF THE AGONY IN THE GARDEN
*San Gimignano, Collegiate Church*

CXLVI    Barna (?) - CHRIST CARRYING HIS CROSS    (Photo. Braun)
New York, Frick Collection

CXLVII       BARNA (?) - DETAIL OF THE MADONNA       *(Photo. Lombardi)*
*Asciano, Church of S. Francesco*

CXLVIII       Naddo Ceccarelli (?) - THE NATIVITY      (Photo. Giraudon)
Aix-en-Provence, Museum

CXLIX     Pietro Lorenzetti · MADONNA OF CORTONA     *(Photo. Alinari)*
*Cortona Cathedral*

CL      P<small>IETRO</small> L<small>ORENZETTI</small>(?) · ST. GREGORY     *(Photo. Lombardi)*
*Siena, Accademia*

CLI    PIETRO LORENZETTI (?) - THE ASSUMPTION    *(Photo. Anderson)*
*Siena, Accademia*

PIETRO LORENZETTI (?) - MADONNA *(Photo. Anderson)*

*Siena, Accademia*

Pietro Lorenzetti - MADONNA
*Settignano, Collection of Bernard Berenson*

CLIV        PIETRO LORENZETTI - ST. AGNES     *(Photo. Anderson)*
*Siena, Accademia*

PIETRO LORENZETTI - ST. CATHERINE    *(Photo. Anderson)*
*Siena, Accademia*

CLVI · PIETRO LORENZETTI - THE MASSACRE OF THE INNOCENTS

*Siena, Servite Church*

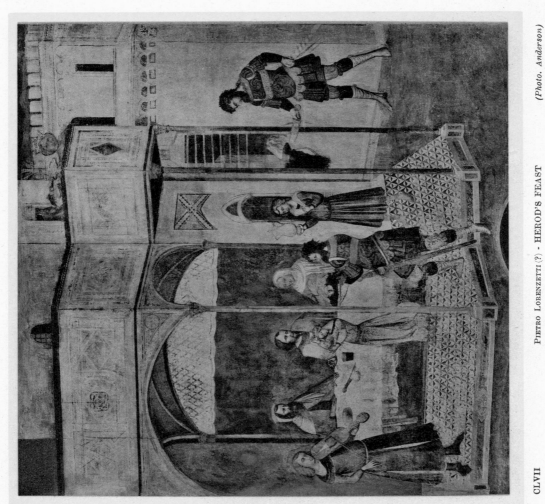

CLVII        P I E T R O  L O R E N Z E T T I (?) - H E R O D ' S  F E A S T     (*Photo. Anderson*)

*Siena, Servite Church*

Pietro Lorenzetti - CHRIST BEFORE PILATE     *(Photo. Anderson)*
*Città del Vaticano, Vatican Gallery*

CLIX          PIETRO LORENZETTI - MARTYR SAINTS
*London, National Gallery*

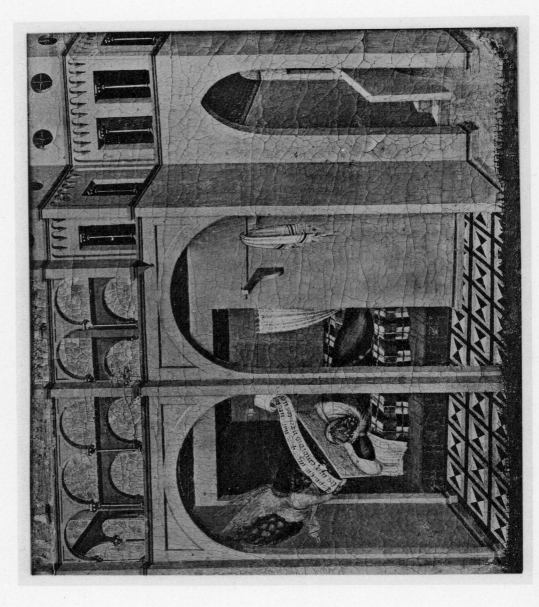

PIETRO LORENZETTI - DREAM OF A MONK (1329?)
Siena Accademia

(Photo. Anderson)

CLXI     Pietro Lorenzetti - CARMELITE FRIARS (1329?)     (Photo. Anderson)
*Siena, Accademia*

Pietro Lorenzetti - HONORIUS IV APPROVES THE CARMELITE RULE (1329?)   (Photo. Anderson)

CLXIII    PIETRO LORENZETTI - THE MADONNA, WITH ST. FRANCIS AND ST. JOHN THE BAPTIST

*Assisi, S. Francesco, Lower Basilica*

CLXIV   Pietro Lorenzetti - THE MADONNA BETWEEN ST. FRANCIS AND ST. JOHN THE EVANGELIST   (Photo. Anderson)
Assisi, S. Francesco, Lower Basilica

(Photo. Anderson)

PIETRO LORENZETTI - DETAIL OF THE MADONNA
*Assisi, S. Francesco, Lower Basilica*

CLXV

CLXVI

Pietro Lorenzetti - The Crucifixion
Assisi, S. Francesco, Lower Basilica

(Photo. Anderson)

CLXVII

PIETRO LORENZETTI · DETAIL OF THE CRUCIFIXION

Assisi, S. Francesco, Lower Basilica

(Photo. Anderson)

PIETRO LORENZETTI - THE DEPOSITION FROM THE CROSS
Assisi, S. Francesco, Lower Basilica

(Photo. Anderson)

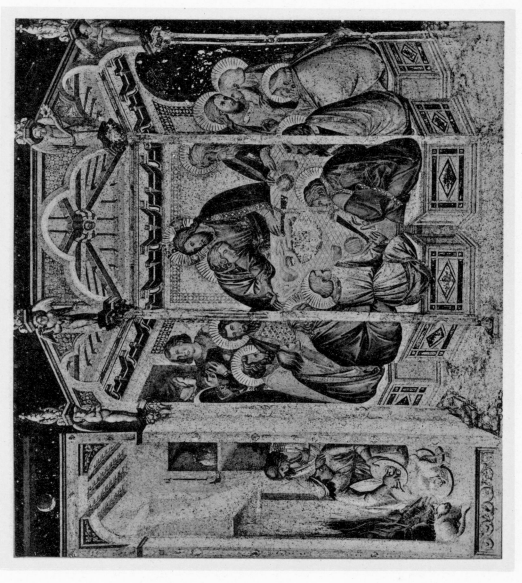

PIETRO LORENZETTI AND PUPILS · THE LAST SUPPER

Assisi, S. Francesco, Lower Basilica

CLXIX

CLXX  Pietro Lorenzetti and Pupils · CHRIST WASHING THE DISCIPLES' FEET  (Photo. Anderson)

Assisi, S. Francesco, Lower Basilica

CLXXI

PIETRO LORENZETTI AND PUPILS · THE SCOURGING

Assisi, S. Francesco, Lower Basilica

PIETRO LORENZETTI · THE CRUCIFIXION (1331?)
*Siena, S. Francesco*

(*Photo. Anderson*)

CLXXIII

PIETRO LORENZETTI (?) - ALLEGORY
*Siena, Accademia*

*(Photo. Anderson)*

CLXXIV     Pietro Lorenzetti (?) - LANDSCAPE     (*Photo. Anderson*)

*Siena, Accademia*

CLXXV

PIETRO LORENZETTI (?) · LANDSCAPE
Siena, Accademia

(Photo. Anderson)

CLXXVI     Pietro Lorenzetti - THE NATIVITY OF THE VIRGIN (1342)

Siena, Opera del Duomo

(Photo. Anderson)

CLXXVII     Pietro Lorenzetti - DETAIL OF THE NATIVITY OF THE VIRGIN     *(Photo. Anderson)*
*Siena, Opera del Duomo*

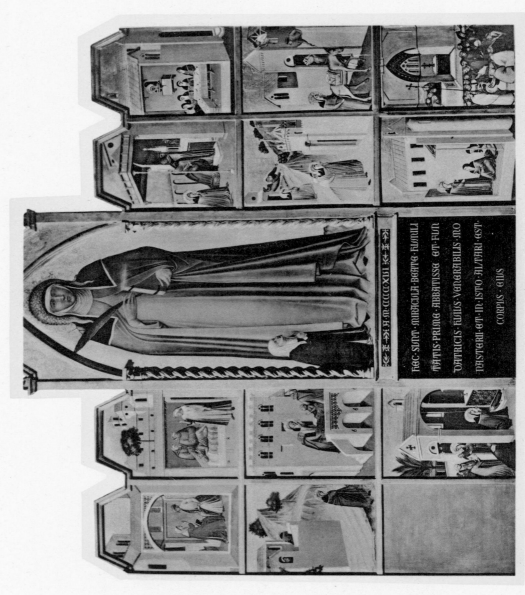

CLXXVIII     Pietro Lorenzetti - Pala of the Altar of Beata Umiltà (1341)

Florence, Uffizi Gallery

(Photo. Alinari)

CLXXIX      Pietro Lorenzetti - ST. LUCY     *(Photo. Alinari)*
*Florence, S. Lucia tra le Rovinate*

CLXXX     Ambrogio Lorenzetti - MADONNA DEL LATTE    *(Photo. Anderson)*
*Siena, Seminary*

CLXXXI    AMBROGIO LORENZETTI · MADONNA OF ROCCALBEGNA (1330?)
Roccalbegna (Grosseto)

CLXXXII    Ambrogio Lorenzetti - MARTYRDOM OF THE FRANCISCANS AT CEUTA (1331)    (Photo. Anderson)

Siena, S. Francesco

CLXXXIII                          AMBROGIO LORENZETTI                       *(Photo. Lombardi)*

DETAIL OF THE MARTYRDOM OF THE FRANCISCANS

*Siena, S. Francesco*

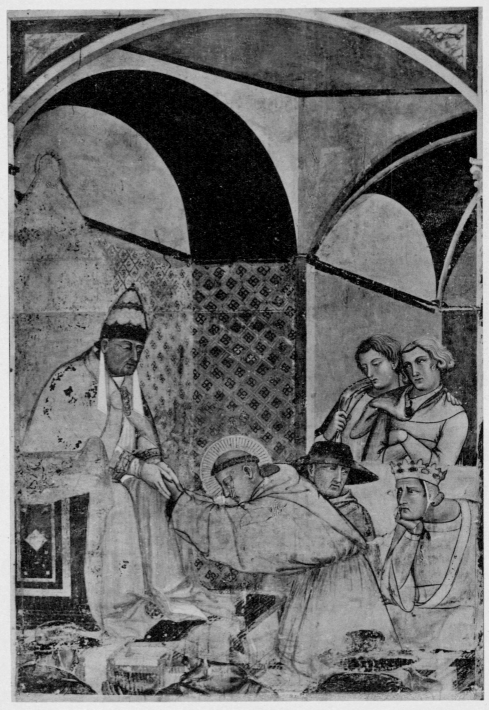

CLXXXIV          AMBROGIO LORENZETTI        *(Photo. Anderson)*

BONIFACE VIII RECEIVING ST. LOUIS AS A NOVICE (1331). Left Part

*Siena, S. Francesco*

AMBROGIO LORENZETTI  *(Photo. Anderson)*
BONIFACE VIII RECEIVING ST. LOUIS AS A NOVICE (1331). Right Part
*Siena, S. Francesco*

AMBROGIO LORENZETTI · DETAIL OF BONIFACE VIII RECEIVING ST. LOUIS    (*Photo. Lombardi*)
Siena, S. Francesco

CLXXXVI

CLXXXVII        AMBROGIO LORENZETTI        *(Photo. Lombardi)*

ANOTHER DETAIL OF BONIFACE VIII RECEIVING ST. LOUIS

*Siena, S. Francesco*

CLXXXVIII        AMBROGIO LORENZETTI        *(Photo. Alinari)*

**EPISODES FROM THE LEGEND OF ST. NICHOLAS OF BARI**

*Florence, Uffizi Gallery*

CLXXXIX        AMBROGIO LORENZETTI

EPISODES FROM THE LEGEND OF ST. NICHOLAS OF BARI

*Florence, Uffizi Gallery*

Ambrogio Lorenzetti · MADONNA AND SAINTS    *(Photo. Anderson)*
*Siena, Accademia*

AMBROGIO LORENZETTI - THE PRESENTATION IN THE TEMPLE (1342)  *(Photo. Alinari)*
*Florence, Uffizi Gallery*

CXCII          Ambrogio Lorenzetti - PEACE          *(Photo. Anderson)*
*Siena, Communal Palace*

CXCIII      Ambrogio Lorenzetti - **FORTITUDE AND PRUDENCE**      *(Photo. Anderson)*
*Siena, Communal Palace*

AMBROGIO LORENZETTI - CONCORD

*Siena, Communal Palace*

*(Photo. Anderson)*

AMBROGIO LORENZETTI - JUSTICE  (*Photo. Lombardi*)
*Siena, Communal Palace*

CXCVI    AMBROGIO LORENZETTI - THE CITIZENS, from the fresco of GOOD GOVERNMENT (1337-1340)

*Siena, Communal Palace*

CXCVII

AMBROGIO LORENZETTI - EFFECTS OF GOOD GOVERNMENT IN THE CITY (1337-1340)

*Siena, Communal Palace*

*(Photo. Anderson)*

CXCVIII        Ambrogio Lorenzetti        (Photo. Anderson)

DETAIL OF GOOD GOVERNMENT IN THE CITY

Siena, Communal Palace

CXCIX        AMBROGIO LORENZETTI - ANOTHER DETAIL OF GOOD GOVERNMENT IN THE CITY        (Photo. Anderson)

Siena, Communal Palace

AMBROGIO LORENZETTI - EFFECTS OF GOOD GOVERNMENT IN THE COUNTRY (1337-1340)

*Siena, Communal Palace*

*(Photo. Anderson)*

CCI     AMBROGIO LORENZETTI · DETAIL OF GOOD GOVERNMENT IN THE COUNTRY     (*Photo. Anderson*)

*Siena, Communal Palace*

AMBROGIO LORENZETTI - BAD GOVERNMENT (1337-1340)
*Siena, Communal Palace*

*(Photo. Anderson)*

AMBROGIO LORENZETTI - DETAIL OF BAD GOVERNMENT    *(Photo. Anderson)*
*Siena, Communal Palace*

AMBROGIO LORENZETTI - SUMMER
*Siena, Communal Palace*

(*Photo. Lombardi*)

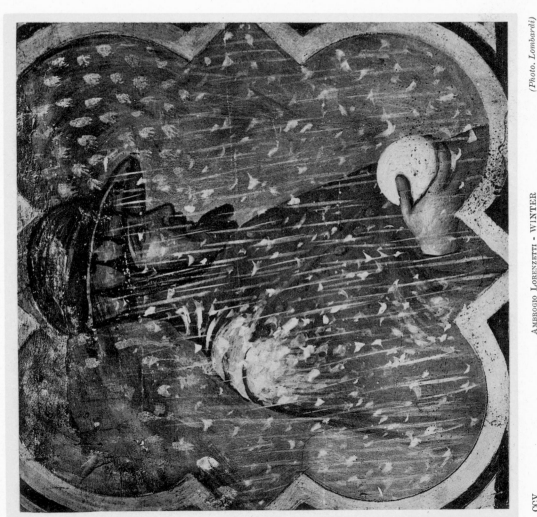

CCV          Ambrogio Lorenzetti - WINTER
Siena, Communal Palace

( *Photo. Alinari* )

AMBROGIO LORENZETTI - MADONNA AND SAINTS

*Massa Marittima, Town Hall*

CCVI

AMBROGIO LORENZETTI - DETAIL OF THE MADONNA AND SAINTS     *(Photo. Alinari)*

*Massa Marittima, Town Hall*

CCVIII    AMBROGIO LORENZETTI - THE ANGEL OF THE ANNUNCIATION (1344)    *(Photo. Anderson)*
*Siena, Accademia*

AMBROGIO LORENZETTI - **MADONNA OF THE ANNUNCIATION** (1344)   *(Photo. Anderson)*
*Siena, Accademia*

CCX        AMBROGIO LORENZETTI      *(Photo. Anderson)*
DETAIL OF THE MADONNA OF THE ANNUNCIATION
*Siena, Accademia*

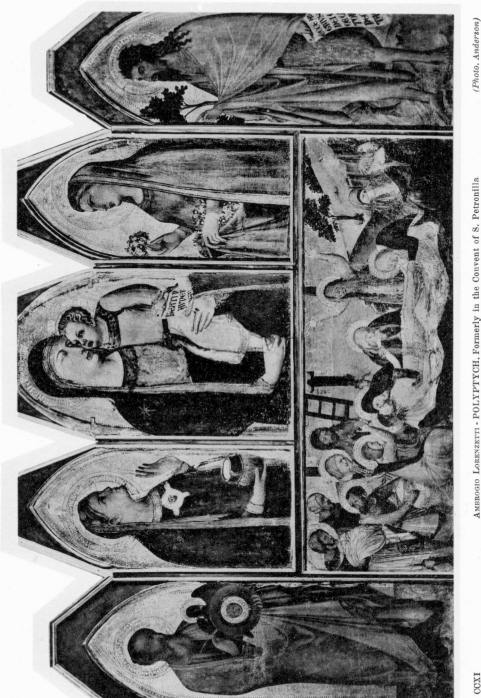

CCXI

AMBROGIO LORENZETTI · POLYPTYCH, Formerly in the Convent of S. Petronilla
*Siena, Accademia*

(*Photo. Anderson*)

CCXII    Ambrogio Lorenzetti - THE DEPOSITION FROM THE CROSS. From the POLYPTYCH of S. Petronilla    *(Photo. Lombardi)*

*Siena, Accademia*

CCXIII       Ambrogio Lorenzetti       *(Photo. Anderson)*
ST. DOROTHY. From the POLYPTYCH of S. Petronilla
*Siena, Accademia*

CCXIV    FLORENTINE FOLLOWER OF THE LORENZETTI - THE STONING OF ST. STEPHEN    (Photo. Anderson)

Città del Vaticano, Vatican Gallery.

(Photo. Anderson)

Florentine Follower of the Lorenzetti

THE BURIAL OF SS. STEPHEN, NICODEMUS, AND COMPANIONS

Città del Vaticano, Vatican Gallery

CCXVII   FLORENTINE FOLLOWER OF THE LORENZETTI - THE SECOND BURIAL   (Photo. Anderson)

Città del Vaticano, Vatican Gallery

CCXVIII        Andrea Vanni - MADONNA       *(Photo. Mansell)*
                *Cambridge, Fitzwilliam Museum*

CCXIX        ANDREA VANNI - **MADONNA**        *(Photo. Anderson)*
*Siena, Church of S. Spirito*

CCXX           Andrea Vanni - **MADONNA**          *(Photo. Anderson)*
*Siena, Church of S. Francesco*

CCXXI      ANDREA VANNI - ST. CATHERINE OF SIENA      *(Photo. Anderson)*

*Siena, Church of S. Domenico*

LIPPO VANNI *(Photo. Anderson)*
ST. PETER MARTYR, ST. DOMINIC, AND ST. THOMAS AQUINAS
*Città del Vaticano, Vatican Gallery*

CCXXIV                    Bartolo di Fredi - THE ADORATION OF THE MAGI        (Photo. Anderson)

Siena, Accademia

CCXXVI        BARTOLO DI FREDI - THE NATIVITY OF THE VIRGIN

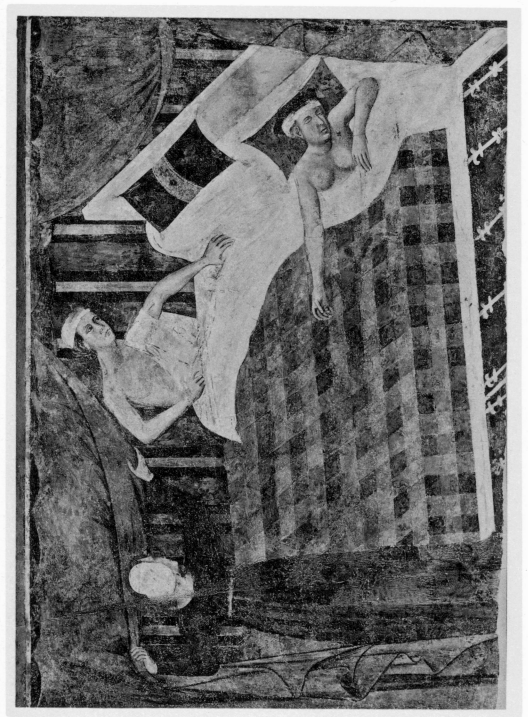

SCHOOL OF BARTOLO DI FREDI - **SCENES OF MARRIED LIFE**
San Gimignano, Tower of the Palazzo Pubblico

*(Photo. Alinari)*

PHOTO BY GIOVANNI FEI . THE NATIVITY OF THE VIRGIN

*(Photo. Anderson)*

CCXXIX      Paolo di Giovanni Fei - MADONNA      *(Photo. Anderson)*
Siena, *Cathedral*

TADDEO DI BARTOLO    *(Photo. Anderson)*

Part of the **ALTAR-PIECE** formerly in S. Francesco (1403)
*Perugia, Art Gallery*

CCXXXI    Taddeo di Bartolo - MADONNA BETWEEN ST. JAMES AND ST. DOMINIC
*Turin, Collection of R. Gualino*

Taddeo di Bartolo - DETAIL OF A CRUCIFIX    *(Photo. Lombardi)*
Siena, Accademia

CCXXXIII        TADDEO DI BARTOLO - ST. JOHN        *(Photo. Lombardi)*
*From the Crucifix in the Accademia, Siena*

CCXXXIV        Taddeo di Bartolo - ST. PETER MARTYR        *(Photo. Anderson)*
Siena, Accademia

Taddeo di Bartolo - JUPITER AND MARS        *(Photo. Lombardi)*
*Siena, Communal Palace*

CCXXXVI          TADDEO DI BARTOLO - THE BURIAL OF THE VIRGIN (1406)          (Photo. Anderson)
                           Siena, Communal Palace

CCXXXVII     Taddeo di Bartolo - THE RESURRECTION OF THE VIRGIN     (Photo. Anderson)

Città del Vaticano, Vatican Gallery

TADDEO DI BARTOLO - THE DAMNED (1393)   *(Photo. Alinari)*

*San Gimignano, Collegiate Church*

CCXXXIX          TADDEO DI BARTOLO - THE DAMNED (1393)          (Photo. Alinari)
                    San Gimignano, Collegiate Church

ANDREA DI BARTOLO - ST. JOACHIM AND THE SHEPHERDS

Città del Vaticano, Vatican Gallery

CCXLI

SASSETTA - THE NATIVITY OF THE VIRGIN. Lower Part

*Asciano, Collegiate Church*

*(Photo. Alinari)*

CCXLIII    SASSETTA - THE NATIVITY OF THE VIRGIN. Central Panel of the Upper Part    (Photo. Alinari)

Asciano, Collegiate Church

(Photo. Hanfstaengl)

SASSETTA - ST. THOMAS AQUINAS
*Budapest, Art Gallery*

CCXLIV

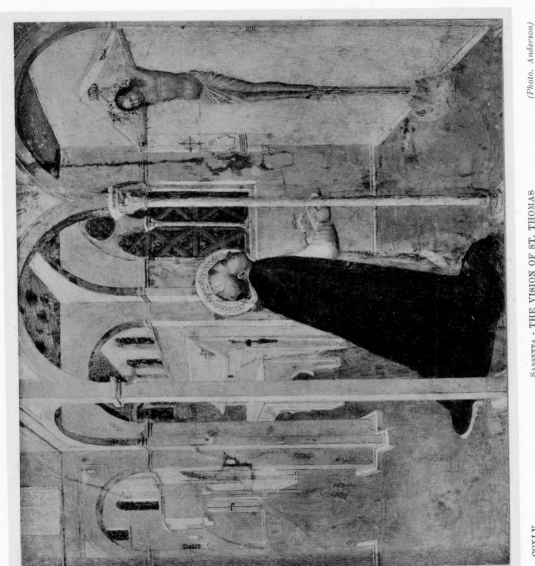

SASSETTA - THE VISION OF ST. THOMAS

*Città del Vaticano, Vatican Gallery*

*(Photo. Anderson)*

CCXLV

CCXLVI

SASSETTA - THE MAGI AND THE STAR

*New York, Maitland Griggs Collection*

CCXLVII

SASSETTA - ST. MARTIN AND THE BEGGAR     (Photo. Lombardi)

Siena, Chigi Saracini Collection

CCXLVIII      Sᴀssᴇᴛᴛᴀ - ST. FRANCIS IN ECSTASY (1444)

*Settignano, Collection of Bernard Berenson*

CCXLIX    SASSETTA - THE BETROTHAL OF ST. FRANCIS (1444)
*Chantilly, Musée Condé*

SASSETTA - THE TEMPTATION OF ST. ANTHONY

*New Haven, U. S. A. Jarves Collection*

CCLI       SASSETTA - A LEGEND OF ST. ANTHONY THE ABBOT
*New York, Lehman Collection*

GIOVANNI DI PAOLO - MADONNA
Siena, Accademia

CCLIII        GIOVANNI DI PAOLO - ST. JEROME      *(Photo. Anderson)*
*Siena, Accademia*

GIOVANNI DI PAOLO - DETAIL OF THE FLIGHT INTO EGYPT
Siena, Accademia

(Photo. Anderson)

CCLIV

(Photo. Lombardi)

SANO DI PIETRO - THE ANGEL AND THE SHEPHERDS
Siena, Accademia

CCLV

CCLVI    Sᴀɴᴏ ᴅɪ Pɪᴇᴛʀᴏ - ST. BERNARDINE OF SIENA PREACHING *(Photo. Anderson)*
*Siena Cathedral, Chapter House*

# GENERAL INDEX

*(Prepared by the Publishers of the English Edition)*